The Object Technology Casebook

Lessons from Award-Winning Business Applications

OBJECT MANAGEMENT GROUP

Paul Harmon

William Morrissey

WILEY COMPUTER PUBLISHING

John Wiley & Sons, Inc.
• New York • Chichester • Brisbane
• Toronto • Singapore

Publisher: Katherine Schowalter
Editor: Robert Elliott
Manager Editor: Frank Grazioli
Text Design & Composition: Publishers' Design and Production Services, Inc.

Designations used by companies to distinguish their products are often claimed as trademarks. In all instances where John Wiley & Sons, Inc., is aware of a claim, the product names appear in initial capital or ALL CAPITAL LETTERS. Readers, however, should contact the appropriate companies for more complete information regarding trademarks and registration.

This text is printed on acid-free paper.

This publication is designed to provide accurate and authoritative information in regard to the subject matter covered. It is sold with the understanding that the publisher is not engaged in rendering legal, accounting, or other professional service. If legal advice or other expert assistance is required, the services of a competent professional person should be sought.

Library of Congress Cataloging-in-Publication Data:

ISBN 0471-14717-6

Printed in the United States of America
10 9 8 7 6 5 4 3 2 1

Contents

Foreword

The Object Management Group (OMG) was founded in 1989. The group is composed of an international assortment of hardware and software companies interested in promoting object technologies. The membership in OMG has grown steadily since its founding and is now in excess of 600 members.

In keeping with its educational goals, in 1991 the OMG established Object World, Inc. to arrange for educational briefings and to sponsor a commercial trade show on object technology. The first show, the Object World conference, was held in San Francisco in June 1991. The second was held in San Francisco in July 1992.

In 1992, *Computerworld,* the weekly newspaper of information systems professionals, came to the OMG and suggested that it would be willing to sponsor a contest that would recognize outstanding applications that utilized object technology in conjunction with the 1992 Object World show. Applications were solicited in the spring, judged in July, and awards were presented at the Object World show in the late summer. In 1993, Paul Harmon and David Taylor, with the assistance of William Morrissey, authored *Objects in Action,* a book that described the finalists in the first contest held in 1992.

The same contest has continued since 1992, and we've included a list of all the finalists and the winners for each contest in Appendix A.

Each year, as new object tools and techniques have become available and as companies have gained experience in the use of object technology, the applications have become more sophisticated. When we reviewed the 1995 winning applications, we decided that the progress evidenced by these applications deserved to be widely publicized. To assure a wider audience, we asked Paul Harmon and William Morrissey to work with the developers of the applications submitted for the 1994 and 1995 Computerworld/Object World contest to prepare a book describing the best of the applications.

We hope this book will help demonstrate the rapid and impressive development of object technology and draw attention to some of the companies and individuals who are finding innovative uses for this major new approach to software development.

William R. Hoffman, President
Object World Corporation
Object Management Group

Gary J. Beach, Publisher
Computerworld

Introduction

The Object Management Group held the first Object World Conference in San Francisco in 1991. In 1992, in conjunction with the San Francisco Object World conference, a contest was initiated to provide recognition to outstanding applications that illustrated the commercial use of object technology. That contest has been held each year since 1992, always in conjunction with the San Francisco Object World conference. The contest is sponsored by *Computerworld,* the weekly newspaper of information systems professionals.

Entries are limited to applications that are actually in use—although in some cases the applications are still being tested in the field rather than fully implemented. A panel of judges evaluates the applications and selects three outstanding applications in each category. Then, one winner is selected from among the three finalists in each category, and the finalists and winners are announced at the San Francisco Object World conference.

ABOUT THE CATEGORIES

When companies submit descriptions of their applications to the Object World Contest Committee, they identify one or more categories for the application. In theory, the same application could win in more than one category, but that has not happened yet, even though some outstanding applications have been selected as finalists in more than one category.

There have always been five categories. The order of the categories and the category names have varied a little over the years, but most have remained unchanged. The categories for 1994 were:

Category 1. Best Object-Based Application Using Non-Object Tools

Category 2. Best Distributed Application Using Object Technology with Legacy Systems

Category 3. Best Application that Demonstrates the Cost/Benefit of Using Object Technology

Category 4. Best Use of Object Technology within an Enterprise or Large Systems Environment

Category 5. Best Application Utilizing Reusable Components Leveraged from or for Use in Other Projects

In 1995, the five categories were:

Category 1. Best Distributed Application Using Object Technology

Category 2. Best Use of Object Technology to Integrate Legacy Systems

Category 3. Best Application Utilizing Reusable Components Leveraged from or for Use in Other Projects

Category 4. Best Application that Demonstrates the Cost/Benefit of Using Object Technology

Category 5. Best Use of Object Technology within an Enterprise or Large Systems Environment

We have used similar categories to cluster the applications described in this book. Applications that appear in one of the sections of this book were finalists or winners in a similar category in either the 1994 or 1995 Object World contest. An application that won in one category, however, may also have been a finalist in another category. Thus, many applications illustrate the features of more than one category.

In Appendix A we have listed all the categories and all the finalists and winners in all the Computerworld/Object World contests since 1992.

INTENDED READERSHIP

This book is designed to provide managers and developers of object technology applications with information about tools and techniques that have worked for others who have been successful in developing important object-oriented applications. The book does not provide the kind of detail that a programmer would be interested in, but it provides detailed information about the nature of the problems, the approach the company took to developing an object-oriented application, and the problems encountered along the way.

HOW TO USE THIS BOOK

Different readers will want to use this book in different ways. If you are new to object technology, you will probably find it rewarding to read straight through the book. The early chapters provide an overview of object technology and prepare you for the discussions that follow. Later, specific sections will provide information on different uses of object technology.

If you are interested in specific types of applications, applications developed with different tools or languages, or applications in specific industries, you can consult the matrix that appears on page *xx*. The matrix lists all of the applications and provides information on the object technology products and techniques used in each application. It also identifies the object technology benefits illustrated by various applications and the industry using each application. The matrix provides the reader with an easy way to identify specific applications with features he or she is specifically interested in studying.

HOW THIS BOOK IS ORGANIZED

Section I provides an overview of the object technology market as it stands at the beginning of 1996. We provide a brief overview of what objects are and then proceeded to consider the overall size of the market and how objects are being used in each of several different areas, ranging from object-oriented network systems and object-oriented tools to object-oriented databases.

Section II focuses on distributed systems. We begin with a discussion of some of the principles underlying object-oriented distributed systems and then consider applications that have been finalists or winners in the distributed systems category.

Section III considers components and reuse. After a description of the various approaches to classes and components and some of the problems of reuse, we discuss applications that have been finalists or winners in the reuse category.

Section IV focuses on enterprise applications. In the introduction we consider how object technology has roots in both object-oriented languages and graphical user interfaces and in artificial intelligence systems and discuss the role that AI is playing in some complex object-oriented applications. Then we consider applications that have been finalists or winners in the enterprise application category.

Section V focuses on legacy systems, the use of non-object-oriented tools to develop object-oriented applications and on re-engineering. Lots of important object-oriented applications have been developed in the context of business process re-engineering (BPR) efforts and we briefly consider re-engineering and its relationship to object technology. Then we consider applications that have been winners or finalists in the legacy systems category.

Section VI focuses on applications that demonstrate the cost effectiveness of object technologies.

A final, brief chapter summarizes the key insights resulting from the study of the winning object technology applications described in this book.

In the appendices we have included a list of the object technology applications that were finalists and winners in each contest held at the San Francisco Object World conference, from 1992 to 1995. There is a separate contest held each year at the

Frankfurt Object World conference in Germany. We did not have time to get detailed descriptions of the applications, but we have provided a list of the winners and finalists in the contest held in the fall of 1995. Finally, we have provided a list of readings for those who want to learn more about object technology.

HOW THE APPLICATION CASES ARE ORGANIZED

Each application description follows the same general format, which, in turn, reflects the way the developers described the applications for the contest committee in their original contest submittals. The following format is used:

Opportunity. What situation the company faced and why they thought object technology might be useful.

Application. A specific description of the application. In addition to describing what the specific application does, we identify the hardware and the software used to create or field the application.

Project Lifecycle. This area includes a discussion of how the application was developed and what problems were encountered. It includes a discussion of how the developers dealt with analysis and design, development, deployment, and maintenance problems.

Benefits. A discussion of the costs and benefits obtained from the application effort.

Conclusions. A summary of the conclusions reached by the managers and developers of the application.

MATRIX OF TECHNOLOGIES AND APPLICATIONS

The matrix that follows (Table I.1) lists each of the applications that are described in this casebook.

To make it easy for readers to find information they are especially interested in, we have listed various products and benefits on the vertical axis and indicated which applications comment on which features. In addition, we have indicated the industry that each application is most closely associated with.

ACKNOWLEDGMENTS

The authors have contributed to the general chapters and take responsibility for the generalizations, opinions, and conclusions expressed there. Each application chapter, however, is based on the contest description submitted by the managers and developers who actually created the application. Thus, the descriptions of problems and the conclusions at the end of each application chapter reflect the opinions of the people who actually developed the applications and not those of the general authors. In a similar way, the final conclusions that the authors have pulled together at the end of the book primarily reflect the work of the many managers and developers who have actually been engaged in creating the specific applications described in this book.

As we have already noted, this book is derived from the work of many managers and developers who created the applications that they then described for the Computerworld/Object World contest. Without the extensive cooperation and editing efforts of these individuals, this book would not have been possible. These individuals include:

Darko Bojanic, MPR TelTech; Bernadette Brooks, The MITRE Corporation; Tom Mowbray, The MITRE Corporation; Allan Douthwaite, Canadian Imperial Bank of Commerce; Walter Ringger, IBM Switzerland; Thomas Buehrer, IBM Switzerland; Daniel Scholz, IBM Switzerland; Les Russell, Naval Computer and Telecommunications Station San Diego; Valerie Hauthaway, Palm Beach County ISS; Greg Smith, Boeing Defense and Space Group; Greg Frierson, IBM Credit Corporation; Richard Goulet, Canadian Tire; Tammy Mead, The Mark Winter Group; Mike Baker, Caterpillar; Ahmad Asadi, AlliedSignal Aerospace; Roland Mathis, Bell Sygma; Eva Podhorska, Bell Sygma; Jules Caza, Nexacor Realty; Katherine Sotka, Blue Cross/Blue Shield of Oregon; Mike Adelson, Chrysler Financial Corporation; Kindle DiGuisto, NeXT Computers; David Pett, Pacific Bell.

In addition, the authors acknowledge the support of many individuals at OMG and Object World, especially Chris Stone, Bill Hoffman, and Richard Soley.

Table I.1   Application/Features Matrix
A Quick Guide to Applications With Specific Characteristics

Column key:
1. MPR Teltech - TRADS
2. MITRE - AF
3. MITRE - DISCUS
4. Con. Imperial - HRA
5. IBM Swiss - ProFormA
6. Navy San Diego - MTF
7. IBM Swiss - Com. Register
8. Palm Beach - Med. Examiner
9. Boeing Defense - PreAmp
10. Boeing Defense - DART
11. Euriware - COGEMO
12. Mount Clemens - Patient Care
13. IBM Credit - FMW
14. Con. Tire - Auto. Kiosk
15. Catepillar - Forging Steel Plan.
16. Navy - TRMS
17. Allied Signal Aero. - SMST
18. Bell Sygma - COORS
19. Blue Cross/BS of Oregon - EMC
20. Chrysler Financial - Branch Auto.
21. Pac Bell - STAC

Features Illustrated	1	2	3	4	5	6	7	8	9	10	11	12	13	14	15	16	17	18	19	20	21
Ada						•						•					•			•	
C++ and C	•	•	•		•	•	•	•		•	•	•		•					•		
Objective C												•								•	
Smalltalk	•		•									•	•	•			•	•			
CLOS			•																		
CORBA and other ORBS	•	•	•		•																
IDL	•	•	•																		
Class libraries/Components	•				•	•	•	•	•			•					•				
Technical objects/Frameworks					•	•	•			•	•	•								•	
Business objects/Frameworks	•	•		•		•		•				•	•	•					•	•	
OO GUI tools	•					•		•	•	•	•		•		•		•		•	•	
O-based 4GL tools			•	•					•												
OO Dev. Env./tools																					
Adv. OO Dev. Env (AI)	•								•	•											
OO CASE tools												•							•		
OO methodologies	•	•			•	•	•						•	•	•			•	•		•
OODB	•											•	•							•	
Benefits Illustrated	1	2	3	4	5	6	7	8	9	10	11	12	13	14	15	16	17	18	19	20	21
Development time saved	•		•	•			•		•			•	•	•	•				•	•	
User time saved			•	•								•						•	•		
Maintenance simplified			•	•				•													
Reuse	•	•		•		•							•				•		•	•	
Distributed applications	•			•																•	
Legacy applications integrated	•	•											•	•			•	•			•
Re-engineering	•		•	•		•						•	•	•				•			
Money saved		•											•		•	•					
Complexity overcome	•					•	•			•	•	•		•	•						
Industry	1	2	3	4	5	6	7	8	9	10	11	12	13	14	15	16	17	18	19	20	21
Telecommunications	•																				•
Finance			•											•						•	
Government/Military		•	•		•	•	•	•									•	•			
Manufacturing										•	•	•				•					
Health													•							•	
Retail														•							
Customer Support														•						•	

The Evolving Nature of Object Technology

Section

The Evolving Nature of Object Technology

Object Technology Today

There is, as almost everyone is now aware, a major transition taking place in corporate computing. The basic elements of business computing, laid down in the late sixties and early seventies, included mainframe-based systems, proprietary operating systems, and procedure-oriented software. Most companies are currently shifting to distributed, heterogeneous systems, open standards and object-oriented software. This shift, unlike the many other "revolutions" that have occurred in computing in the past twenty years, is very serious because it is so comprehensive. Mainframes have hardly disappeared, but they are rapidly being marginalized by networks of personal computers, workstations, and powerful database servers. Similarly, open APIs (application programming interface) are gradually making it easier to link software running on different platforms. At the same time, new languages capable of supporting component and class-based development have appeared. New object-oriented client/server 4GL tools, and new object-oriented CASE tools are proliferating and new object-oriented databases are gradually establishing a place for themselves in the database market.

More important than the new techniques and new software development tools, however, is a whole new way of approaching the software development process. The open, distributed object-oriented paradigm offers companies a chance to change their computing infrastructure while radically improving the speed and the productivity of their software development organizations.

All of this has come at an opportune time. Broad changes in the world economy are forcing companies to re-engineer themselves to be more effective users of information. Indeed, in many cases, the core business of the company has changed to the point that information is now the main product the company is selling. Equally important, as companies merge and develop a worldwide presence, instantaneous communications are imperative to survival. Similarly, as companies eliminate support staff and empower lower-level employees, it becomes important that every employee be able to access and manipulate critical information that might reside on other computers and in databases anywhere in the world.

Distributed object technology provides the basis for the major information system changes the companies desire. Such significant change can hardly be accomplished overnight, but the possible benefits have motivated leading companies to initiate efforts that should result in radical improvements by the end of this decade.

THE ESSENCE OF OBJECT TECHNOLOGY

Many readers will already have a good grasp of the basics of object technology and should probably simply skip this section. For those who are new to the subject, however, we want to provide a very brief guide to the essential elements of object technology.

An object is a complex data type that contains other data types, usually called attributes, and modules of code, usually called methods or operations. The attributes and associated values are "hidden" inside the object. Any other object that wants to obtain or change a value associated with the first object must do so by sending a message to one of the first object's methods. Each object's own methods manage that object's attributes. This is called *encapsulation.* If encapsulation is enforced, it means that objects don't know or care how other objects store or process data. One object sends a message to another object's method and that method, in turn, replies or takes action (see Figure 1.1).

To appreciate objects, you must contrast them with the basic elements of conventional programming. A conventional software system is comprised of a block of procedural code—the program—and data, which is independent of the procedural code and is stored in flat files or a database. In a conventional application, all of the procedural code is stored as a single module and any changes in the program must be carefully made to assure that changes at one point in the code don't have unwanted side effects elsewhere. Similarly, since the procedural code calls the data, any changes must be carefully made to assure that one procedure

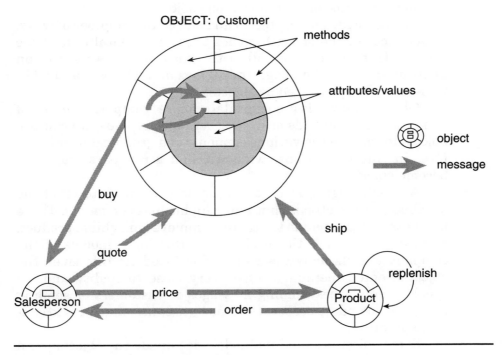

FIGURE 1.1 Objects and messages.

doesn't change the data in inappropriate ways before another procedure can use the data. It's possible to modularize a conventional program—that's exactly what the structured methodologies were aiming at—but the very nature of the approach guarantees that modularization will usually be limited and that modifications will be difficult.

Figure 1.2 contrasts a conventional application and an object-oriented application. Unlike the monolithic procedural application, an object-oriented application is modularized in the sense that each object is independent of any other. Moreover, the procedural code is modularized in the sense that each object contains several independent methods. A message usually only triggers a single method. If a change needs to be made, the developer often only needs to change one method. If changes are made to the internal data structures, the developer can be confident that the only procedural code changes that need to be made will involve the methods associated with that one object.

The basic idea of an object can be used in a number of ways. In some cases, the object becomes the fundamental unit of the system. In this situation, all of the basic concepts used in an application—including bags and strings and numbers and addition—are all represented as objects.

Objects may also encapsulate more complex groups of attributes and methods or even other objects. Thus, we can use objects to capture the various elements of a graphical user interface. In this case, icons, windows, and scroll bars and tools become objects.

At a still higher level, an object can encapsulate all of the attributes and methods that make up business elements. These business objects include things like employee, machine, product, plan, and customer. Using objects of this kind, models of the company and its activities can be developed. At this level, the object-oriented metaphor comes very close to reality and we speak of employees sending messages to customers or sending messages to update corporate plans or to cause machines to generate products.

Some object-oriented methodologies divide the objects in an application into interface objects, business objects, and database

A Conventional Application

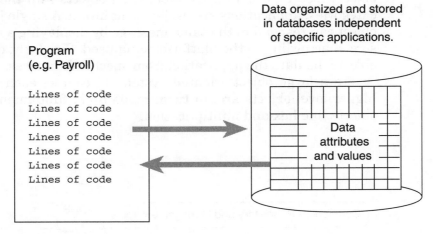

Data organized and stored in databases independent of specific applications.

Program
(e.g. Payroll)

Lines of code
Lines of code
Lines of code
Lines of code
Lines of code
Lines of code
Lines of code

Data attributes and values

An Object-Oriented Application

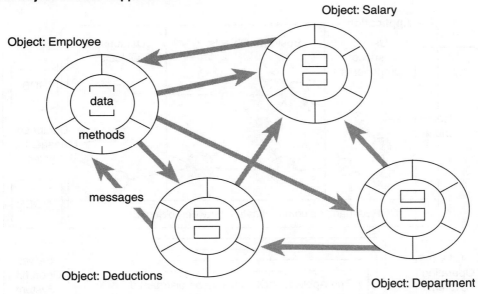

Object: Salary

Object: Employee

data

methods

messages

Object: Deductions

Object: Department

FIGURE 1.2 A conventional procedural application contrasted with an object-oriented application.

objects (see Figure 1.3). By separating objects into these three categories, applications are easier to maintain. A single interface object can respond to the same message by displaying a different screen according to the platform being used. Similarly, database objects insulate the application from specific databases.

In a large object-oriented system, of course, each of these higher-level objects are, in turn, made up of fundamental code objects like hex and multiplication.

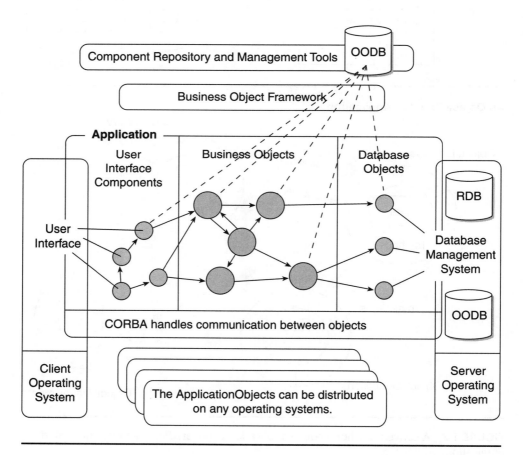

FIGURE 1.3 An application composed of three broad groups of objects: interface, business, and database objects.

Objects can also be used to encapsulate existing programs. Thus, if a company needs to continue to use a large legacy system—say the application that handles the company payroll— the entire application can be placed inside an object and access to the system can henceforth be managed by methods associated with the legacy application. In fact, although we speak of the application as being placed inside an object, normally an object simply serves as an interface to the legacy application, taking messages directed at the legacy application, causing the application to run and then sending the results back to other objects. In a similar way we can encapsulate databases with objects that stand between other objects and the database.

At an even higher level of abstraction, computer platforms can be considered objects. This is, in a sense, what an object request broker (ORB) does. It treats each platform as an object with a set of methods and manages the messages that are sent between the different platforms.

Some of these different uses of object technology are illustrated in Figure 1.4. The variety of different ways that object concepts can be used might make them confusing at first. Once the basic concepts are understood, however, object technology becomes a very powerful technology because the same basic concepts can be used at many different levels of abstraction and in many different situations. In fact, object technology can become the great unifying concept underlying all software systems.

Objects are much more complex than their basic structure and the fact that they communicate via messages. We can subdivide objects into classes—templates that have methods and attribute types but no actual values—and instances that are generated by the classes and that actually contain the values.

Objects can be arranged in hierarchies so that more concrete classes and instances obtain data structures and methods from more abstract classes. This is called *inheritance*. By adding new attributes and methods or changing the code associated with inherited methods, more concrete classes can be specialized. Thus, we might begin with a class that describes employees and then create two subclasses that are each specialized so that one represents hourly employees and the other represents salaried employees. Because we reuse most of the code that is associated

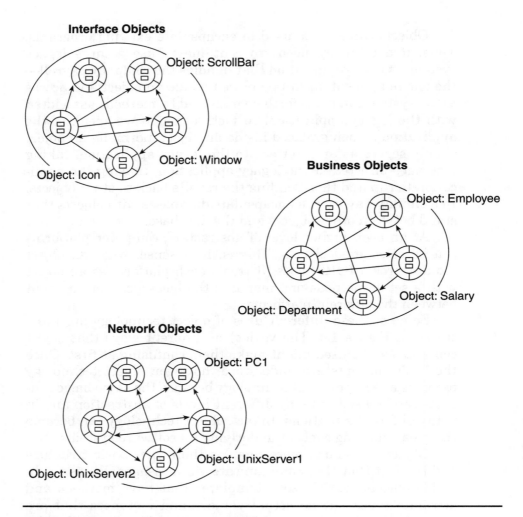

FIGURE 1.4 Objects used in different kinds of systems.

with the employee class and only need to add a few refinements to the classes for hourly and salaried employees, object-oriented development tends to go faster than conventional programming.

Different objects can have methods with the same name. This means that an object can send a PRINT message to several objects and each object will use its own method to execute the

Classes are templates that can be used to generate instances.

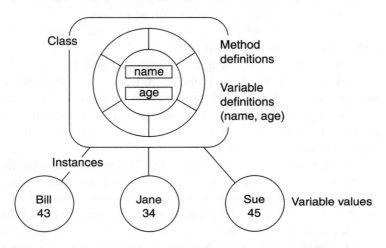

Classes can be arranged in hierarchies. Subclasses inherit attributes and values from superclasses.

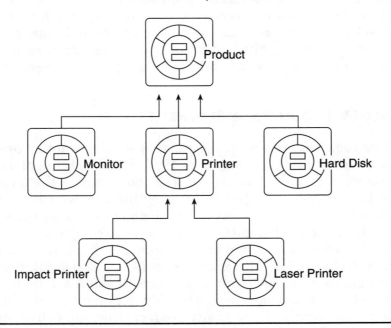

FIGURE 1.5 Some basic object concepts.

PRINT command. This ability of objects to respond in different ways to the same command is called *polymorphism*.

Figure 1.5 illustrates some of these basic object technology concepts in a very general way.

Of course it gets much more technical than we have suggested here but we don't want to go into any more detail because we expect that most of our readers already understand the basics. If you would like more detailed information, we recommend that you read some of the introductory books we have listed in the Bibliography.

All we wanted to do in this brief section is to provide enough of an overview of object technology to help someone new to object technology understand how it facilitates modularization. We also wanted to emphasize how the same basic concepts can be used to develop operating systems and applications, to create networks, and to model high level business process. This, in turn, should convince the reader that object technology is fundamentally new and a very basic approach to software development. Moreover, object technology is a very comprehensive approach that allows developers to reconceptualize how to create and manage everything from coding bits and bytes to coding large applications or designing worldwide networks of heterogeneous computers.

TECHNOLOGY, PRODUCTS, AND BENEFITS

This book has been written for managers who want an overview of where object technology is in 1996. Space does not allow us to provide a detailed technical discussion of any of the more specialized aspects of object technology. Instead, we have stressed the approaches to application development taken by the various finalists and the benefits obtained by each company.

Developers are often excited about the intrinsic qualities of new technologies. Managers, in general, aren't interested in technologies, as such, but in the benefits that accrue from the use of one technology or another. Vendors tend to mix different technologies in order to create products that can deliver desired benefits. Technology purists may decry the compromises incorporated in products, but the compromises are often necessary to

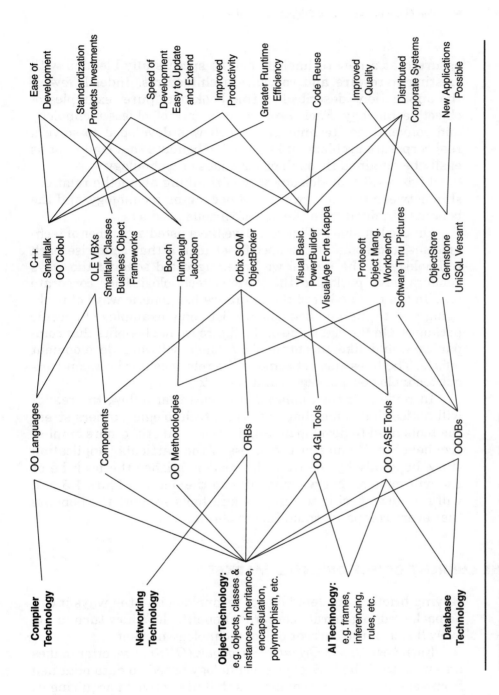

FIGURE 1.6 Technologies, products, and benefits.

assure that a new technology can be successfully blended with existing hardware and software architectures. Indeed, few of the applications described in this book are "pure" examples of object technology. Each represents a mix of object technology and conventional technologies. Each was developed to solve a real corporate problem and to provide benefits that could not as easily be obtained through other mixes of technology.

Figure 1.6 provides one way of thinking about the relationship between technology, ways of packaging technology, and the benefits obtained from the use of various products.

On the left side of Figure 1.6 we have listed a number of technologies and some of the specific elements that comprise each technology. In the middle we have suggested some of the ways vendors have packaged the various technologies for corporate use. To the middle-left of the figure we list generic ways of packaging and to the middle-right we list some examples of specific packages. On the right side of the figure we list benefits that companies would like to obtain from their software development efforts. The lines suggest some of the relationships between various technologies, packages, and benefits.

In reviewing the application stories that follow, the reader will notice that some chapters stress technologies, others stress the tools used to develop an application, and still others emphasize benefits. No matter the stress of the particular application story, hopefully by the time the reader finishes the book he or she will have an overview similar to the one in Figure 1.5 and will see how specific techniques and tools support the benefits that every company would like to obtain.

THE CURRENT OBJECT-ORIENTED MARKET

Having briefly considered object technology and the ways it can be packaged to generate corporate benefits, let's now turn to the overall size of the current object technology market.

Each year *Object-Oriented Strategies (OOS)* newsletter makes an estimate of the U.S. object technology based on data obtained from vendors and from companies that are active in acquiring it. Anyone who has made an effort to estimate a market as diverse as object technologies will know that any figures are only approximations and estimates. The figures developed by *OOS* are rather conservative. By believing everything the vendors say, or by including products like Microsoft Windows, which contains OLE and other object-oriented technology, for example, one can easily generate much higher figures. Given that all projections of new software markets involve quite a bit of guesswork, however, we believe that the *OOS* figures give a reasonably accurate account of what is happening in the object technologies marketplace.

The *OOS* projections were generated in 1995 and describe the object technologies market as it stood at the beginning of 1995. According to *OOS*, total worldwide sales of all object-oriented development products sold by North American vendors and foreign vendors selling object-oriented development products within North America amounted to $915 million in 1994. This represented an increase of $244 million in sales compared to revenues generated from sales of similar products in 1993. Overall sales of object-oriented development products increased by slightly more than 36 percent over an approximate one-year period.

Figure 1.7 provides a breakdown of the total sales in 1994 for all object-oriented software development products by their respective market niches. Summarizing these figures, we see that at $376 million, the market for object-oriented languages is still the largest niche in the overall object-oriented marketplace. Ranking second are sales of object-oriented application development environments and tools (object-oriented ADTs), which accounted for $282 million in sales in 1994. The third largest niche in the object-oriented market is for object-oriented databases. Sales of object-oriented database products accounted for $150 million in 1994. Object-oriented CASE tools, which include object-oriented A&D and integrated object-oriented I-CASE environments (model/object-oriented methodology-based tools) generated $76 million in sales in 1994. Object-oriented class libraries and object-oriented framework products accounted for $30 million in sales in 1994.

Figure 1.8 provides an overview of overall sales of object-oriented development products for the four years that *OOS* has tracked them. The findings indicate that sales of these products

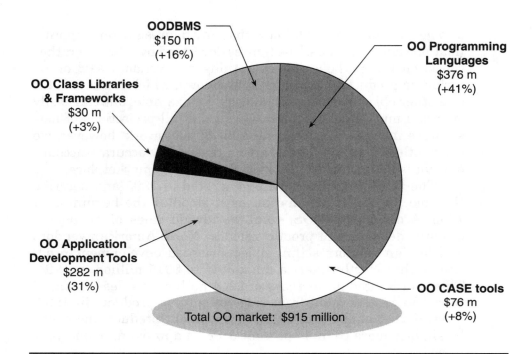

OODBMS
$150 m
(+16%)

**OO Programming
Languages**
$376 m
(+41%)

**OO Class Libraries
& Frameworks**
$30 m
(+3%)

**OO Application
Development Tools**
$282 m
(31%)

OO CASE tools
$76 m
(+8%)

Total OO market: $915 million

FIGURE 1.7 The object-oriented development tools market in 1994 by market segment (all numbers in millions).

have increased every year from 1991 through 1994. In comparing yearly sales for this period, we see that revenues increased 25, 90, and 36 percent respectively over each preceding year.

In 1991, Geoffrey Moore wrote *Crossing the Chasm,* in which he described the lifecycles of several new technologies. Successful technologies tend to follow an adoption pattern that resembles a bell-shaped curve. In each case, however, Moore notes that the progression up the curve isn't as smooth as one might expect. The move from the labs to companies that are willing to experiment with new technology goes smoothly enough. A gap occurs, however, between the early adapters and widespread acceptance. Figure 1.9 illustrates the gap or chasm, as Moore called it, that typically occurs. Successful new technologies cross the gap. Unsuccessful technologies fall into the gap. I'm sure we can all think of some

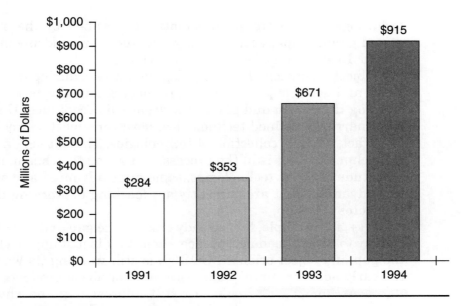

FIGURE 1.8 Growth of the object technology market.

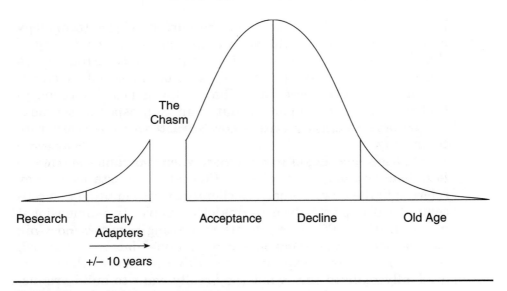

FIGURE 1.9 Object technology is beginning to cross the chasm.

technologies that were given a fantastic reception by the press, gained ground rapidly for several years, and then suddenly disappeared. In effect, they fell into Moore's chasm.

Object technology has enjoyed great success during its early years and some object-oriented products are in the process of crossing the chasm and gaining widespread acceptance. Unlike more narrowly defined technologies, however, object technology is, in fact, a whole collection of technologies. Thus, it isn't a single technology that is in the process of crossing the chasm, it's a multitude of object technologies, some more advanced and some less advanced, that are currently approaching or working their way across the gap.

C++, for example, has already crossed the gap and is well on its way to widespread acceptance. Smalltalk is just approaching the gap and object-oriented COBOL is still working its way up the early adapter curve. Object-oriented database products and object-oriented CASE tools are still approaching the chasm, while object-oriented methodologies seem ready to jump across.

CORPORATE COMPUTING INFRASTRUCTURES

Returning from the specifics of the current object technology market to the broader themes we laid out at the beginning of this chapter, the major transition that has occurred in the nineties does not involve the acceptance of any specific technology, but the broader acceptance that computing can be reconceptualized and that companies that want to prosper in the next decade must begin to create a new infrastructure for corporate computing.

At the beginning of the nineties, when companies started to focus on building networks of PCs and workstations, they referred to the new approach as client/server computing and conceptualized it primarily in terms of a simple, two-dimensional model in which PCs were clients requesting services and Unix workstations were servers on which relational databases resided. As companies have experimented with this model, they have gradually realized that what they really want to build are distributed systems that can link a wide variety of different types of platforms together. Moreover, architects increasingly realize that they don't want to be limited to clients and servers—they want every computer to function, as occasion demands, as either a client or a server. Systems designers are also increasingly aware that object-based networks provide the best middleware to use to tie all the various parts of a distributed system together.

In the next chapter we'll go on to consider how object technology is being used in each of several specific areas of computing. Later, we'll consider specific applications that will illustrate the variety of ways object technology is being applied. For the manager, however, the most important thing to take away from this discussion is the fundamental nature of object technology: the fact that object technology, when properly understood, provides a powerful new way to conceptualize the entire software effort.

The Various Uses of Object Technology

This chapter will provide the reader with an overview of the current activity in the commercial object technology market. We'll consider several different areas, and, in each case, try to define the role that object technology is playing within that area and what role it is likely to play in the near future. Later, when we consider specific applications, we'll discuss how the applications discussed in this book illustrate the general comments in this chapter.

One major trend in object technology is to break down any sharp barriers and to mix together categories that have previously been considered separately. This occurs because object technology tends to focus on the object or component and form larger units by combining components. Thus, where in the past there was a reasonably well understood distinction between an operating system and an application, that distinction is becoming increasingly blurred as people develop applications that incorporate components that are provided by the operating system. We'll try, in the following discussion, to discuss each of the following niches without overlapping too much, but the reader should realize that sharp distinctions are no longer as valid as they once were. We'll consider eight areas where object technology is being used:

- Object-oriented operating systems
- Object-oriented networks, middleware, and Internet products
- Object-oriented class and component libraries and frameworks
- Object-oriented languages and environments
- Object-oriented client/server application development tools
- Object-oriented CASE and object-oriented BPR tools
- Object-oriented methodologies
- Object-oriented and object-oriented/RDB databases

OBJECT-ORIENTED OPERATING SYSTEMS

Many people are talking about object-oriented operating systems, but none of the currently popular operating systems are based on an object-oriented design. The closest anyone comes, at the moment, is NextStep, and that is probably better classified as an object-oriented framework rather than an operating system. Taligent originally claimed that it was developing an object-oriented operating system but have since decided to focus on creating a framework. Microsoft claims that its 1998 successor to Windows, which is code-named Cairo, will be an object-oriented operating system, but it probably won't be. Instead, it will probably be a framework sitting on top of a DOS/Windows kernel.

The main trend in the operating system market is to convert monolithic operating systems to kernel-based operating systems along the lines pioneered by Carnegie-Mellon's Mach version of Unix. This results in a modular operating system design and makes it easy to mix and match framework components from other sources with the core or kernel of the operating system.

We don't expect to see a real object-oriented operating system in the near future. We expect that all the real action will be focused on creating object-oriented frameworks that can work with the non-object-oriented kernel architectures that appear within the next two to three years.

OBJECT-ORIENTED NETWORKS, MIDDLEWARE, AND INTERNET PRODUCTS

A major trend in corporate computing is toward distributed systems. An even broader trend is toward Internet-based systems where each computer becomes a node in some larger network. In either case, to make this happen, we need to develop a technology that allows an application running on one computer to find any resources it needs from other computers. Moreover, to work efficiently, resources must be found without the user needing to know where the resources are located or having to specify the path the computer needs to follow to access them.

In 1990, when companies first began to consider how to build distributed computing environments, they initially turned to simple client/server designs. A simple client/server design links a number of clients, usually PCs running Windows, to a server, usually a workstation running Unix. A relational database management system (RDBMS) on the server provides data to each client, as needed. There are various ways to link the clients to the servers, but most early systems relied on remote procedure calls (RPCs). In other words, the clients were "hardwired" to the server in a rigid, procedural manner that makes the client/server system difficult to modify. Simple client/server systems are satisfactory to simply link some users to a RDB, but they don't provide the basis for more complex distributed systems.

Client/server systems have been extended beyond the simple systems I described by incorporating departmental servers and linking those, in turn, to a mainframe server in so-called "three-tiered" client/server systems. These systems, while more complex, are still, however, really only database access systems and they are generally linked by procedural code that is hard to modify.

Once companies satisfy the need for simple or three-tiered client/server systems to access established RDBs, they usually arrive at the real challenge: creating distributed or peer-to-peer systems. In a distributed network, any node can be either a client or server, as occasion demands. A distributed system should allow any user to access applications or data on any other computer in the network. Moreover, it should allow a user to access programs or data on several different systems, as needed. In addition, most enterprise-wide distributed systems require that the architecture be flexible to allow for the constant addition and subtraction of nodes and for mobile nodes (i.e., laptop systems that may want to access the network for services from almost any location). When companies focus on these kinds of problems, they usually turn to object-oriented approaches to provide the flexibility they require. In effect, instead of thinking of each computer as either a client or server, distributed object systems tend to conceptualize all the data and programs on the network in terms of objects and use the network to pass messages between these objects. Distributed object systems typically separate the client object from the server object and store routing information in an intermediate object system called an object request broker (ORB). An ORB provides the flexibility that large distributed systems require. It eliminates the hardwired links between specific clients and servers and make it easy to add and subtract nodes from the network.

An ORB is a kind of middleware that stands between clients and servers. Unlike the various procedural types of middleware that are popular at the moment, an ORB supports flexibility. Most of the middleware that most companies are currently using simply creates hardwired systems that will rapidly become the next generation of legacy applications with all the maintenance problems that the older legacy applications typically have.

At the moment there is one established standard for ORBs —the Object Management Group's Common Object Request Broker Architecture (CORBA). This standard is still evolving. When the applications described in this book were developed, the various implementations of CORBA did not talk with each other. That problem has now been overcome with the CORBA2 specification; a new generation of ORB applications will begin to appear in 1996, consisting of distributed systems in which several different versions of CORBA are used. In addition, the OMG is continuing to define ORB support services that will facilitate the development of more complex distributed applications.

The alternative to CORBA is Microsoft's promise to introduce a distributed version of its OLE2 product, which we'll consider in the next section. The pervasiveness of Windows and Windows/NT, which will include OLE2 by 1996 and will probably include the distributed version of OLE in 1997, has led many to expect that OLE2 will establish a de facto ORB at some point in the future. We doubt this. First, OMG has a considerable head start. Moreover, CORBA2 is an open standard that runs on every possible hardware platform and it is supported by almost every major hardware and software vendor. Distributed OLE may become an option for smaller companies and departments that only use Windows and Windows/NT operating systems, but companies that are serious about enterprise-wide, distributed systems are surely going to opt for CORBA. Microsoft is trying to resist this trend in an effort to preserve its proprietary lock on the desktop operating system market, but we expect that once Microsoft perceives the problems with this approach they will become more supportive of OLE-CORBA links and companies will proceed to build CORBA enterprise systems that can connect to Windows applications, when necessary, via OLE.

We'll consider ORBs in more detail when we discuss some of the distributed applications in Section II.

The Internet is the most dynamic phenomena on the current computing scene. As the Internet is currently configured, it lacks middleware that is capable of supporting more complex uses. We won't go into detail at this point, since none of the applications considered in this book involve the use on the Internet. We note, however, that new object-oriented languages, like Java, and extensions of Internet protocols to incorporate ORBs will be necessary if the Internet is to continue to grow and realize its full potential.

OBJECT-ORIENTED CLASS AND COMPONENT LIBRARIES AND FRAMEWORKS

Much of the interest in object technology has always been motivated by the promise of reuse. Object-oriented promoters have argued that in the future applications would be assembled from standardized code components rather like today's computers are assembled from standardized parts. Some of the applications described in this book will provide a good illustration of how this goal is in the process of being realized. In general, however, the development of the infrastructure necessary to support component-built applications is still being put in place and it will be several years before component-based development becomes a common practice.

One key issue involves the size of the components that will be used. At first, since many object-oriented developers were focused on object-oriented languages, they assumed that reuse would be based on small-scale classes that are used in Smalltalk and C++ development. Recently, more attention has been focused on mid-sized components like those used in linking and embedding standard PC applications. Increasingly, however, object-oriented gurus are focusing on the development of very large-scale components, usually termed business objects or domain objects, that encapsulated all of the functionality required for a major business concept—objects like "machine," "employee," "customer," and "product." In fact, for the foreseeable future, object-oriented applications will be built by combining various kinds and sizes of components, as the applications in this book illustrate.

The component market is especially confusing because there are so many different things going under the name of components. Figure 2.1 provides an overview of the component market.

On the horizontal axis we have classified components according to size. The vertical axis focuses on the difference between what a single component is called and what a larger set of the same components is called.

Small components tend to be used in object-oriented language-based application development. An individual component tends to be called a class and a group is called a class library. Class libraries may be generic groups of classes or they may be designed to support specific programming functions. The class libraries that come with Smalltalk are good examples of small components.

The typical class in a Smalltalk class library has about 40 bytes of data. Most small objects are designed to facilitate the rapid coding of applications in a specific programming language. Classes like Hash, Bag, Max, and Date are included in class libraries accompanying Smalltalk, C++, and other object-oriented

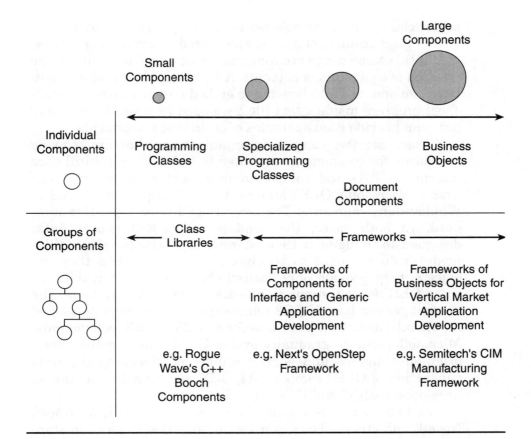

FIGURE 2.1   An overview of components.

languages. The class libraries accompanying object-oriented languages also tend to include classes (often called Widgets) to assist in the development of graphical interfaces—classes like Button, PushButton, Window, and ScrollBar. C++ libraries like those provided by Microsoft and Rogue Wave provide similar capabilities.

In the mid-sized range are specialized programming classes— classes and class libraries designed to support more specialized programming functions like database access or expert system development. A framework of classes like IBM's SOM, designed to implement CORBA and provide an easy way to import and export classes from one object-oriented language to another, provides a good example of a set of specialized programming classes.

In this same range are components designed to facilitate the creation of compound documents. A set of OLE2 or a set of Open-Doc components that allow me to embed a figure from a spreadsheet program inside a text file developed by a word processing program provide good examples of document components.

There are two competing organizations that are offering standards for components designed to facilitate graphical user interface (GUI) and compound document development. The first is Microsoft's OLE2 standard, which is primarily used in Windows environments. The second is CI Labs' OpenDoc standard. In both cases, the vendors talk about the modules designed to implement their standards as components. OLE2 modules do not need to be objects, and even when they are objects, they provide only limited object-oriented capabilities, since OLE doesn't support inheritance or polymorphism. The current generation of OLE2 components are typically developed in Visual Basic and are sometimes called VBX components. Microsoft plans to gradually evolve OLE2 into a more object-oriented standard and is increasingly emphasizing the next generation of OLE2 components, OCX components that can be developed with Visual C++ 2.0.

CI Labs is a consortium of vendors, including IBM, Apple, Novell, and others. The OpenDoc specification is an open standard and is fully object-oriented. (An OpenDoc component is a SOM object that has a specific set of sixty methods added.) A number of different vendors are creating OpenDoc components for a wide variety of operating systems.

Some object-oriented experts combine specialized class libraries and document components and call them, collectively, technical objects or technical components.

Groups of specialized programming classes are sometimes called class libraries, but it is currently more common to refer to them as frameworks. Similarly, groups of document components are also referred to as frameworks.

The largest components are those that encapsulate the major concepts of a business and they are typically called either domain or business objects. Groups of business objects are called frameworks.

It's important to distinguish between frameworks of technical objects that are typically used in generic application efforts and frameworks of business objects that are only used for developing domain-specific applications. Thus, a technical framework like Next's OpenStep can be used for any application development effort since it provides components for GUI development, database access, and so on. On the other hand, a business framework like Semitech's CIM Manufacturing Framework is more specialized and is really only useful for developing semiconductor applications.

As a generalization, you get more reuse and faster application development as you use large components. This occurs because most of the effort in a typical application effort occurs in the analysis and design stage and not in the coding stage. In effect, a business object framework contains an implicit analysis and design approach and significantly reduces the analysis and design effort required on an application development team. A Smalltalk class library, on the other hand, although it certainly saves time and effort, is only helpful during the coding phase of the application effort and thus cannot have the impact that large components have when they significantly reduce the analysis and design phases of the effort.

Another aspect of component-based development that should also be considered involves creating components that encapsulate or serve as gateways for existing legacy applications. Objects in the system send messages to other objects that stand for the legacy application. The legacy application object then passes necessary parameters to the legacy application, obtains the results once the legacy application has done its thing, and passes the results, via a message, back to the original object. In effect, the legacy system becomes a special kind of business object that performs some large-scale task, like payroll generation. One very powerful feature of object technology is its ability to easily integrate existing legacy applications with new object-oriented applications. Some companies encapsulate entire legacy applications as a single object and simply leave the legacy application as it was. In other situations, a company will modularize a legacy application so that it can systematically begin to replace modules and transition from the legacy application to an object-oriented replacement in easy steps.

To date, most reuse stories involve the use of class libraries. Those who have used class libraries are happy that the coding effort goes much faster. Managers who have evaluated the overall saving, however, have not been so impressed. To obtain the productivity increases that object-oriented advocates have promised, object-oriented development will need to group class libraries and technical objects together into business objects that can, when used, reduce the overall development effort by orders of magnitude.

Unfortunately, while class libraries and components are available from vendors, most companies are forced to develop their own business objects. Some industries have created consortiums to help with this process, but it still requires a major commitment. Moreover, it must usually wait until after a company has developed several object-oriented applications and learns exactly what concepts are best packaged as business objects for reuse. To make matters worse, the use of business objects requires that a company change its basic IS operations. Individuals must be made responsible for creating and maintaining business objects. Other individuals must be responsible for cataloging and storing business objects. Incentive systems must be changed to assure that programmers are rewarded for writing less code rather than more code, for example.

None of this is to suggest that object technology will not deliver on its reuse promises, but it will take longer than some early enthusiasts suggested.

OBJECT-ORIENTED LANGUAGES AND ENVIRONMENTS

As we noted earlier, most companies began to explore object technology by developing applications in object-oriented languages. This tendency is well represented in this book where most of the applications were developed via object-oriented languages. Currently, there is a move toward object-oriented 4GL tools and object-oriented CASE tools, but it will be two or three years from now before large applications developed in tools become the rule rather than the exception.

The two dominant object-oriented languages are C++ and Smalltalk. C++ has over 65 percent of the overall object-oriented language market, but Smalltalk is increasing its share very rapidly. Initially, most object-oriented applications were developed on workstations, where C was well entrenched, and thus C++ developed a strong lead. As companies have begun to develop larger, enterprise-wide applications, however, they have begun to pay more attention to Smalltalk. Many of the large applications are being developed by programmers who have a COBOL rather than a C background, and it turns out that it's a lot easier to learn Smalltalk than C or C++. Smalltalk is also popular with developers who want to create complex graphical interfaces on PCs or workstations.

The major complaints against C++ is its complexity and its difficulty. In addition, C++ is not an interpreted language and hence is not so flexible; it allows developers the opportunity of mixing C and C++ techniques to create truly awful code. The major complaints against Smalltalk are that it is interpreted and therefore runs slightly slower than C++ and that it takes up so much room on machines. Newer machines and newer versions of Smalltalk have reduced the speed problem so that it is negligible in most cases. Moreover, the latest versions of Smalltalk are being modularized, which should significantly reduce the memory they require in runtime environments. The applications described in this book are nearly evenly split between C++ and Smalltalk. In at least one case, the developer reports starting in C++ and then moving to Smalltalk to take advantage of its easier development environment. In another case, the developers used both C++ and Smalltalk, using Smalltalk for rapid interface development and C++ in areas where speed was very important.

There are several other good object-oriented languages, like Objective C and CLOS, and there are also object-based languages, like Ada, which is used by the U.S. military. Both CLOS and Ada are represented in this book.

The key is dynamics and how much you value it. Smalltalk, Objective C, and CLOS are all interpreted languages and they are all more dynamic, making complex programming much easier.

The major unknown in the object-oriented language arena is the role that object-oriented COBOL will play. Object-oriented COBOL has only recently become available and was not used for any of the applications in this book, but it will undoubtedly be used more in the near future. Just as most C programmers prefer to move to C++ rather than Smalltalk, it may turn out that most COBOL programmers will prefer to move to object-oriented COBOL rather than Smalltalk.

There is another new object-oriented language, Java, that is getting a lot of attention at the moment. In the abstract, it seems like a poor time to introduce a new object-oriented language. Java is an interpreted object-oriented language, like Objective C and Smalltalk, that uses a C-like syntax. It is designed to be used for Internet applications. In conventional Internet commerce, I send a name to a site and get a file back. Using Java, I can send a name and get a program back. This means that individuals can sign on to company systems and access applications they need to interact with via Internet. Equally important, Java is designed to run in a self-contained space on each platform. Thus, it doesn't make any different what hardware or what operating system I'm running when I request an applet from a server. I get a Java applet that will run on my machine. This has lots of people excited. Moreover, some of the people who have been using Java for Internet applications have begun to wonder why they shouldn't be using it for general applications as well. It's a long shot, but Internet is attracting such attention that it might just launch a new object-oriented language as a side effect.

We have discussed object-oriented languages because that's the most common way to develop object-oriented applications. It's important to keep in mind, however, that object-oriented development can be done in any Turing language, as one object-oriented application written in COBOL demonstrates. Object orientation lies in the design of the application, not in the language, as such. Most developers, however, won't want to go to the trouble of creating lots of special and idiosyncratic functionality in an established language when they can use an object-oriented language that is specifically designed for object-oriented development.

OBJECT-ORIENTED APPLICATION DEVELOPMENT TOOLS

Many of the object-oriented languages (compilers) come with extensive class libraries and development utilities and could just as well be called object-oriented development environments. When we use the term "tool," we suggest that the product is configured more like a program and less like a language compiler plus browsers and class libraries—but we admit that it's a rather fuzzy distinction.

The object-oriented application development tools (object-oriented ADTs) niche is one of the most difficult because there are a lot of rather different products that can be put under this umbrella. It is also difficult because the products in this category are often the most difficult to classify as object-oriented, object-based, or simply object-wanna-be products.

When you consider any product in the object-oriented ADT area, you need to consider several things. First, you need to consider if the tool provides an internal or scripting language that provides a full complement of object-oriented techniques. Does it support inheritance and subclassing, for example? If it doesn't, then it's probably best to call it an object-based product.

Next, you want to consider the degree to which the developer can actually access any object-oriented capabilities the tool is alleged to have. Some vendors will suggest that because their product was written in an object-oriented language it should be called an object-oriented product. I refer to this difference by asking if the object-oriented capabilities are on the dashboard so that a developer or an end user could access them, or if they are under the hood so that only the people who developed the tool can access them.

You should probably mentally divide the tool into three parts: a part that can be used to develop and manipulate user interfaces, a part that can support object modeling and contains application logic, and a part that accesses data from databases. Any one of these parts could be object-based or object-oriented. One can use an object-oriented ADT that relies on SQL to access RDBs or one can use an object-oriented ADT that provides database objects. In the second case, the developer simply arranges to send a message to a database object and that object handles the links between itself and an RDB. Figure 2.2 illustrates this.

You should also consider whether the tool runs on a client or a server, or whether it is distributed and can run on a combination of clients and servers. Some object-oriented ADTs help the developer distribute the application across various platforms. Some provide CORBA to handle distribution.

Finally, if you are considering a complex application that will entail very complex logic or the use of lots of business rules, you should consider if you will need inferencing and the rule capabilities of an object-oriented tool that has AI (artificial intelligence) components.

There are many ways to subdivide the object-oriented application development environments. We tend to divide them into the following five groups:

1. GUI development tools
2. Simple object-based client/server tools
3. Object-oriented client/server tools
4. Object-oriented distributed tools
5. Object-oriented AI tools

The matrix illustrated in Figure 2.3 illustrates how we might distinguish the five categories. On one axis we consider the nature of the internal language of the tool. Does it provide some or all of the object-oriented techniques one finds in a complete object-oriented language? At the extreme, does it provide inferencing and rule techniques as well. On the other axis we consider how well the tool handles distribution. Simpler products like the GUI tools and the simpler object-based tools are platform specific, or at most they support rather rigid client/ server models. The object-oriented client/server tools tend to support more flexible client/server models. A few tools support

The extent that object techniques are used in Powersoft's PowerBuilder

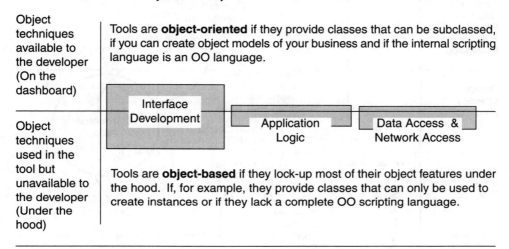

The extent that object techniques are used in IBM's VisualAge/Smalltalk

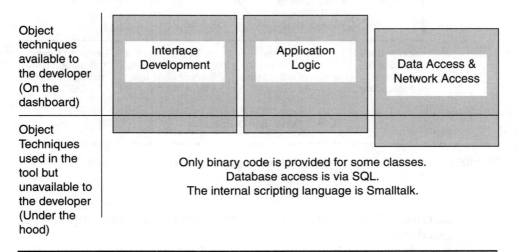

FIGURE 2.2 One way of analyzing application development tools.

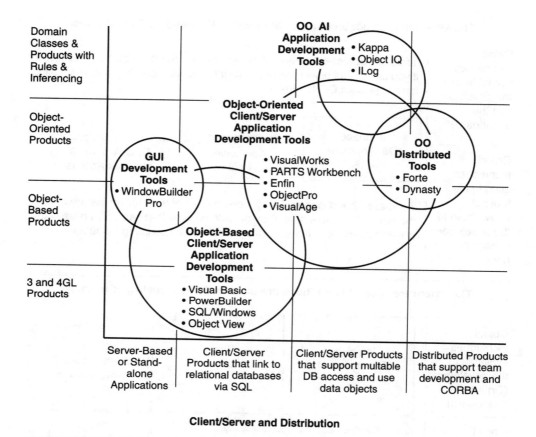

FIGURE 2.3 A classification of object-oriented application development tools.

distributed object-oriented environments and a few support AI capabilities.

■ Object-based or object-oriented GUI development tools are specialized products that make it easy to develop an interface for one or more operating systems. They are used because the current generation of operating systems make it very difficult to program interfaces. At some point in the future the operating systems will be supplemented by frameworks of interface components or will be object oriented and the market for these tools will disappear, just as windows tools have disappeared now that

DOS and Unix have been enhanced by standardized windows interfaces.

When the market first developed an interest in client/server applications, products that could support GUI development on Microsoft Windows 3.x and link to standard RDBs became very popular. PowerBuilder is probably the best example of a tool that falls in this group. In effect, these products were modern fourth generation languages (4GLs) and they proved very popular with departmental developers.

As companies have tried to tackle larger client/server problems, they have turned to more sophisticated ADTs, usually with complete object-oriented capabilities. They have also begun to use ADTs specifically designed to support distributed application development.

The ADT market is very unstable, however, because it is pressed on the one side by component frameworks, OLE2 products and OpenDoc implementations, and on the other side by distributed OLE and CORBA products that will form the new basis for distributed computing. The most we can be sure of is that all the tools in this category will continue to evolve and change in the years ahead.

OBJECT-ORIENTED CASE AND OBJECT-ORIENTED BPR TOOLS

Object-oriented application development tools, as we use the term, refers to tools designed for an incremental approach to object-oriented development. Using an ADT, one frequently begins by developing user screens or by arranging links to a pre-existing RDB. You can use object-oriented methodologies with these tools to assist in developing the application logic, but methodologies play a minor role in most ADT development efforts.

Object-oriented CASE tools, on the other hand, rely heavily on object-oriented methodologies. Object-oriented CASE tools are designed for a top-down approach to application development. One normally begins with an analysis of the object model that will guide the application process. The best object-oriented CASE tools allow the developer to specify the entire application in object-oriented diagrams and then generate code from those specifications. Most object-oriented CASE tools aren't so comprehensive: They allow the developer to create an object model and then generate skeletal code—leaving the developer to write the actual code that comprises the methods.

We usually divide object-oriented CASE tools into three categories:

1. Object-oriented analysis and design tools (generate diagrams)
2. Object-oriented CASE tools (generate skeletal code)
3. Comprehensive object-oriented CASE tools (generate complete code)

Most object-oriented CASE tools support several of the current object-oriented methodologies. Some "metaCASE" tools are designed so the developer can define the methodology the CASE tool will support. Most object-oriented CASE tools generate a single type of code (usually C/C++), although some generate more than one type of code.

Object-oriented BPR and object-oriented workflow tools constitute a new and rapidly expanding area for object technology developers. Business process re-engineering began in the early nineties and has been accumulating momentum since then. For some, BPR is just a new name for software development. Instead of saying that the company is going to automate the payroll function, some would say that they are going to re-engineer the payroll function. Others, however, use the term to mean something more like Hammer and Champy meant when they coined it. For these folks, BPR is a radical redesign of a business process. It usually involves a software development effort, but it typically involves many other changes as well, and the emphasis is on a very serious revision of an existing business process. In most cases, serious BPR efforts involve using new methodologies that have been created to help corporate managers radically rethink how a business process is accomplished. Several software vendors are in the process of creating software tools to assist in BPR analysis and design efforts. Some of these new software tools are object-oriented BPR tools. In addition, several existing object-oriented vendors have repositioned their products and suggested that they can be used in BPR efforts. The object-oriented CASE vendors and some of the AI object orientation vendors have been particularly active in this repositioning effort.

Three applications described in this book involve serious BPR efforts. One involves an effort to lay a BPR methodology on top of an object-oriented methodology to create a hybrid methodology. We predict that this trend will continue and that future ObjectWorld contests will see more and more large object-oriented applications that were created as byproducts of BPR efforts.

Object-oriented CASE tools and object-oriented BPR tools are becoming increasingly popular for large object-oriented projects. There are only two examples of applications developed with object-oriented CASE tools in this book, but the use of object-oriented CASE tools will undoubtedly grow as newer applications are fielded.

OBJECT-ORIENTED METHODOLOGIES

The early nineties witnessed a proliferation of new object-oriented methodologies. Some were derived from earlier Ada methodologies. Some were informal and designed for incremental Smalltalk development. Others were very formal and designed to support object-oriented CASE tools.

When the applications in this book were developed, the developers had to choose which of several competing object-oriented methodologies to use. Many companies chose to use a hybrid of several methods or even to create their own object-oriented methodology. Those that chose among the popular formal object-oriented methodologies usually chose Rumbaugh and colleagues' OMT (object modelling technique) methodology, Booch's OD (object design) methodology, or Jacobson's Use-Case methodology. Those that considered the less formal methodologies often tried Wirfs-Brock's Responsibility-Driven Design or the Coad-Yourdon methodology.

In 1994 Booch and Rumbaugh joined forces at Rational to create a new unified methodology. A first draft of that new methodology is now in circulation. As the book goes to press, Rational has acquired Objectory and added Jacobson to its staff, assuring that the unified methodology they create will combine the best of three of the leading object-oriented methodologists. It's easy to imagine that the resulting unified methodology will rapidly become the de facto standard and that by the end of 1996, most object-oriented methodology efforts will involve specializations or niche-oriented versions of this unified methodology.

Thus, the applications described in this book illustrate more variety in terms of object-oriented methodology than we expect to see in applications developed for future ObjectWorld contests.

OBJECT-ORIENTED AND OBJECT-ORIENTED/ RELATIONAL DATABASES

Object-oriented databases have been around since the mid-eighties. Sales of object-oriented databases have been increasing rapidly in the nineties, although, to date, sales only constitute a tiny fraction of the annual sales of relational database (RDB) products. In the nineties, the object-oriented database vendors have been joined by vendors offering products that seek to combine object orientation and RDB capabilities. One way to do this is to use an object-oriented database as a front end for an RDB. Another way is to have a front-end application that takes objects and reduces them to pieces that can be filed in RDBs and in files. There are now several different object-oriented/RDB approaches. Moreover, the major RDB vendors are currently preparing their own object-oriented/RDB products for release to begin in 1996.

Historically, new database approaches don't replace the older databases; they are used for new applications. Thus, although many companies swear by their RDBs, most corporate data is still stored in flat file and hierarchical databases. The same trend will probably apply to the object-oriented database transition. Companies will continue to use RDBs for applications where they are appropriate and use object-oriented databases only when they encounter new applications that the RDBs really can support. Clearly the next generation of multimedia applications will fall in that category. Meantime, as companies build object-oriented applications that rely on data currently stored in RDBs, we will continue to see applications that combine object-oriented and RDB capabilities.

Most of the applications in this book have relied on RDBs for data storage. A couple have used object-oriented databases for more specialized applications.

In 1994 the object-oriented database vendors agreed on standards that they are in the process of implementing in new releases of their object-oriented database products. In 1996 companies can expect to begin to move data from one object-oriented database to another without a lot of trouble. Thus, we expect subsequent applications will report more complex object-oriented database usage patterns than any illustrated in this book.

The ODMG-93 standard addresses five issues:

1. **A common object model.** The ODMG supports the OMG core object model. The OMG model was extended to support relationships and has been accepted by the OMG.
2. **An object definition language.** The ODMG supports the OMG's Interface Definition Language (IDL) and extends it to support persistence.
3. **An object query language.** The ODMG defined an object language for querying object-oriented databases. In effect, OQL is an extension of SQL-92. (There is an ANSI committee—X3H2—working on the next version of SQL—SQL3—which will include object-oriented support. OQL is not exactly the same as the early versions of SQL3, but ODMG is working with the SQL committee to attain convergence. SQL3 is not expected before 1997.)
4. **A C++ language binding.** The C++ binding will support portable persistent C++ code. In effect, the C++ binding is an extension of the ODL that uses C++ syntax.
5. **A Smalltalk language binding.** The Smalltalk binding supports portable Smalltalk by providing a Smalltalk extension of the ODL.

ODMG is currently working on a certification suite that can be used to audit object-oriented databases and certify that they conform to ODMG-93. ODMG plans a new release of the standard in 1996.

Although not an object-oriented database standard as such, the recent transaction processing service formalized by OMG will probably play a role in the object-oriented database market in 1996. Many companies think of their RDBs as a necessary part of any transaction processing architecture. If it turns out the object-oriented developers can deliver significant transaction processing applications that rely on object-oriented databases that will probably increase the willingness of IS departments to seriously consider them.

Some object-oriented databases and object-oriented/RDBs are being used as CASE repositories. R&O's Rochade Information Repository is a good example. Rochade supports several CASE tools. This reflects the lack of a standard, open object-oriented repository that all object-oriented development products could rely on. Unisys has made an object-oriented repository available, IBM has one in the works, and Texas Instruments and Microsoft are working on an OLE-based repository that is being designed to support Texas Instruments' OLE CASE products. The growing object-oriented CASE market will either reach some general agreement to store objects in standardized object-oriented databases—extended to provide management functions needed by CASE tools—or they will create a niche for an object-oriented repository, which will, in effect, be a specialized object-oriented database. Several applications in this book discuss the use of object-oriented database or tool-based repositories. These repositories save the information generated in the process of developing the specific application, but don't provide generic storage for information generated from multiple object-oriented development efforts.

Beyond object-oriented databases lie still more powerful databases that will incorporate AI techniques to make more intelligent queries and richer semantic content possible. We expect that the cutting edge object-oriented database vendors will not only add RDB elements to their current products, but will also add intelligent elements as well in the course of the next few years.

SUMMARY

The applications we will look at in the subsequent chapters represent a snapshot of work done in 1993 to 1995. The tools available for object-oriented analysis, design, and development are changing rapidly. Undoubtedly the developers of these applications would choose some different tools if they were to redo the applications. In this chapter we've outlined some of the trends to suggest what choices a developer starting a new object-oriented application might have. This, of course, in no way negates the choices of developers who used what was available several years ago. It suggests, however, that the reader will want to study the stories that follow with an open mind. These applications suggest problems to be overcome and approaches that have resulted in successful object-oriented applications. They do not, however, represent a definitive template for object-oriented development.

Section II

Object Technology and Distributed Systems

OVERVIEW OF SECTION II

When we refer to distributed systems, we generally think of systems that go beyond the simple client/server models to create networks of platforms that can alternatively function as either clients or servers as occasion demands. Moreover, we go beyond the idea that data must reside in a database and be accessed by a client system and begin to think of applications that send messages to other objects that may reside in databases or on other client machines in other applications, anywhere in an organization. Distributed systems are clearly the end toward which most corporations are heading as they seek to create worldwide networks and allow individuals throughout the company to access whatever data they need to solve problems as they occur.

At the moment, the best approach to the developing distributed systems relies on object technology. Specifically, it relies on the object request brokers (ORB) architecture developed by the Object Management Group. The OMG's ORB is called CORBA and it has gone through two major iterations. The first OMG standard allowed vendors to create self-contained CORBA systems. The second version, CORBA2, expands the initial standard to assure that any CORBA system can exchange information with any other.

At the moment, most client/server systems rely on one of three approaches: SQL, transaction process monitoring (TPM), or e-mail-based groupware.

When most developers think of client/server systems, they imagine a client with an interface and some application logic and a server with a relational database. In between lies SQL. SQL started out as a declarative language for manipulating data in RDBs. In 1986, Sybase extended SQL to enable it to manipulate stored procedures, and today, most SQL/database vendors support SQL with extensions to support stored procedures. Unfortunately, the extensions that support stored procedures are proprietary and hence the use of SQL normally ties the user into a specific vendor's product. Moreover, there's no standard middleware. It's relatively easy to develop a simple client/server system with a tool like PowerBuilder, but once you do you are locked into PowerBuilder. And, it's very hard to extend PowerBuilder applications to support enterprise-wide applications. More important, SQL depends on a clearly defined link between the applications running on the client and the data management system residing on the server. In effect, when you change anything, you need to recompile everything. Finally, SQL, like the RDB, really isn't designed for handling complex data types or data located on multiple servers. Every effort to extend SQL to make it more effective in these areas simply results in a more proprietary version of SQL and actually makes matters worse. For all these reasons, SQL isn't adequate for distributed computing.

Luckily, SQL can be encapsulated with object wrappers. Thus, the move from SQL to CORBA2 won't be nearly as difficult as it would be if companies had to stop using SQL entirely.

Another approach to distributed computing relies on transaction processing monitors (TPMs). TPMs come out of the mainframe tradition and have been used for many years in large mainframe systems. In effect, TPMs link applications and regulate the flow of information (transactions) between different applications. Using transactions, TPMs are capable of hiding one application from another and regulating the flow of information to assure that the operation system isn't overwhelmed by large volumes of data. Unlike SQL, TPMs are capable of scaling up to support very large systems. So far, however, TPMs haven't fared very well in the era of client/server computing. They are overkill for small LAN systems and the large hardware vendors that understand them have been slow to make them available in easy-to-understand packages.

In fact, however, CORBA has many of the characteristics of a TPM. Rather than disappearing, TPMs are about to be reborn in the form of CORBA.

The third approach to simple client/server development has relied on e-mail-based groupware tools like Lotus Notes. Notes has proved quite popular from a wide variety of simple applications. The key to Notes is the replication of databases. To get information out quickly, Notes simply replicates data and broadcasts it. Of course, this is anathema to SQL developers who are concerned with locking and data integrity, but it's proved quite popular for groupware applications where security and control aren't so important. Moreover, via DataLens, Lotus Notes can easily access data stored in SQL databases; it also lets SQL applications get data from Notes via ODBC APIs.

Clearly Notes and other groupware systems like it have a bright future. Unfortunately, Notes and groupware cannot serve as the basis for large-scale distributed systems development. To begin with, they're proprietary. More important, its middleware can handle large volumes of data or legacy applications. In fact, it's likely that Notes and other groupware products will be subsumed by CORBA. An ORB provides the right middleware for the types of applications that Notes provides. It's easy to imagine that IBM will combine Notes with OpenDoc and CORBA to provide a much more robust and powerful type of groupware for the era of distributed computing.

Having suggested why the technologies that have dominated the early years of client/server computing won't scale up to distributed computing, let's consider how an object request broker (ORB) like CORBA can overcome the problems that limit these other technologies.

First, CORBA is open. It's been developed by the OMG, a consortium of some 500 companies. Second, it's based on object technology and uses encapsulation and a broker to avoid direct linkages between applications. In effect, the boundaries between applications disappear and each object in an enterprise-wide environment can locate any other object without having to know where that object is located. There's nothing simple or easy about creating a CORBA system, but once it's in place, a company can change any one application without having to worry that any other application will be affected. CORBA lays the foundation for large, easily extensible systems that can be maintained and modified much more easily than any of today's client/server systems. Third, object techniques make it possible to encapsulate existing legacy applications and other client/server techniques (e.g., SQL). Thus, a company doesn't have to abandon existing techniques and legacy applications when it moves to CORBA. It can encapsulate existing things and treat them as objects as it moves into the world of distributed object computing.

Figure II.1 illustrates the familiar CORBA model that the OMG has been using. The ORB and the network is represented as a software bus and objects and applications are clustered in three boxes, each linked to the bus.

One box of objects is labeled object services. Object services are low-level middleware utilities. They are not a required part of CORBA, but they provide developers with functions often needed for application development. Some services include:

- **Naming Service.** Allows objects on the bus to locate other objects by name. This service also allows objects to be bound in existing network directories or naming contexts like ISO's x.500 or OSF's DCE.
- **The Persistence Service.** Provides a single interface for storing objects on a variety of servers, including simple files, RDBs, and object-oriented databases.
- **The Event Service.** Allows objects on the bus to dynamically register or unregister their interest in specific events. Using an object called an event channel, this service collects and distributes events to objects that otherwise know nothing of each other.

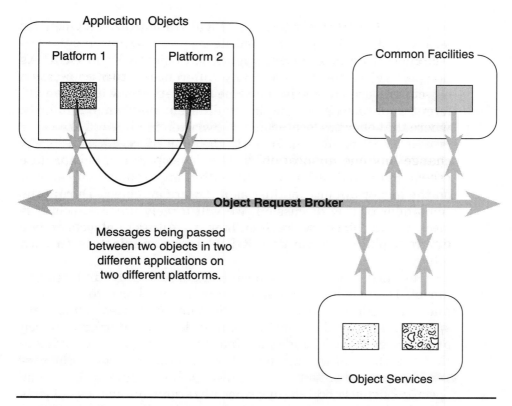

FIGURE II.1 The early OMG model of the CORBA architecture. We will be focusing on the process whereby one object in an application sends a message to another.

The OMG is in the process of standardizing about a dozen services.

A second box includes common facilities. Common facilities are higher-level components that provide services that can be directly used by application objects. Some of the common facilities are referred to as horizontal facilities and can be used with a wide variety of applications; others are vertical facilities and are designed to be used with applications in vertical markets—like telecommunications and finance. Two horizontal facilities are User Interface and Information Management. Both of these facilities make it possible for developers to create compound documents. It seems likely that OMG will standardize on OpenDoc as a way of providing these facilities.

The third box includes application objects. From CORBA's perspective, it doesn't make any difference if two application objects are located within the same application or within two different applications on completely different platforms. Similarly, CORBA doesn't care if one object is written in C++ and the other is written in Smalltalk. In fact, one "object" could be a legacy application written in COBOL. The developers can encapsulate the COBOL application and thereafter, any application can call on the legacy application just as if it were an object. During the remainder of this discussion, we will largely ignore object services and facilities and focus on how two different objects on two different platforms can use CORBA to communicate with each other.

Recently, the OMG has been using a new OMG architecture model. The new model breaks the application box into two boxes and discriminates between application interfaces, which are specific to particular companies and domain interfaces, which are more generic. The idea behind this new model is to indicate that the OMG is willing to work with industry groups to standardize domain interface frameworks, but assumes that some specific business objects and specializations of business objects will always be proprietary and unique to individual companies. For the purposes of our discussion in this section, we'll simply use the old model.

CORBA'S TWO MODES OF INVOCATION

When the OMG was first developing its ORB, there were two different approaches proposed. One approach was static and assumed that the layout of the environment was well understood. The other was a dynamic approach that didn't make any prior assumptions about the environment. The common ORB architecture combines both approaches and gives developers a choice. The static approach is easier and faster. The dynamic approach is more difficult to program and slower to execute, but indispensable when you are faced with a rapidly changing environment.

Static Invocation

Figure II.2 provides an overview of a static invocation. In this case, an object within an application on one platform wants to call an object on another platform.

In the process of creating CORBA, a jargon has grown up that is sometimes useful and sometimes simply idiosyncratic. For example, CORBA isn't concerned with clients and servers the way developers of simple client/server systems are. In effect, all objects and applications associated with CORBA are peers. At any point in time any specific object on one platform can either request information or respond to a request. Nonetheless,

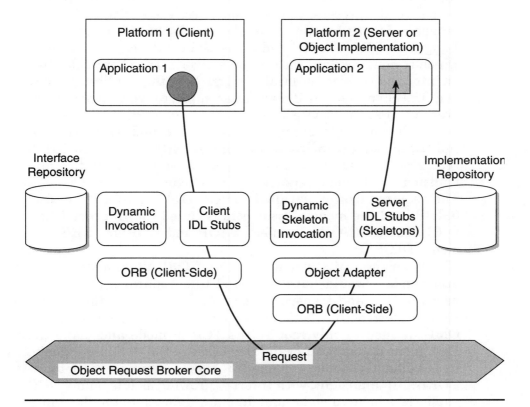

FIGURE II.2 An overview of the elements that can be used to pass a message from object 1 to object 2. The static invocation path is illustrated.

the OMG refers to the object making the request as a "client." Following this logic, they should probably call the object that responds to the request the "server." Instead, however, they speak of the respondent as the "object implementation." In a similar vein, OMG talks about the code stubs inserted in the client application as "client stubs" but they refer to the code stubs inserted in the responding application as "skeletons." We'll normally call them server stubs and we'll call the responding object the server object to keep things a little clearer.

When the client object needs another object to perform some function, it sends a message requesting that the function be performed. That message is intercepted by the CORBA client stub that represents the server object that is associated with application 1. In the process, the message is converted from whatever language it was written in to the OMG's Interface Definition Language (IDL). The IDL code is passed via the client-side ORB, which resides on platform 1 to the network. The client-side ORB or interface consists of local services that the application may use. The client-side ORB may, for example, convert an object reference to a string or vice versa.

In the past the message syntax and the mode of transportation were left up to the individual CORBA vendor. CORBA2 requires that every vendor support a standard syntax and transport so that one version of CORBA can talk with any other. The required syntax is called the General Inter-ORB Protocol (GIOP) and the mode of transport is called the Internet Inter-ORB Protocol (IIOP). In effect, GIOP and IIOP are ORB versions of TCP/IP.

When the OMG was working on CORBA2 standards, several vendors would have preferred to standardize on a DCE-based syntax and transport mode. At a minimum, they would have preferred that both modes be required. In the end, the OMG decided to only require the TCP/IP mode and make the DCE mode optional. They did this because they wanted to make it possible for some vendors to make minimal versions of CORBA. In hindsight, with Internet growing as it is, many DCE supporters have come around and now appreciate the flexibility this provides to CORBA. Major vendors who are interested in creating versions of CORBA for large distributed environments will be implementing and relying on an ORB version of DCE running on either TCP/IP or on OSI. They will also support the GIOP/IIOP version, however, and thus ensure that a large corporate system will still be able to interact with objects distributed on the Internet or in other smaller CORBA environments.

Once the message arrives at platform 2, it is picked up by the client-side ORB and passed to the object adapter. The object adapter provides the runtime environment for instantiating server objects and passing requests to them. The object adapter keeps track of all classes and their runtime instances and registers them with the implementation repository. OMG requires that each version of CORBA must support a basic object adapter (BOA). Some individual vendors will differentiate their products by also supporting more specific object adapters.

The BOA passes the message to the server stub, which translates the IDL code into the message format and code of the server object. The server object then performs whatever it is asked to do. If it can't, for some reason, or if the message requests that it be provided with data, CORBA reverses the process and passes appropriate information back to the sender.

Dynamic Invocation

Figure II.3 illustrates dynamic invocation. In this case, the client object does not know the object to which it wants to send a message. In this case the message is passed to the Dynamic Invocation utility. This utility accesses an interface repository— a runtime database—that contains descriptions of the methods associated with various objects (i.e., their interfaces). The dynamic invocation utility identifies one or more objects that have methods that could satisfy the message request and proceeds to route the message to one of those objects. Once again the message is in IDL code and it is passed via the client-side ORB to the network. Similarly, it is received by the server-side ORB and passed via the object adapter to the appropriate object. If the appropriate object on the server has an IDL stub, the message is passed via the server stub and thereby translated into the code of the target object. In the more complex case, when the message is sent to a server that has an object that lacks an

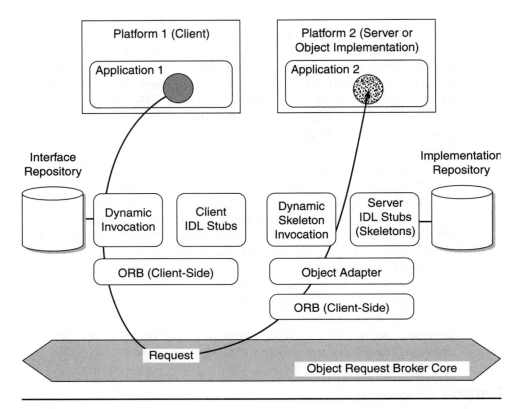

FIGURE II.3 An overview of the elements that can be used to pass the message from object 1 to object 2. The dynamic invocation path is illustrated.

appropriate stub, the Dynamic Skeleton Invocation utility dynamically creates a stub for the target object and then translates the message, and so on.

As we already mentioned, dynamic techniques require more programming and are slower, but they make it possible to use CORBA in situations where the environment is constantly changing without requiring recompilation. In effect, when new objects are added to an environment, they send messages to register their interfaces with the interface repository and, thereafter, they are available to receive messages, even though the object sending the message was created before the new server object, server application, or server platform were added to the system.

In both Figures II.2 and II.3, we've highlighted the elements of the CORBA system that were added to the CORBA2 specification. They include the interface repository, the core ORB—in effect, the standardized message syntax and transport mode (GIOP, IIOP, TCP/IP), and the Dynamic Skeleton Invocation.

A key technology used by CORBA is the OMG's interface definition language (IDL). IDL is a purely declarative language. IDL is a subset of ANSI C++ with some extensions to support distribution. IDL uses C++ syntax for constant type and operation definitions, but it does not include any control structures or variables.

CORBA separates one object from another and uses the broker architecture to assure that the objects don't need to know anything about each other. That's what makes CORBA an ideal basis for large-scale distributed computing. The key to enforcing the separation is IDL. In effect, any specific object (or application, for that matter) can be written in any language. The message generated by the object is captured by the ORB and translated into IDL. If it is necessary to check the interface repository to see if there is any object that can respond to the message, the descriptions of all the possible server objects are described in IDL. Once the message arrives at the server application, the IDL message is then translated back into the language of the target object. In effect, all the problems associated with trying to get different object-oriented languages and different class libraries to talk to each other are eliminated by CORBA.

At the moment, the OMG has standardized the translations between C, C++, and Smalltalk and IDL. Groups are currently working on standard translations between Ada, CLOS, object-oriented COBOL and other object-oriented languages and IDL.

Figure II.4 illustrates the steps a developer needs to go through to create a CORBA system.

To keep things simple, let's assume our developer is creating a static system. The developer creates all of the interface definitions for all the objects in the systems. In effect, he or she speci-

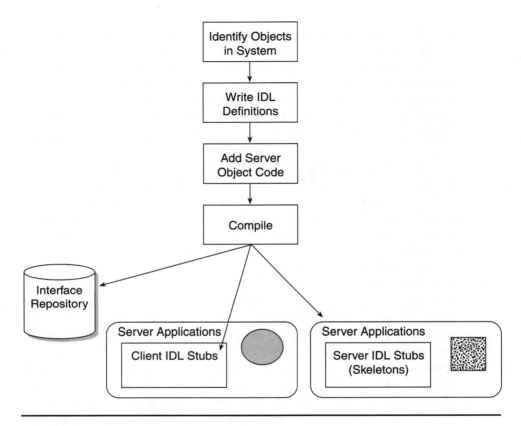

FIGURE II.4 Steps in developing a CORBA application.

fies the methods supported by each object and the arguments that need to be passed if those methods are to be invoked. The developer creates the specifications in IDL.

Next, the developer adds the actual code of all the server objects. Then using an IDL compiler, the developer generates client applications with stubs for all possible objects that objects within that application might call. Similarly, the compiler generates server applications with stubs (skeletons) for any messages the objects in that application might receive. The stubs are translated into the language of the client or server application and compiled with the application. At the moment, CORBA compilers support the generation of C, C++, and Smalltalk applications. In the near future they will support all of the other major object-oriented languages and could support non-object-oriented languages.

In addition to generating the stubs and applications, the compiler also generates the IDL interfaces that are stored in the interface repository.

The developer also needs to make decisions about the implementation repository and object adapter. When an application is started, the object adapter obtains information about object names from the implementation repository and generally prepares to respond to any messages it might receive.

In the early days of object-oriented development, one of the problems developers encountered involved the incompatibility of different object-oriented languages. Typically, class libraries developed for one object-oriented language wouldn't work with another. CORBA solves this problem by providing a neutral interface between languages and classes. Thus, a Smalltalk application on one platform can use CORBA to call a C++ class residing on the same platform or on a different platform. Since the message from the Smalltalk application is changed to IDL when it passes through CORBA and from IDL into C++ when it is finally sent to the C++ class, no problems occur.

Distributed OLE2, being developed by Microsoft, might become an alternative to CORBA, but it hasn't been released yet and probably won't be available until 1997. Even then, distributed OLE will probably only run on a limited number of platforms. Thus, although we may see distributed OLE applications in the future, they will probably be limited to departmental applications. Bridges between OLE and CORBA will allow organizations to construct enterprise applications that combine the two approaches to distributed object computing.

APPLICATIONS

Section II includes descriptions of three applications, winners or finalists in the Object World contest, that illustrate the use of ORBs. One relies on an ORB developed for that specific application before the CORBA2 specification was published. The other two applications rely on CORBA.

MPR Teltech's TRaDS (Telecommunications Repair and Diagnostic System) Finalist, Category 2, 1995

This application is a diagnostic tool used by repair center clerical staff to diagnose and solve customer-reported phone service complaints. The system was written in Smalltalk and C++ and interfaces with legacy systems. The application relies, in part, on a case-based reasoning (CBR) utility to manage sessions. It depends on an ORB, based on DCE, that the company developed on its own since the application was developed prior to the publication of the CORBA2 standard. The system accesses a number of different relational databases and an object-oriented database. The application is distributed and runs on PC and Unix Workstations and uses some databases on mainframes.

This application was developed as part of a re-engineering effort at MPR Teltech. It uses some AI elements, two object-oriented languages, an object-oriented database, and a proprietary ORB. It used domain objects and legacy applications. It solved a problem that would have been difficult to solve otherwise and it was developed faster as a result of object-oriented techniques. In other words, this application could have just as well been placed in any one of the sections in this book. It illustrates most of the trends that are present in the latest object-oriented applications.

Center for Advanced Aviation Systems Development and MITRE Corporation's Air Traffic Control Framework (AF) Winner, Category 1, 1995

In effect, the AF is a business object framework that is designed to facilitate the development of new applications. This application is thus a very good example of reuse, as well as an example of object-oriented distribution.

To prove the usefulness of the AF, MITRE proceeded to develop three actual applications to demonstrate how the AF facilitated reuse and the rapid development of aviation applications. The AF relies on Iona's version of CORBA to handle distribution. The AF itself was written in IDL, C++, and with Rogue Wave's class libraries. The initial analysis of the AF was done in Coad-Yourdon's object-oriented methodology, supplemented by Ralph Johnson's methodology for frameworks.

MITRE Corporation's DISCUS
(Data Interchange and Synergistic Collateral Usage System)
Finalist, Category 1, 1994

This application is based on a generic framework for linking and integrating legacy applications. It was created to support both government agencies and internal MITRE application development efforts. The framework was subsequently used to create a demonstration system called DISCUS. The framework and DISCUS both rely on Digital Equipment's ObjectBroker version of CORBA and on OMG's Object Services and IDL. Both use Domain (Technical) Objects, Smalltalk, C/C++, and some CLOS. (This is thus another example of a complex system that adds a touch of AI to object-orientation to handle a very complex problem.)

DISCUS uses 3000 lines of code to integrate legacy applications that contain some 2 million lines of code. The developers argue that DISCUS was developed for some $35,000 using the framework and that it would have cost about $2 million dollars to develop a similar system without the reuse provided by the framework.

This application illustrates a solution to a problem that all companies face as they embark on serious object-oriented efforts. To take advantage of reuse, you need frameworks and business objects that are broadly applicable to applications you want to build. Some companies try to obtain classes for reuse by building one application after another and systematically refining their growing class libraries. Others turn to outside specialists, as the government did in the case of this application, or join with industry consortiums to develop business class libraries. However they approach the problem, it takes several years to develop high quality business objects that can drive a serious corporate reuse program.

TRaDS: Telecommunications Repair and Diagnostic System

MPR Teltech Ltd.

THE OPPORTUNITY

MPR Teltech Ltd,. headquartered in Burnaby, British Columbia, Canada, provides advanced telecommunications systems and products to an international portfolio of customers.

With the advent of competition, the provision of high quality repair service has become an imperative in order for telephone companies to retain their customer bases. At the same time, competitive pressures are mandating that the cost of providing customer service be continually reduced. Many telecommunications service providers are re-engineering their customer service processes to meet both requirements. One specific target is the diagnosis of customer requests for repairs.

THE APPLICATION

TRaDS is the system used by repair center staff to diagnose and solve customer-reported phone service complaints at the first point of contact. The need for such a product was identified by the client's repair process re-engineering initiative.

One of the main criteria that had to be satisfied was the provision of data and diagnostic results to the user while the customer is still on the line. Data and diagnosis display had to be coordinated with user entry of the reported problem symptoms in order to provide a "smooth" contact session with the customer. This was achieved by allowing the case-based expert system (diagnostic engine) to continuously perform diagnosis and then re-evaluate that diagnosis as more data became available.

TRaDS also takes over the complex task of legacy systems communication, integrating the data from multiple sources across the company. The user interacts with one system (TRaDS) instead of the five they previously used.

Object technology was a natural choice for an application estimated to be approximately 100,000 lines of code. Since many users were to use a single source of data, client/server architecture was also a natural choice.

One of the issues considered when developing TRaDS was performance. Having a customer on the line makes this application very demanding for the data retrieval. This was the main reason for implementing the server using C++. Also needed was something that would provide real multiplatform support, a pure object-oriented language, a powerful GUI builder, and the possibility of interfacing with other languages. The ParcPlace Visual-Works implementation of Smalltalk satisfied these requirements.

System Architecture

TRaDS consists of the following components.

DCE-Based Data Server

The server is a DCE-based multi-threaded server that accesses data from diverse data sources such as ORACLE, mainframes, and VT100-based legacy systems. It serves its data using the relational paradigm, regardless of the source. This server has a simple API based on the SQL verb set, tables, rows, and attribute value pairs. The server is written in C and C++ and uses dynamic SQL to access data from relational databases such as ORACLE. The server also incorporates a generic "screen scraper" mechanism that allows simple screen definitions to be automatically converted into templates for relational transactions. By this mechanism, connections to numerous IMS and Tandem-based legacy systems are supported over SNA and TCP/IP. The data server hides the sources from the client.

Transactions

The transaction objects are mappings of SQL statements used to get information from various data sources through the Data-Server. This is the interface for Smalltalk to the C++ world.

Database Objects

The next layer hides the transactions from the rest of the application. There are several objects here that behave as if they were object-oriented databases. Requests come in to instantiate domain objects and the database objects know which transactions to create and how to populate them in order to retrieve or store information in the outside world. Database objects also know how to create and populate domain objects from transactions.

Domain Objects

The domain model contains objects that map into real-world telephony and telephone trouble-related objects. Most of the objects have a potential diagnostic function. Objects such as Customer, Access Line, Switch, Service Order, Telephone Products, and Telephone Test Systems are modeled and instantiated here.

Session

The session object holds the current domain objects that are being viewed by the user.

Session Manager

The session manager controls access to the diagnostic engine and manages the session objects. Upon receiving triggering messages, which may be changes in state of domain objects or GUI events, a SymptomList may be created and sent to the diagnostic engine.

Symptom List

This is a snapshot of the session at the time a triggering event occurred.

Diagnostic Engine

This is the engine that diagnoses the problems and identifies any additional information required for diagnosis. Given the SymptomList prepared by the SessionManager, it arrives at a diagnosis based on the most up-to-date information available. A list of diagnoses is passed to the Scripter that displays them on the GUI. The diagnosis can include requests for more information (e.g., questions), suggested solutions to the problem, and simple text messages. The diagnostic engine is currently implemented using case-based technology built in Smalltalk.

Scripter

The scripter controls the GUI. Any diagnosis that is returned from the diagnostic engine will be interpreted by the scripter for display in the GUI. The scripter may choose the appropriate manner of obtaining requested data such as asking a question or highlighting a field.

Graphical User Interface (GUI)

The GUI displays the domain objects to the user and contains objects that represent various GUI entities such as screens, buttons, and text entry fields. The automatic update mechanisms provided by Smalltalk are used to ensure that the data displayed on the screen is synchronized with the objects in the domain model. The GUI can also display diagnostic information, including suggested actions, questions and suggested outcomes.

Figure 3.1 shows the TRaDS main customer screen. It integrates data from multiple legacy systems and from other sources. Figure 3.2 shows the TRaDS diagnosis window.

Distributed Objects

TRaDS's solution for distributed objects is based on OSF distributed computing environment (DCE). The effective encapsulation

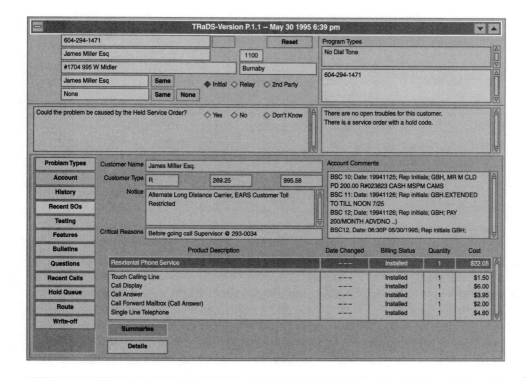

FIGURE 3.1 TRaDS main customer screen.

of DCE provided the freedom to think about more important design issues. It also provided advantages of using DCE features such as naming services, security services, time synchronization, and other administration utilities. DCE was viewed as an industry standard in the distributed computing area, with a clear advantage over new and not very standardized CORBA solutions in the areas of stability and multiplatform support.

Once CORBA is standardized and becomes more mature, future releases of TRaDS will use CORBA.

Currently the database layer simulates an object-oriented database. It does this by using transaction objects, each of which represents a single predefined data request or update. Each

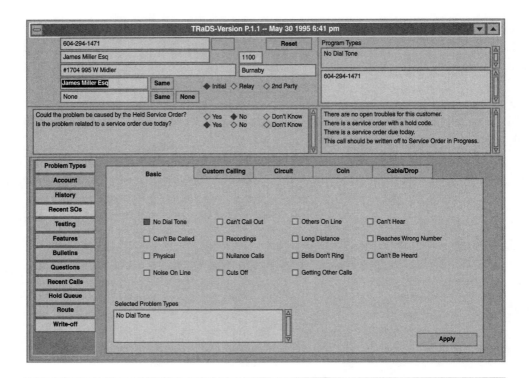

FIGURE 3.2 TRaDS uses customer provided information in conjunction with information it has acquired from legacy and test systems to perform diagnosis of the reported problem.

transaction object presents itself as a stream and constructs itself from a stream. So, to instantiate one transaction object, the interface will pass a request to the server, which will respond with the stream that transaction object will use to build itself. The whole mechanism is fully threaded, using Smalltalk threads on the client side and DCE threads on the server side.

Each distributed object in TRaDS is a subclass of a transaction. At present, there are more than fifty different subclasses, addressing specific representations of data received from different legacy systems.

Legacy Systems Interfaces

People involved with legacy systems know that interface definition, implementation, and, most of all, maintenance can be a real nightmare.

Even with direct access to some of the data, more than 70 percent of it was accessible only through existing user interfaces. Therefore, a generic screen scraping mechanism was created, allowing developers to emulate the user performing a specific task. Object technology provided the opportunity to inherit from transaction, while specializing specific interfacing mechanisms.

Currently the legacy system interface supports the following:

- IMS Cobol Transactions (run over LU6.2)
- VT100 terminal emulation
- Tandem terminal emulation
- IBM mainframe terminal emulation

In addition to interfacing to a number of legacy systems, another design goal was to make sure that changes to the legacy systems would not put a maintenance burden on TRaDS. Developers introduced a number of scripts that address legacy application definition, screen definition, and transaction definition. The screen and application definition scripts describe where to find certain data on the screen or certain screens inside an application. In contrast, a transaction definition describes the sequence of steps that the user of that specific legacy system would have to perform to accomplish the same task.

Keeping these descriptions in easily changeable scripts means that maintenance can be performed much more easily than if code needed to be changed and recompiled.

This script approach has already proven itself in handling several legacy system changes, usually taking just a few minutes to change the script, without recompiling or even shutting down the server. With an average of one new release of a legacy system per year, and having in mind the need to talk to five of them, developers are confident that this solution will continue to be an effective maintenance cost reducer.

Hardware and Software Used

	Hardware	Software
Interface		DCE (PC-DCE)
Core Code	RS6000, PC	AIX, Windows 3.1 (NT)
Data Base	RS6000	Oracle
Development	RS6000, PC	ParcPlace VW, IBM XLC, MS Visual
Environment		C++, DEC CVS

PROJECT LIFECYCLE

The project was managed using the iterative lifecycle approach. The team started with a number of prototypes, closely monitored the customer reactions, and with each iteration moved closer to the final release. By using this approach, developers could refine the requirements as they went along. By maintaining constant connection with users throughout all the phases of the process, the development team minimized the risk of customer surprises with the end product. Requirements analysis was performed by a combined MPR/customer team.

For design the team used its own methodology, using available tools. First design drafts were made using OOATool. Later in the project they moved to Rational Rose, which matched their needs more closely.

In the implementation phase, several parts were developed independently and tested before integration. This resulted in a robust application, despite the size and the number of interfaces to other applications.

Overall, the TRaDS team used the following:

- The Smalltalk class library that was provided with ParcPlace VisualWorks
- The customer's existing DataServer application
- TCL as a generic scripting language, Tools ++ class library for the C++ side of the project

- Some existing code for the DCE server developed in a previous project in the department

For release control UNIX-based CVS was used because it is the departmental standard. It is used successfully to manage Smalltalk, C++ and C code, scripts, and documentation.

The developers have been happy to find that most of the maintenance issues to date have been related to keeping the channels to legacy applications open and operational. That was expected considering the size of the average telephone company and the diversity of the hardware and software being used throughout the company.

BENEFITS

The TRaDS Team cites the following benefits provided by their system.

Productivity Improvement

Problem Resolution at Point of Contact

A significant percentage of problems can be attributed to switch programming errors. TRaDS can diagnose and automatically correct these errors while the customer is on the line.

Diagnosis Improvement

Since diagnosis is performed while the customer is on the phone, all relevant information is obtained and used by TRaDS to make the best diagnosis possible, resulting in fewer repeat problems.

Cost Reduction

Skill Efficiencies

TRaDS permits clerical personnel to respond to customers reporting problems. These personnel can then be selected for their interpersonal skills, rather than for their ability to repair problems.

Training Efficiencies

TRaDS can interface with operational support systems, electronic test equipment, and switches, eliminating training of front line staff on the use of many different systems.

A Framework for Distributed Interactive Simulation

The MITRE Corporation

THE OPPORTUNITY

The Center for Advanced Aviation System Development (CAASD) is a federally funded research and development center sponsored by the Federal Aviation Administration (FAA). CAASD uses models, simulations, and prototypes to evolve new functions and minimize the cost of developing air traffic control automation. CAASD resources include several laboratories such as the Integration and Interaction Laboratory (I-Lab). The I-Lab uses simulations and prototypes developed or under development by various FAA programs in En Route, Terminal, Tower, and Traffic Flow Management automation. Prototypes or simulations developed in support of specific vertical programs are integrated with general purpose models and simulations to provide a means for evaluating alternative operational air traffic control concepts. This framework is under consideration to be integrated with the existing conventional techniques used in the I-Lab and to facilitate the rapid configuration of air traffic control simulations.

The first goal of the framework is to increase the cost effectiveness of distributed interactive simulation and prototyping work not only at CAASD but at MITRE in general and in areas other than civil aviation as well.

71

The I-Lab needed to be more productive. To meet this demand, a need was identified to move towards developing smaller, lightweight reusable components within a consistent framework.

The I-Lab currently uses several conventional approaches for building distributed interactive simulations. First, it is limited to one style of interaction, reliable asynchronous message passing. The new framework uses synchronous message passing that handles exceptions. Second, the I-Lab lacks a locator that finds objects easily across a distributed system of hosts. Orbix uses a locator service that uses configuration files to locate servers. A client program that knows the unique, systemwide Identifier for an Orbix object can use that object regardless of its location. Third, data marshalling is performed in an ad hoc manner and by hand. IDL-generated code, on the other hand, performs all data marshalling according to a set of standards for the programmer. Finally, the I-Lab uses unreliable mechanisms to start processes. The reliable activation of object servers provided by CORBA is a great help.

It is well known that object orientation facilitates software reuse through encapsulation and the clear expression of software architecture, thereby leading to increased productivity. The object management architecture (OMA) of the Object Management Group (OMG) extends this assertion to distributed systems. This project demonstrates the benefits of combining the OMA with a special-purpose protocol for simulation, the Distributed Interactive Simulation (DIS) protocol of the Department of Defense, to produce a framework for distributed interactive air traffic control simulation. The encapsulation of DIS as distributed objects overcomes inefficiencies in current implementations of the OMA while allowing simulations to be constructed in a purely OMA environment.

THE APPLICATION

The framework adheres to and relies on the OMA. Its components appear as distinct objects in the classic sense, with distinct identity and internal state, and not just as stateless services or servers. The interfaces between distributed objects are defined in OMG Interface Definition Language (IDL). We have used CORBA services wherever possible. Our framework is structured in terms of the services it provides.

The framework is a set of objects used together to create a simulation. The objects and the rules for their use define an architecture that persists from one application of the framework to the next. The intent is that the simulation programmer, by programming in the context of the framework and adhering to its rules, is able to construct a simulation more quickly. The simulation programmer can also exploit other application objects that adhere to the framework.

The framework is partly "white-box" in that the simulation programmer must be aware of much of the simulation control protocol to make use of the framework. The earliest versions of the framework presented the application programmer with classes to inherit from. A desire to decrease what the application programmer must know, that is, to move to a "black box" design, have led us to replace some superclasses with objects that are aggregated with application objects. The current design thus mixes inheritance with aggregation. The framework, like most such efforts, is evolving with use. It may not be possible or desirable to shield the simulation programmer entirely from the simulation control protocol; thus the framework may remain partly "white box." The framework objects are used in several ways: by interaction with framework objects according to a prescribed protocol, by composition, and by extension.

Interaction with Framework Objects

Applications acquire some services by interaction with framework objects according to a prescribed protocol. An example of this is the Registry, an object created and maintained by the framework, which can be asked by an application for the object reference for any Aircraft in a simulation.

The OMA support of distinct objects, rather than mere servers, was very useful to us. It allows distinct simulation-specific objects, like Aircraft. It also supports distinct objects that represent simultaneous, distinct simulations: Each simulation session is under control of a separate Manager object, whose state includes the identity of all the other objects participating in the session.

Programming in the OMA context means that the CORBA services are available (where implemented) both to the framework developer and to the application developer. From the application developer's point of view, these services are part of the benefit conveyed by use of the framework.

Composition or Aggregation of Framework Objects

Some application behavior is gained by making a framework-provided object part of an application object. An example is the Flight Plan Subscription. Each aircraft in a simulation typically has a flight plan that expresses its intended route of flight. The plans change as aircraft routes are amended by air traffic controllers. An object that wishes to receive flight plans and amendments for certain aircraft can instantiate a Flight Plan Subscription object, which maintains a local database of flight plans by interacting with remote objects that manage the flight plans.

Extension of Framework Objects

Much of the behavior of application objects in the present state of the framework is acquired by inheritance from a framework object. An example is the Component, which embodies the unit of simulation control. The simulation Manager—which is responsible for establishing a simulation—creates, controls, and disposes of Components. The inheritance feature of IDL allowed us to abstract the simulation control protocol. The Manager deals with Components through polymorphism. The Component implementation is decoupled from its interface. With support for implementation inheritance, a common implementation of Component was abstracted and inherited by application implementations.

Extension of the Framework Itself

The framework itself can be extended by the addition of new application protocols. As the need arises to add new kinds of simulation entities, new objects and protocols can be defined to represent them. For example, the framework presently contains an Aircraft class that can perform certain basic maneuvers. If the need arose, one could add a Vehicle class to represent traffic on an airport surface, which might implement a very different set of operations. Like the Aircraft class, the Vehicle class could be abstract and be specialized for various purposes.

Services

The behaviors and information provided to an application object by the framework may be described as "services." Each service is represented by one or more objects with published interfaces with which the application object interacts. The services are a convenient way to describe the framework's functionality. The sum of the services defines the application object's interface with the framework.

The framework-provided services fall into two groups: infrastructure services and application support services. The framework also provides some applications that exploit these services. The infrastructure services (simulation control, time, entity ID, aircraft state) are independent of the simulation domain. They correspond to OMG CORBA facilities and might be standardized eventually. The application support services (site data, flight data) are specific to air traffic control. They are less likely to be standardized. Application objects must adhere to the framework interface for each service if they are to interact; the process of defining and implementing these services has been most beneficial in clarifying the definitions and exposing the problems that arise in standardizing these services.

The services may also be classified in terms of the kinds of objects they support. Simulations in the framework are composed of "coarse-grained" objects that exist for the sake of simulation control and are really artifacts of configuring and conducting a simulation. Simulations also contain "fine-grained" objects that correspond to things in the domain being simulated. An application process may support many fine-grained objects of a given type. An example of this is the Aircraft Manager. It instantiates as many Aircraft objects as the simulation scenario calls for. It performs state updates on the Aircraft objects as a batch for the sake of efficiency. However, each Aircraft object has its own CORBA object reference, and operations (commands to maneuver) may be invoked on them individually through CORBA. The Aircraft Manager itself is a subclass of Component and is managed by the simulation Manager.

Infrastructure Services

The simulation control service is used to instantiate, activate, initialize, and dispose of the coarse-grain objects that manage the simulation objects. Instantiation and activation have the important effect of starting the necessary object server processes on the desired simulation hosts. An application programmer participates in this service by subclassing Component and Component-Factory.

A simulation is begun by instantiating a Manager and providing the Manager a list of objects (derived from Component) to be instantiated. The Manager first instantiates (or merely activates, in the case of persistent objects like the Adaptation object) all the simulation infrastructure objects required for the simulation, and then invokes the appropriate factory objects (all derived from ComponentFactory) to create the coarse-grained Components. The Manager later deactivates and disposes of the Component.

CORBA's ability to start object server processes on given simulation hosts and its exception reporting turn out to be particularly valuable in establishing a simulation. We were able to program a reliable Manager in a several weeks; earlier conventional implementations of a simulation controller took months to program and debug and never performed altogether reliably.

Each Component (or derived instance) in a simulation must know the initial simulation time and when the simulation clock is started and stopped. The time service is provided by objects acting together. Each derived instance of Component inherits a member instance of an Event Handler that maintains local simulation time. A Component instance can determine the simulation time and state of the clock by consulting its Event Handler. The Event Handler is kept up to date by messages from a single

Time Manager instance that is an infrastructure object created by the Manager. Part of the behavior inherited with Component is that each Event Handler registers itself with the Time Manager during initialization; thereafter, clock state changes are commanded by the Manager to the Time Manager, which forwards the commands to the Event Handlers registered with it. The Time Manager is a simple example of a CORBA implementation of a publish-and-subscribe service. The OMG Event Service might have been used for this purpose had it been available.

The aircraft state service provides the position, velocity, and orientation of vehicles in the simulation to any interested participant. This service is described in more detail below.

The entity ID service is an artifact of the use of DIS. Each vehicle whose state is to be reported through the aircraft state service must have a unique entity ID assigned to it. Components that wish to create entities (vehicles) request a block of unique IDs from the entity ID server. This central server is an infrastructure object. Writing this server was an afternoon's exercise.

Application Support Services

These services are peculiar to the simulation domain of air traffic control. The Adaptation service is provided by a persistent object, that is, one that exists before and after a simulation session. The Adaptation object contains the location of navigational aids, airports, and other geographical data of interest to simulation components. The current implementation is rudimentary; the team intends eventually that the Adaptation object will be a front end for a complete database.

The flight data service provides an application with Flight Plans that represent the plans submitted before aircraft fly in the air traffic control system. Flight Plans are "flyweight" objects maintained by Flight Plan Managers. Applications desiring Flight Plans subscribe to one or more Flight Plan Managers, which send their current plans and later amendments to subscribers. To the application programmer, the service takes the form of an object to be instantiated and initialized with the names of one or more Flight Plan Managers. The subscription mechanism is encapsulated in the local object, which appears to the application programmer as a collection of Flight Plans. Here CORBA is being used to implement a locally replicated data base.

The Registry is an infrastructure object that, if queried with a flight ID or entity ID, replies with the CORBA object reference of the corresponding Flight Plan or Aircraft object. This allows an application to interact with one of these objects directly without knowing what Component may have responsibility for it.

Applications

To demonstrate the framework, the MITRE team built three applications: an Aircraft Manager that populates a simulation with simple Aircraft; a Situation Display that depicts the current position of the Aircraft; and a simulated pilot, with which one can maneuver an Aircraft.

They created a NewtonsAircraft that flies in a straight line until given one of a set of simple maneuvers: turn to heading, climb, descend, accelerate, or decelerate. The NewtonsAircraft Manager creates sets of NewtonsAircraft corresponding to vestigial "flight plans" that state their initial conditions. The Aircraft Manager updates the NewtonsAircraft flight models periodically and reports their current state through an entity interface.

It would be possible to subclass the Aircraft IDL interface to include more sophisticated aircraft models. It would also be possible to create an Aircraft Manager subclass that would represent a cockpit simulator as an Aircraft in a simulation.

The goal of the Situation Display was to demonstrate reception of Aircraft positions through an entity interface, the combining of that information with Flight Plan data from a Flight Plan Manager, the use of the Adaptation object for geographical information, and the integration of an X Windows interface with an object server. The Situation Display simply plots the positions of all Aircraft in the simulation (regardless of the Component generating the aircraft). The Situation Display uses Flight Plan in formation to put flight IDs on the plots.

The simulated pilot is strictly a client. It is started manually after a simulation is begun. When given a flight ID of an Aircraft to maneuver, it extracts the corresponding object reference from the Registry, and then invokes maneuvers on the Aircraft object. Its purpose is to demonstrate the fact that Aircraft are CORBA objects and may be invoked regardless of what process implements them.

The framework has two distinct class hierarchies: an interface hierarchy expressed in IDL and an implementation hierarchy. The two hierarchies are not identical, as illustrated in Figures 4.1 and 4.2. The implementation class hierarchy represents how the objects are in fact implemented. The user of the framework employs both the interface and implementation hierarchies.

Encapsulation

Aircraft states (position, velocity, attitude) change rapidly and must be conveyed to many applications. The design pattern used is akin to the publish-and-subscribe pattern offered by the OMG Event Service. However, there is no implementation of the Event Service efficient enough for this application. Nor do any of the Event Service implementations deal with the creation and destruction of the objects whose states are reported.

The entity interface object encapsulates a commercial implementation of the DIS entity state protocol. An entity interface object is instantiated on each simulation host; all application objects on a host that require the service interact with the local interface. The interface offers these services: create/update aircraft state, create/update aircraft state for a set of aircraft, give state information about a given aircraft in the simulation, and list all existing aircraft and their states.

Encapsulation of the DIS entity state protocol allows us to handle large numbers of aircraft efficiently. Nevertheless, Aircraft are genuine ORB objects, addressable through object references.

Polymorphism

Polymorphic interfaces appear as abstract base classes: Component for simulation control, Aircraft for maneuvers using various flight models.

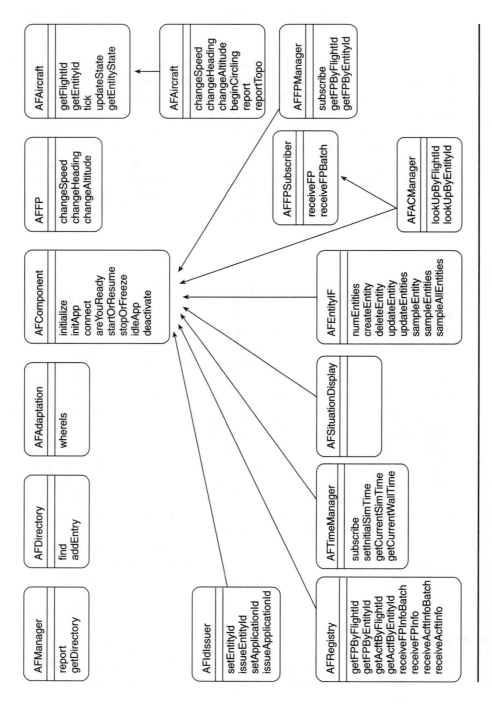

FIGURE 4.1 AF interface class hierarchy.

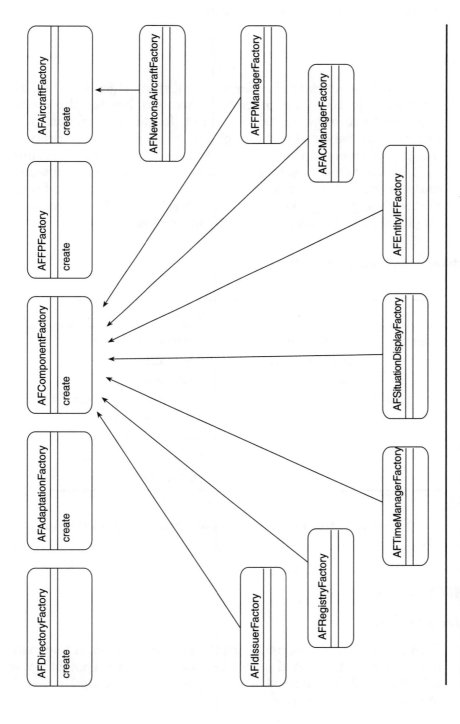

FIGURE 4.2 AF interface factory class hierarchy.

Persistence

Orbix uses loaders to implement persistent objects. When an invocation arrives at a process, Orbix searches for the target object in the process table. If not found, an exception is returned. However, if a loader object is installed in the process, it is informed about the object fault and provided an opportunity to load the target object and resume the invocation transparently to the caller. Our framework includes a persistent adaptation object that provides site information such as latitude, longitude, and altitude of airports and navigation aids.

Hardware and Software Used

	Hardware	Software
Interface	Sun SPARCstation 10, SGI Indigo R4000 with Elan Graphics	Xt/Motif, Mak Stealth Viewer, ICS BuilderXcessory
Core code		Solaris 2.4, Irix 5.32, SunSoft DOE, Orbix MT 1.3, SunSPARCompiler C++ 4.0, RogueWave Tools.h++, MaK Technologies' VR-Link

The size of the Framework is approximately 11,000 lines of code.

PROJECT LIFECYCLE

Analysis/Design

CAASD had some experience with object orientation. It had evaluated an object-oriented prototype in an air traffic control tower in 1989, and has fielded a prototype object-oriented network management system since then.

The problem was identified through the experience of building interactive simulations in the I-Lab. There was increasing desire for rapid reconfigurability.

Lab managers and technical leads had to sell object orientation to their superiors. According to Frederick Kuhl, project leader: "It still needs to be sold. CORBA may finally make object orientation a significant part of our development activity."

The methodology employed was Coad/Yourdon with frameworks according to Ralph Johnson.

According to Kuhl, the major benefit of object orientation in this phase was the clear analysis of simulation management protocol.

Development

Development was iterative. It involved two technical staff members and one co-op student—Bernadette Brooks, Glenn Waldron, Prashant Sridharan—full time for ten months.

For development software, an Early Developer's Release of Project DOE was chosen initially, and Orbix later, because they are well developed in regard to features considered to be essential for the framework:

- Support for activation of servers and objects, including the launching of implementation processes
- Static invocation interface
- Speed of invoking an active object
- Support for "flyweight" objects, allowing efficient access to many instances of the same classes, for example, Aircraft and Flight Plans

Kuhl assesses the benefits and drawbacks of object orientation in the development phase:

"We have a much richer set of services to support simulation than anything built previously.

"Our simulation manager took three weeks to program and has worked reliably; its conventional counterpart required four months and has remained a source of difficulty for years.

"The learning curve of ORB implementation inheritance was fairly steep."

Deployment and Maintenance

An initial version has been released for experimentation. Development is still underway.

BENEFITS

Benefits from deployment will depend not only on the usefulness of the framework but also the stability and reliability of the ORB and associated tools. Initial experience is encouraging where it is possible to compare development times for similar functions with development using conventional techniques.

CONCLUSIONS

Kuhl offers the following conclusions:

"We have proved that a simulation framework can be built that exploits the strengths of CORBA and supplements them with a special-purpose protocol. Implementation inheritance is essential to design a framework that is easy to use and easy to modify.

"What this project means to CAASD's overall approach to computing remains to be seen. ORB is no longer mere idle chatter, but it has not been proven yet. CAASD architects are considering incorporation of our framework into a significant air traffic control prototype. The success of this effort could determine the extent of the influence of our framework on CAASD.

"Programmers need a solid C++ base, and a solid understanding of concurrency. The architectural problems of distributed systems don't disappear in the face of CORBA; the project will need architects who understand the problems and can guide a development team. However, CORBA appears to be an effective tool for building distributed systems more easily."

5

Data Interchange and Synergistic Collateral Usage System (DISCUS)

The MITRE Corporation

THE OPPORTUNITY

The lack of interoperability of multiple legacy systems indicated that productivity benefits could be achieved by providing data interchange. The need for this capability was validated by an extensive survey of end users, and later by end-user testing using the DISCUS software.

DISCUS is an object-oriented system built by a nonprofit research organization (MITRE) for government furnished release on a no-fee basis to the government computing market as a reference technology. DISCUS is a not-for-resale system that is used by internal MITRE users, government software projects, and contractors on their independent research and development initiatives. The DISCUS system is a complete functional application system, as well as an object-oriented framework for advanced technologies to populate. The various development users of DISCUS have repopulated the framework with alternative sets of applications to meet their domain-specific requirements. As such, DISCUS has achieved one of the key object-oriented benefits of software/design, reuse, and acceptance of a common object-oriented framework by a multiorganization community of developers.

THE APPLICATION

DISCUS is a distributed object-oriented system integrating multiple legacy applications. The DISCUS system is a comprehensive end-user environment including operational information sources and application tools. For example, the end user can step through a complete work cycle, starting with initial task assignment, data retrieval, examination, analysis, annotation, and reporting. The tools work together seamlessly to interchange information with transparent format conversions. An extensible set of data types includes text, database tables, imagery, maps, spatial overlays, and documents. Data retrieval is automated through the exchange of end-user task context. For example, spatial coordinates from a database are used to automatically retrieve map coverage and other relevant information. In the final step, the end user can merge all the data items into a report, which is a final form information product that can be instantly transmitted to information consumers.

Early in the DISCUS project, the developers identified a synergistic commercial technology initiative, coordinated by the Object Management Group. DISCUS utilizes the OMG's standards including CORBA, the Interface Definition Language, and the Common Object Services Specification. In DISCUS, CORBA enhances the flexibility of the architecture through its support for distributed objects. CORBA provides location transparency and simplifies the programming of distributed objects. The essence of DISCUS software architecture is the OMG IDL (Interface Definition Language) specification. At less than 200 lines, the specification provides an implementation independent object-oriented encapsulation for all DISCUS applications and exchangeable data. The simplicity and portability of OMG IDL specification is a major source of DISCUS's success, since it clarified the object encapsulation requirements and simplified the development and maintenance of applications. The COSS (Common Object Services Specification) specifications provided essential guidance for implementation of life cycle services, in a manner that supports multiple languages (Smalltalk, C, CLOS, and C++) and distributed objects on multiple platforms (UNIX, Macintosh, and Microsoft Windows).

The custom application, DISCUS, was responsible for reducing the cost of legacy software integration. The system comprises a fully functional installation. The system will also be used for end user testing and evaluation of preoperational systems and R&D prototypes. The DISCUS testbed demonstrates the integration of both commercial software packages and legacy software. The DISCUS system was developed with the reuse of five legacy software applications.

DISCUS is an electronic desktop environment that supports end-to-end automation support for end users. The end users are primarily information scientists who require access to multiple forms of information: text, images, maps, and relational data. Figure 5.1 shows the application objects integrated to the DISCUS framework. The framework is entirely independent from

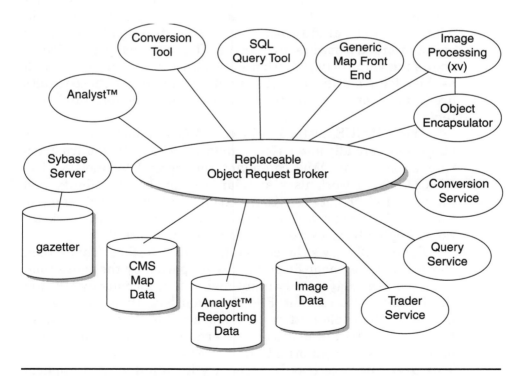

FIGURE 5.1 DISCUS applications.

the specific applications that comprise the integrated DISCUS systems, so that any or all of these applications can be replaced by the developers.

The legacy applications include the CMS mapping system, the imagery database, a document processor, an image processing tool, and several relational databases. DISCUS encapsulates these legacy applications using an object-oriented API specified in OMG IDL. DISCUS also adds some new generic services such as multidatabase generic map query tool, a conversion service, and the Trader service. The conversion service provides transparent translations between all of the various data formats used by the applications (or perform complex data transformations that were beyond the abilities of most end users).

DISCUS is a multiyear project chartered to create innovative solutions to interoperability problems. The current demonstration represents a third generation of the DISCUS framework, which has been carefully designed to embody a highly extensible object-oriented software architecture. The current system clearly shows the value of object-oriented software architectures, as well as the effective utilization of computing standards. These results are very supportive of framework-based object-oriented systems.

The DISCUS testbed utilizes OMG standards and many other commercially supported standards. The testbed infrastructure is based on OMG compliant commercial technology. The DISCUS framework uses standards to enable portability and interoperability between commercial platforms. For example, the DISCUS framework currently runs across UNIX workstations, Apple Macintoshes, and Microsoft Windows PCs.

Figure 5.2 shows the conversion user interface. This screen shows all of the image format types supported by the conversion tool. The user may specify input and output formats by clicking the format button in the File Selection box, then clicking the mouse on the radio button for the desired format. When possible, the software automatically determines the input file format based on available information such as the file name extension. This user interface is only necessary for unintegrated application. Applications that are integrated with the DISCUS system can exchange formats transparently using the same conversion services in a background software-controlled mode.

The Smalltalk Analyst Document System is a legacy word processing tool. It contains a DISCUS map data object of the UK, which was retrieved using the Generic Map Front End application shown in the background. GMFE can retrieve information from several map data sources, in this case the GMFE has retrieved a vector map of the UK coastline and rivers from CMS, a legacy application. Prior to DISCUS, these applications were unable to interchange data, and end-users had to go without map information in their documents, or wait for hardcopy layout services from a professional graphics shop.

DISCUS demonstrates interoperability between multiple legacy software projects and commercial software packages. MITRE achieved an unprecedented level of interoperability between these systems, but the real achievement was the simplicity of the solution, representing a substantial reduction in integration time and cost.

Overview of the Classes

Figure 5.2 shows the classes, attributes, and methods for the class hierarchy in the DISCUS framework.

Figure 5.3 shows an independent object class hierarchy for the property values of data objects. The separation of these hierarchies adds to the flexibility of the DISCUS framework to incorporate new properties without changing encapsulation code for the remaining applications and data objects.

DISCUS makes extensive use and inherits from pre-existing class definitions as contained in the CORBA specification, including NVLISTS and the class Object. The data object properties classes were inherited from a pre-existing object-oriented schema for application domain attributes.

The size of the total system, including legacy code, is about 3 million lines. The size of the integration code added to implement the encapsulations of legacy applications and new software includes about 3000 lines of code. The majority of this code

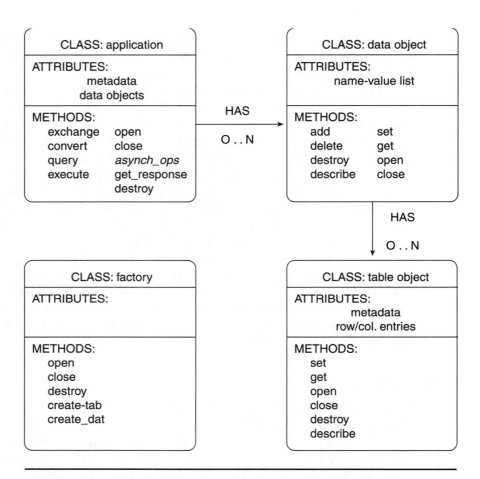

FIGURE 5.2 Application and data object class hierarchy.

is in C and Smalltalk, but selected functions were written in C++ and the Common Lisp Object System (CLOS).

Object-oriented features exploited in DISCUS include:

1. Use of OMG CORBA to implement the system. DISCUS is religiously compliant with CORBA and related OMG standards. The implementation architecture is described entirely in OMG IDL. The project used CORBA APIs and the COSS Life Cycle service.

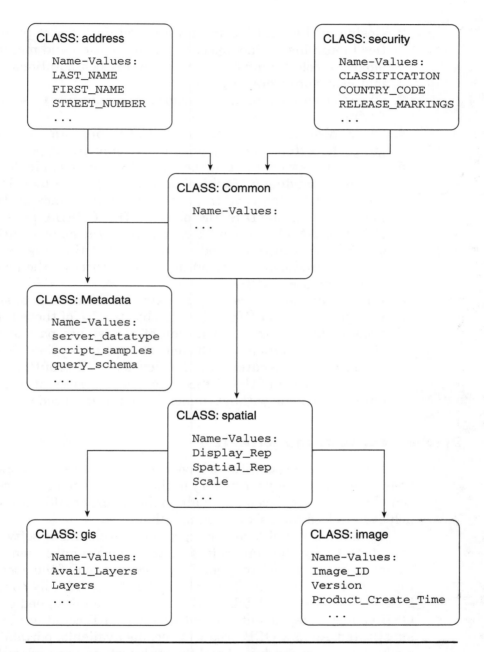

FIGURE 5.3   Data object property class hierarchy.

2. Design of the DISCUS framework and data object properties hierarchies using object-oriented notation and methodology. An eclectic mixture of Coad and Booch notations and methodologies were employed.

3. Object-oriented languages including Smalltalk, C++, and CLOS.

4. CLOS, also, as a functional or applicative programming language, for extended development environment support.

5. Various tools were built by the DISCUS team to aid in development, including a graphical data object inspect tool. They also coded testing code to provide a detailed trace of data flow through the DISCUS objects. The CORBA product, DEC ObjectBroker, provided control flow tracing by printing out messages in trace mode that indicated the progress of dynamic bindings of method invocations through the object request broker (ORB).

6. Implementation of the project team's own functions to support persistence of DISCUS data objects. Use of these functions makes the implementation of persistence part of the object encapsulation and the actual implementation of persistence is transparent to the developer. Retrofitting an implementation of the COSS Persistence service at a later date can be done without impacting application code.

Development Costs and Software

The total project expenditures have been less than seven person years over the three-year history of the project. The most recent complete reuse (replacement of all applications) of DISCUS was achieved in less than six person months.

In many cases of legacy integration, development software was dictated by the constraints of the legacy application, for example, the choice of compiler, language, version of the operating system, and so forth. The CORBA ORB was initially chosen based upon early availability. DISCUS has been designed to be ORB vendor independent, so that another ORB could easily be substituted. As new ORB products became available, portability evaluations were conducted and the architecture was updated to reflect different interpretations of the standard. The team has hands-on experience with most of the available CORBA ORBs and they are confident that they can port to other ORBs with minimal application impact.

According to Tom Mowbray, specific benefits of using object orientation in DISCUS are:

- **Design Reuse.** The DISCUS framework design has been reusable across most types of applications that have been encountered. The addition of some new data object properties has been all that was needed to support new application types. DISCUS supports the introduction of new data format conversion services and new data object properties without modification to previously integrated application.
- **Polymorphism.** The DISCUS framework uses a polymorphic data object definition that allows applications of all types to share common base properties, and allows specialization to create unique domain specific properties. Due to object orientation, the new properties do not interfere with the base class methods and properties. This greatly increases interoperability between applications in DISCUS.
- **Abstraction through Encapsulation.** A primary example of how abstraction benefited DISCUS is the conversion services. DISCUS defined a common encapsulation for conversion services that was used to encapsulate all types of conversion services, regardless of legacy APIs or parameter conventions. As a result, the initial conversion service included three libraries of format conversions that combined allowed over thirty data file formats to be interchanged. This combined the power of multiple disparate APIs through a common encapsulation. Software clients of conversion services have a consistent simple interface to any type of conversion, even conversions that are introduced to the system after the application code is written.

Mowbray cites some drawbacks to object orientation experienced in DISCUS:

- **Fragmentation of the object-oriented CASE Market.** The abundance of object-oriented methodologies and notations made it difficult to choose one. Initially they were hoping that an object-oriented notation could help document the system for maintainers and reusers. A market survey revealed that due to the fragmented object-oriented notation, none of the existing notations provided any leverage towards creating universally understandable documentation. So, we chose to document DISCUS for intracompany consumption using more conventional techniques, such as prose descriptions, examples, and UNIX-style manual pages.

■ Encapsulation. Access to data hidden behind an encapsulation layer was sometimes awkward for the programmers. It was sometimes difficult to utilize the dynamic ORB type "any," but compiler-generated type code handles for user-defined types will make this easier in the future.

■ Early ORB Products. The early ORB releases were divergent from the written CORBA standard in many ways. In order to realize the goal of ORB portability in DISCUS they were forced to layer CORBA compliant features in several places over the ORB product, such as the typecode mechanism and the exception values. More recent releases of ORBs have virtually eliminated this issue. This eliminates the need for CORBA layering code, reducing maintenance cost.

BENEFITS OF DISCUS

A primary DISCUS benefit is the reduction of software development cost. One of the constituent legacy applications was integrated for a cost of less than $35,000 versus an estimated $2 million. Given that six comparable legacy applications were integrated, the potential cost savings would be over $10 million. However, such a cost would have made the effort fiscally unfeasible. None of this could have been achieved without the use of CORBA-based distributed objects.

Since DISCUS integrates six legacy systems that were formerly unable to communicate, the end user saves considerable rekeying time.

Applications Developed with Reusable Components

OVERVIEW OF SECTION III

In Chapter 2 we discussed the wide variety of objects, components, and frameworks that companies are using to facilitate the reuse of code. Before considering applications that demonstrate the value of reuse, let's consider the more common types of reuse and the components that facilitate it.

To date most reuse has resulted from the use of class libraries that accompany object-oriented languages like Smalltalk and C++ or application development environments like PowerBuilder or VisualAge. If you were accustomed to developing an application in an older language like COBOL and instead used Smalltalk, you would be impressed by how much less code you had to write. Lots of things that you would need to write in COBOL comes prepackaged in the class libraries that accompany any Smalltalk language package.

In spite of the real time savings that results from reusing code stored in class libraries, however, class libraries have not significantly reduced the overall time it takes to develop applications. When you consider that most of the time in application development is consumed in analysis and design and relatively little in the actual coding process, you realize that even if you cut the coding effort in half, you wouldn't speed the overall development process up very much.

To get the significant increases in productivity that object-oriented theorists have promised, you need to consider larger components. When you develop an application using business objects, you use them initially when you are analyzing the problem and creating a business model. If you already have a library of business objects, you can probably significantly reduce the time it takes to do an analysis and design effort. Moreover, if your business objects have already been tested, you can significantly reduce the time it takes to test the new application. Reuse based on development with business objects can result in major increases in developer productivity. Unfortunately, most companies don't have libraries of business objects and are only beginning to create them.

In the meantime, many companies are exploring the use of specialized programming frameworks and document components. These components lie about halfway between the smaller classes contained in class libraries and the larger business objects. We predict that developers will be impressed with how much faster development goes with these mid-size components, but that, in the longer run, companies will still turn to business objects for really major increases in productivity.

With that overview, let's consider what's happening in each of the component niches.

CLASSES AND CLASS LIBRARIES

Most class libraries are acquired along with an object-oriented language or an object-oriented application development tool. The classes that accompany object-oriented languages tend to be more generic, while class libraries accompanying tools are often written in the internal or scripting language of the tool and are hard to use outside that context. Even language-based class libraries have historically been difficult to use with any other language, although CORBA is making it much easier to mix class libraries and languages.

In addition to the class libraries that are packaged with object-oriented languages and application development tools, there are some independent class library vendors. The best known, perhaps, is Rogue Wave that sells several C++ class libraries. Smaller vendors who have been positioning themselves as class library vendors are now generally repositioning themselves as document component vendors.

SPECIALIZED PROGRAMMING CLASSES
AND FRAMEWORKS

Specialized programming classes are larger and tend to be grouped together to provide some type of advanced functionality. Indeed, almost all specialized programming classes are sold as frameworks. We have already mentioned that the word framework can be used to refer to either groups of specialized classes or document components, or it can refer to a collection of business objects. When the term framework is applied to specialized classes or document components, it is often called an application framework—suggesting that the framework contains all of the classes needed to develop an application.

Historically, the most important application framework has been the MacApp framework. For years Macintosh application developers have used this framework to create Macintosh applications. Its use accounts for the consistency of Macintosh applications. There has never been anything like it, until very recently, for DOS, Windows, or Unix, and thus, applications running on those platforms tend to be very inconsistent. Different approaches to windowing and tool bars make it hard to move from one application to another.

Packages are now available to help developers create consistent Unix and Windows applications, but these aren't object-oriented environments and, in any case, many companies are now interested in developing consistent applications that can run on a variety of different platforms.

Next began by offering a computer and an object-oriented development environment, NextStep, that made it very easy to develop applications for Next machines. Some applications in this book were developed by taking advantage of the NextStep environment. A few years ago, Next realized that it wasn't going to succeed as another hardware vendor and shifted its strategy. They have stopped selling hardware and focused on software. More specifically, they have changed the name of their object-oriented application development framework to OpenStep and are now implementing it on various platforms.

Next's strategy is very similar to the strategy that Taligent evolved. Taligent originally started out to be an operating system vendor, but changed and is now focusing on creating an object-oriented application development environment, Common Point, that a developer can use to create applications that will run on any of several different platforms.

In effect, both Next and Taligent are trying to sell generic application frameworks that companies can use to develop object-oriented applications that will run on any of the major platforms.

DOCUMENT COMPONENTS

When most people think of document components, they think of Microsoft's OLE2 components or CI Labs' OpenDoc components. Both Microsoft and CI Labs have created specifications for components that can be used to integrate documents. As vendors develop specific components and companies begin to use them, a whole new approach to PC and departmental application development will come into being.

The usual way of explaining document components is to talk about wanting to embed a figure in a word processing text file. It would be nice if you could combine the features of a word processing program and a drawing program so that you can edit them as if they were a single file. Or, to think of it a little differently, think how many PC programs you have that each has its own spellchecker. It would be nice if you could link whatever text processing program you want to use to your favorite spellchecker. The way to facilitate this sort of thing is to modularize everything so that the user can link modules together, as needed. That was what OLE2 and OpenDoc are designed to do.

They provide a way of breaking procedural PC programs (like Word, Lotus, and Draw) into components so that they can later be assembled by users to satisfy their specific requirements.

At the moment there are two organizations that have developed standards for components that can be used to link documents and create GUI. Many different vendors are working on actual document components that implement each of these two models. (There are other groups working on document component models, but I expect these two groups will dominate the market.) The two organizations proposing standards are CI Labs (OpenDoc) and Microsoft (OLE).

The CI Labs/OpenDoc Strategy

CI Labs is a consortium whose members include hardware and software companies—IBM, Apple, H-P and DEC—as well as Novell and Lotus and corporate consumers like Citibank and American Airlines.

Figure III.1 provides an overview of some of the elements that make up the OpenDoc "family." The OpenDoc standard is based in IBM's distributed SOM standard, which, in turn, is based on the OMG's CORBA2 standard, which is ultimately grounded in OMG's Object Model. The OpenDoc standard provides complete object-oriented support. An OpenDoc component is a SOM object with some sixty methods added to it. You can add more methods, but the specified sixty methods guarantee that the component has a standard interface that will allow it to interact with other OpenDoc components. At the moment, several different vendors are readying sets of OpenDoc components for release in 1996.

To give a hint of the future, we have included IBM's Visual-Age tool and Taligent's CommonPoint framework. VisualAge is a visual programming environment that includes a number of components. At the moment these components are based on SOM objects, but are not exactly compatible with OpenDoc standards. IBM will change the components (parts) in VisualAge to make them compatible with the OpenDoc standard so that anyone using VisualAge will be able to use any OpenDoc component in a VisualAge application. Other tool vendors will do the same

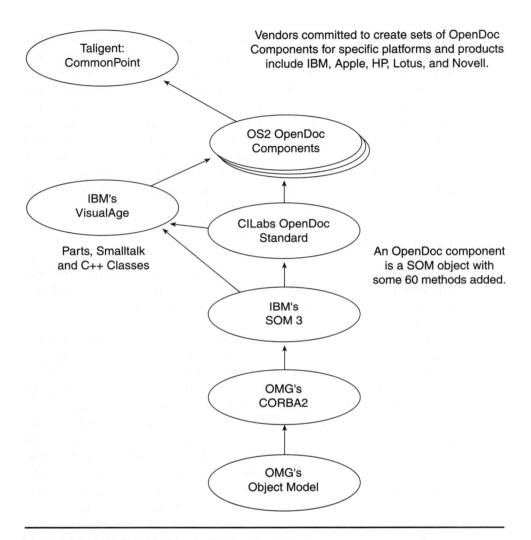

FIGURE III.1 The OpenDoc component standard.

thing. Tools supporting OpenDoc components should begin to appear in 1996.

Taligent (which has recently become a subsidiary of IBM) has released its CommonPoint framework for OS/2—in essence a large set of classes and components that support application development. Taligent currently uses SOM to handle the distribution of objects, but does not support OpenDoc components. Taligent will probably change its internal standard to bring it into line with the OpenDoc standard in the 1996-1997 time-frame. This will mean that tools and developers working with Taligent will also be able to use any other OpenDoc components.

All the companies supporting OpenDoc believe in object-oriented technology and they all want an open component standard that can be used to create multiplatform systems. In addition, of course, several of the vendors regard Microsoft as their major competitor and are determined to support developments that will prevent Microsoft from developing a proprietary standard for component-based development.

In an attempt to assure that the OpenDoc approach is open, Novell (WordPerfect) has developed a set of OpenDoc components for the MS Windows environment that function, in effect, exactly like OLE components. Thus, while you cannot develop an OpenDoc component in OLE, you can develop OLE components in OpenDoc. Moreover, it's easier to develop OpenDoc components than OLE components. In addition, OpenDoc components are truly object-oriented and can support greater functionality than OLE components. Thus, it would seem that OpenDoc developers can have the best of both worlds, while, at the moment, OLE only runs on Windows and doesn't provide a complete object model.

We also believe that CI Labs recognizes that OpenDoc components will serve a limited function and that eventually business objects will play an even more important role in the overall components market. Everyone we have discussed business objects with is convinced that the business objects market will depend on an open distributed computing environment and on the development of interface standards. No one that we have talked with who is active in business object development believes that OLE can support business objects.

The actual component vendors in the case of OpenDoc, are, initially, the various hardware vendors who are implementing OpenDoc on their platforms, and subsequently, everyone else who wants to encapsulate a component in an OpenDoc interface. As we have already suggested, we expect that most of the Class Library vendors and most of the object-oriented tool vendors will migrate to OpenDoc in the course of the next two to three years. The widespread availability of OpenDoc components in 1996-1997 should begin an exciting new era in object-oriented component development.

The Microsoft/OLE Strategy

Microsoft is a single company and has the advantage over CI Labs that it can move faster and coordinate its considerable resources to promote its approach to document components. Figure III.2 provides an overview of the OLE family. OLE presents a much more inconsistent picture. To begin with, Microsoft created OLE1, which was an elementary document linking system. Then it broadened its sights and produced OLE2, which has little in common with OLE1.

OLE2 does not currently support inheritance or polymorphism and is not truly object-oriented, although it does support encapsulation. Nor does OLE2 currently provide any way for documents to travel through networks while retaining their ability to be edited. Moreover, OLE's overall approach is procedural and requires that OLE clients or servers be well defined and that communications between them be precisely specified in advance. Microsoft claims that it will make OLE available on other platforms and evolve it to support distributed computing, but it's hard to see how Microsoft will do this, given OLE's current limitations.

Microsoft's popular VisualBasic product allows developers to create components that conform with the OLE2 standard, and they are popularly called VBX components. Many companies that rely on Windows extensively are very excited about VBX components and they are rapidly developing VBX libraries. Similarly, several new software vendors are busy creating VBX components. Most tools claim to support OLE, but most, in fact, support OLE1 and are only now preparing to support OLE2.

Microsoft's original OLE2 standard was based on its component object model. Recently, Microsoft signed an agreement with Digital and they have created a new Common Object Model than can serve as the basis for a bridge between OLE and CORBA. At the same time, Microsoft is developing a new ver-

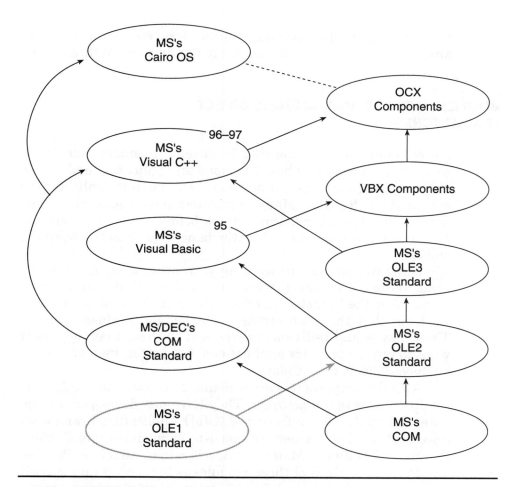

FIGURE III.2 The OLE component standard.

sion of OLE for distributed computing and promoting the use of their Visual C++ product as a way to create OCX components that will be more sophisticated than VBX components and will work with future versions of MS's operating system. At some point, Microsoft will, presumably, align their upcoming Cairo operating system (which is supposed to be object-oriented) with OCX components and with their new COM model.

It is hard to develop OLE systems. They are not, at the moment, object-oriented, capable of supporting distributed systems, or capable of supporting multiplatform environments. They are going to change over the course of the next two to three years.

BUSINESS OBJECTS AND BUSINESS OBJECT FRAMEWORKS

Many companies are working to develop business objects. In some cases, a company has developed an application and is now using some of the classes it developed for the first application in a second application. Many companies have found that they need to develop several applications before they can determine exactly what attributes and methods need to be in the business objects.

Some companies are working with other companies in the same industry to develop business objects that can be used throughout the industry. In effect, these business object consortia hope that they can create a market for business objects. Then they would tell vendors who sell to them that they don't want to buy proprietary applications, but prefer, instead, to buy business objects from them.

A good example of this is the Semitech consortium made up of semiconductor manufacturers. They have just developed a Computer Integrated Manufacturing (CIM) Application Framework Specification. The framework consists of modules like Factory, Planner, Scheduler, Material, Specification, Machine/Process, and Personnel. Each of these modules is broken up into specific classes and each class is defined in terms of attributes and methods. The specification allows each company or vendor to implement the classes as it sees fit. Thus, one company might code the framework in C++ while another might code it in Smalltalk, using specific class libraries from a specific Smalltalk vendor.

There are a few vendors who are already selling business objects for specific industries—specifically in finance.

Companies that are serious about reuse are beginning to assign managers to keep track of company component libraries and they are working out procedures to determine who has ownership of specific components and how they should be updated. Similarly, companies are developing indexes to their component libraries and they are modifying personnel policies to reward developers for reusing code whenever they can.

A few companies are becoming quite sophisticated in software reuse, but most companies are just beginning to learn about reuse. The applications discussed in this book range from applications where developers obtained reuse from class libraries to more complex applications that relied on a wide variety of components. Two applications involved the development of application frameworks as a prelude to specific application development efforts. Still, all these applications only illustrate the beginning phases of the corporate move to software reuse. We expect that as companies develop better frameworks and accumulate business class libraries, reuse will continue to emerge as a major focus of all object-oriented application development efforts.

APPLICATIONS

Section III considers five finalists in the Object World contest that focused on reuse.

Canadian Imperial Bank of Commerce's Human Resources Application (HRA)
Finalist, Category 3, 1995

This application is a suite of some twenty discrete human resource applications developed as the company sought to re-engineer its human resources process. This application was developed as part of a major re-engineering effort undertaken by Canadian Imperial Bank. Specific applications included Job Evaluation, Open Staffing, Pensions, Payroll, and Compensation Administration. To facilitate the development of the suite, the company developed business objects that could be reused in various specific application. Business objects included: Buys, Unit, Branch, Salary, Job Level, Performance, Compensation, Position, and so on. The actual development was done in Sapiens' object-oriented Application Development Tool for mainframe use. The bank used Sapiens' ObjectPool as a repository for the business objects. The application is fielded on an IBM 3090 and on PCs.

The developers estimate that the effort took only one-quarter of the time it would have taken had they used a conventional approach and not obtained significant reuse. Like the first application in Section II, this application could have gone in almost any category. It involves the use of object-oriented tools, business objects, and an object-oriented repository. It was done as part of a corporate re-engineering effort, was distributed, and combined object-oriented code with legacy code to create a large system in a relative short time.

Swiss Cantons of Zug and Solothurn and IBM Switzerland's Professional Forms Application (ProFormA).
Finalist, Category 3, 1995

ProFormA is a new tax declaration application for two cantons. It allows canton officials to modify forms as tax laws change. The original effort was to use a conventional approach, but it was decided that such an approach would not provide adequate flexibility for updates. ProFormA was designed with the Booch methodology using Rational's Rose object-oriented analysis and design product. The application used IBM's SOM implementation of CORBA to handle distribution. It was coded in C++. The application obtained reuse from a variety of sources ranging from C++ class libraries and SOM objects through some sixty-four business objects developed specifically for the project. This application provides a very good example of the various ways an object-oriented development effort can obtain reuse from a variety of different sized components ranging from class libraries associated with object-oriented languages through technical frameworks to business objects. The group reported that this effort was 40 percent more productive than an earlier similar effort that had not taken advantage of reuse.

Here's another one of those complex object-oriented applications that could have been a finalist in any of several categories. It involves a bit of everything: re-engineering, reuse, significant cost savings, ease of maintenance, and distributed computing.

Naval Computer and Telecommunications Station in San Diego's MTF (Message Text Format Editor)
Winner, Category 3, 1995

This application helps format messages as required by the Navy. A wide variety of messages must be formatted in a specific way to ensure efficient communication. This application sees that each message is formatted correctly and is without omissions. The application was analyzed and designed via the Booch methodology. The actual coding was in Ada and C++. The developers relied on AdaSAGE, a large Ada component library. The authors discuss the problems of trying to find new components for reuse as compared with simply writing them—suggesting the need for centrally managed component libraries and good indexing systems. This is an example of an application that completely solved a problem that had previously resisted a complete solution. The main credit for this goes to the object modeling effort. This application illustrates how even a partial use of object technology, especially in the analysis phase, can be very useful.

Swiss Cantons of Zug and Solothurn and IBM Switzerland's Commercial Register
Winner, Category 5, 1994

IBM Switzerland, Business Government Solutions division, developed a second application for the Swiss cantons of Zug and Solothurn. In this case the application was called the Commercial Register, and it helps canton clerks record information about new corporations registering with the cantons. IBM started with a conventional 4GL, but found it inadequate and switched to C++ and made extensive use of C++ class libraries. IBM began its analysis using the Coad methodology, but switched to Booch to handle the complexity of the application.

This case provides a nice example of the different types of components that can be used in an application. Language class libraries are used. A variety of interface, database, and technical components are used. General application objects and specific business objects are used. All of these classes and components taken together make up most of the code used in this application.

This system is fielded on OS/2 and AS/400 hardware.

This is a second application that resulted from the re-engineering effort undertaken by two Swiss cantons. It is also another example of an effort that began with a conventional approach and then turned to an object-oriented approach to simplify the development effort.

Palm Beach County's ISS Medical Examiner System
Finalist, Category 5, 1994

This application tracks deaths that must be investigated by the Coroner's Office. The application was developed in PowerBuilder 3.0 and SQL*Net. The developers used PowerCerv's PowerTool template and object-oriented library as a foundation. This isn't a large application, but it illustrates how classes can reduce development time of client/server applications developed in object-based tools. It also illustrates how class libraries can be integrated with an object-based tool to solve a well-defined problem. This isn't a major object-oriented project, but it's probably very similar to many of the mixed object-based client/server applications that companies will be undertaking in 1996 and 1997.

Human Resources Applications

6

Canadian Imperial Bank of Commerce

THE OPPORTUNITY

Canadian Imperial Bank of Commerce considers its greatest resource to be its 50,000 employees. The bank saw a need to better manage that resource, because of the belief that their people make the business difference. In dealing with people, the bank identified immediate needs—needs that kept changing, yet had to be addressed almost immediately. Even without the full picture of what was needed, the bank had to implement and change quickly.

Deregulation was bringing new competitors into the financial services industry in Canada. The rate of change in the industry was increasing, and going higher. CIBC needed to address its short-term needs now and integrate them later. Traditionally, it used to take six months just to write requirements. Then they went through a process of having them checked. Finally, they would develop the application. If developers would take twelve months to develop one of these applications, it would be out of date before it was actually implemented.

Often, the schedule required managers to submit annual compensation increases before assessing performance. Employees had little way to mentally link their performance to the increases they were given for review and possible adjustment.

CIBC's 38,000 employees in Canada work in 1,400 branches and a number of Head Offices/Regional Offices. To handle the needs of these employees required a large staff of human resource professionals. The concern was the cost of the HR resources and the increasing number of HR business functions that were being provided.

THE APPLICATION

Human Resources Applications is a knowledge-based environment, containing approximately twenty discrete business functions (applications). Some of these applications include:

- Compensation Administration
- Job Evaluation
- Open Staffing
- Competency
- Administration
- Pension
- Payroll
- Benefits
- Employment Equity
- Health & Safety

Some applications are massive, others are small. However, they all are tightly interwoven and feature business objects that have proven highly reusable.

The original task was re-engineering three major business functions: Compensation Administration, Job Evaluation, and Open Staffing. Among the goals were to move administration of several HR functions to the line managers, and to give employees more responsibility for pursuing and developing their own career paths. During the process, additional functionality was provided in a number of business areas (approximately twenty). Some examples follow.

In the area of Compensation Administration, a program was introduced in 1991 that was nicknamed the "thin edge of the wedge." It was part of a plan to make every manager a people manager. It consisted of such functions as annual payroll increases and performance bonuses. Figure 6.1a shows a 3270 snapshot of the screen that displays the components used to determine an employee's bonus amount. Figure 6.1b shows the same information through the new GUI. It is the same application, using the same data objects and rules, with a different presentation layer.

In 1993, a program called Job Evaluation was introduced. The goal simply was to get the right people into the right jobs. The situation at hand was a listing of nearly 4,000 jobs throughout the corporation. There was, however, no consistency in job descriptions and no framework for comparing work within the organization. The results again were most favorable. The total number of "official" jobs was reduced from 4,000+ to about 500. Jobs now are described consistently using terms currently valued by CIBC. As a result, pay is consistent for similar types of work, and the number of job levels reduced from 35+ to 10.

Another program developed is the Competency Administration System. In it, current job skills of all employees are kept and updated. With that done, if you have a perfect model of the corporation and the skills of its individuals, you can then talk rationally about development needs. With this system, managers know what training has been supplied to each employee, and what training is needed by each, either for their current position, or for advancement.

In the area of Open Staffing, prior to 1993, employees generally found out about open positions through the corporation by word of mouth or the "old boys network." HR slated the jobs and moved people—a high administration cost. Employees had little feeling of career development. After building the 500 job descriptions, the system added functionality to allow managers to post open positions on-line (a policy requirement for all positions of vice-president and below).

Using the on-line job catalogue, a manager selects the appropriate job and adds any local needs. Overnight, the job posting is converted into a computer generated voice ad and placed on the Staffing Network. Employees can then dial into

```
CIBC HR - TRANSACTIONS           TM DOLLARS CALC              (753015)
COMMAND =>
  S.I.N.   SURNAME                    INIT  TITLE  KNOWN AS         REC CAT
  440302370 SMITH_____   __   MR._   JOHN_____      1 1 0

  JOB CODE    JOB TITLE                       JOB LEVEL
   123_       MANAGER, PRIVATE BANKING CTR._    8_

  EARNINGS    MKT MULT %    (1)                MARKET RATE
  76517___ x    10.00_ =    7652__   <=======  CALCULATION

                           (1)      MULT %  WGT %    (2)
  CIBC_____   7652_ x  95.00_ x 25.00_ = 1817_  <=
                           (1)                       (3)    BUSINESS
  P&C_____   7652_ x  95.00_ x 25.00_ = 1817  <= RESULTS
                           (1)                       (4)      CALCULATIONS
  OTTAWA EAST_____   7652_ x 101.53 x 50.00_ = 3885_  <=

  (2)+(3)+(4)   PPM %   TEAM$   AMENDMENTS   TTL TEAM $    PERSONAL
    7519_     x  100 =  7519_ +   31___  =    7550__    <== PERFORMANCE
                                                            CALCULATION

  ==   INPUT   ==..................... R0009 S MF RL15   18/12/95 12:10:51
  1-HELP 3-QUIT 9-FRANèAIS 24-ZOOM
  ⌗⌗⌗            Aa   A Session1   R 2  C 13          13:16  12/18/95
```

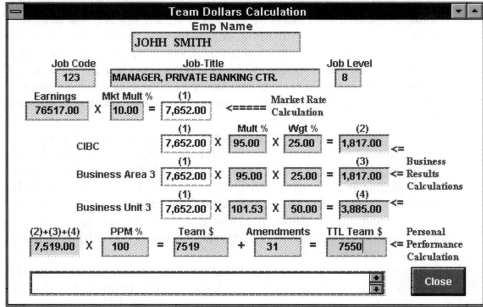

FIGURE 6.1 Bonus information. Top (a) 3270 version. Bottom (b) GUI version.

the Staffing Network, using an 800 number. By pressing appropriate codes for job experience and career path, they can access the computer voice ad summary. If interested, they can leave their fax number, and the complete job description is sent to them. Figure 6.2 shows a job listing on the HRA system.

There is an extremely high reusability of data objects between applications. Presentation objects are assembled using Sapiens built-in classes from the repository.

Size of the System

Human Resources Applications, with approximately 4,000 online users (line managers, administrators, and others), consists of 1,500 screens, 840 tables, and 15 interfaces to external systems. It also contains 13 DB-DASD (for example, one of the DB2

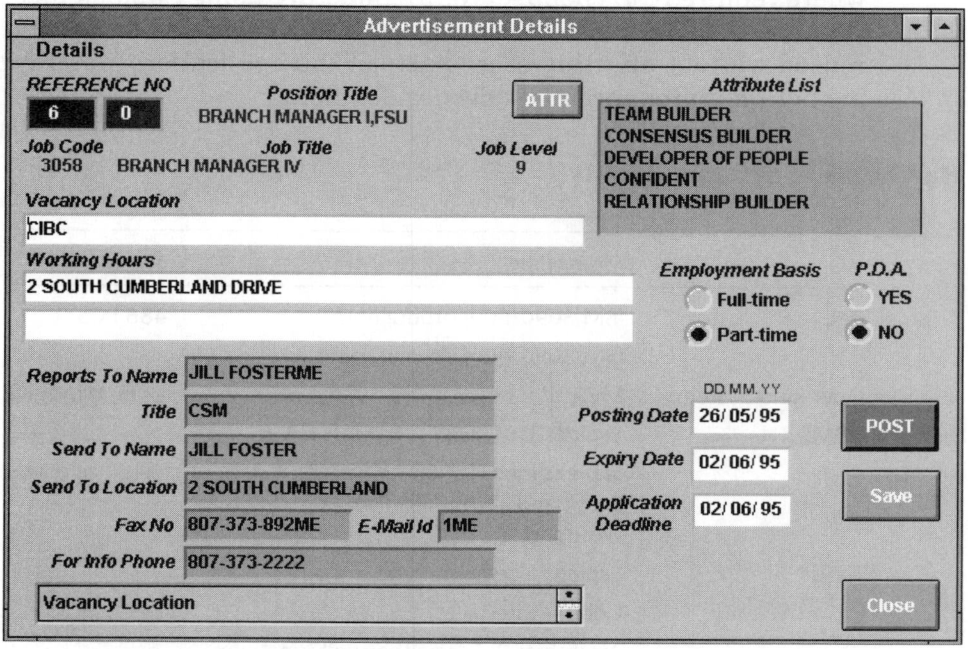

FIGURE 6.2   Job listing.

tables contains 10 million rows). On-line, there are 6,000 IMS DC transactions per hour (peak), which corresponds to 60,000 business transactions per hour (peak), with a 16-hour day, plus 360,000 batched transactions per night.

Object-Oriented Features Used in the System

The development tool (Sapiens) provides a complete environment for rapid development of centralized mainframe applications, including a high-level rule language and an object-oriented structure for attaching rules to data definitions. Applications are built by assembling and editing business objects. Objects are stored in Sapiens ObjectPool. The ObjectPool provides database-independent access to IMS and Sapiens DB1 and DB2. In addition, by triggering the rules attached to the objects, the ObjectPool environment leverages mainframe processing power and allows distribution of presentation objects (and distribution of processing where required), to client/server architecture using Sapiens Ideo. Because they are discrete, the objects can be changed easily and reused without affecting other parts of the application, simplifying both maintenance and new development.

Hardware/Software Used

	Mainframe	*Server*
CPU	IBM 3090/600J production	486 PCS
	IBM 3090/400J development	
Operating Systems	MVS	DOS, Windows
DBMS	Sapiens/DB1, DB2, VSAM, IMS-DB	
	Sapiens Ideo, Sapiens IQ, Lotus 1-2-3, Excel, and TP monitorIMS/DC, TSO, Wordperfect	
Tools	Sapiens—development & maintenance,	
	Cobol—interfaces,	
	Assembler PL1—off-the-shelf functions,	
	QMF—ad hoc reporting on DB2 tables	

ObjectPool supports three classes of Objects: Data, Program, Presentation. Objects have messages and methods associated with them. The application is event-driven and datacentric—action in a data object causes a reaction to be triggered. Messages are passed between the data objects, or data object to program object (3GL). It also can trigger methods specific to the presentation layer based. If you push it a little, the message itself can be viewed as an object, since it too can have methods attached to it, triggered before or after passage to the presentation layer (EDITTRAN and ISSUETRAN rules).

There is some inheritance in ObjectPool—PF keys in 3270 presentation (and ZOOM and SELECT functionalities) can be inherited from predecessors, data objects can inherit keys of its parent and grandparent, and so on.

More examples of inheritance are found in Sapiens Ideo. For example, buttons and column displays (fields from the database) inherit the characteristics of the display template used for the window. The same is true of virtual methods. Ideo methods can be modified on the fly. Methods are encapsulated as part of the object. They can be reused by (encapsulated) more than one object, either directly or by calling.

Sapiens Object Modeler generates some methods for referential integrity. Data access in both ObjectPool and Ideo is built dynamically, based on the attributes of the data object. ObjectPool generates default presentation objects (DETAIL, ZOOM, and SELECT), it generates automatic application flow and presentation controls, that is, submenus based on table relationships and PF key assignments. Both ObjectPool and Ideo have built-in constraint handling that automatically validates and presents a list of values without programming effort. This list of values automatically becomes cursor sensitive documentation. Other object-oriented features of the Human Resources Applications include:

■ Extended Programming Environment. Human Resources has five types of TOL methods: check, local, derive, call, and fetch. SmartGL for Ideo is presentation object oriented. ObjectPool has "positive thinking," an inference engine. Ideo can invoke program objects on the mainframe through the

ObjectPool by sending a message (transaction) that causes an update to a mainframe data object.

- In a PC environment, everything is basically point and click. The browser is GUI. Ideo has editors for the objects. Ideo is portable across MAC, PC, and UNIX.
- ObjectModeler and SapiensWorkstation are GUI. The language is tokenized. SapiensWorkstation graphical browser can put all the information in the KnowledgeBase into a graphical context.
- Mainframe development can be done either in 3270 mode or using PC GUI workstations. Mainframe ObjectPool is portable across all mainframe operating systems, TP monitors, and DBMSs.
- Storage Management. Sapiens ObjectPool has a very powerful, active repository with many built-in features that are inherited for every object. It offers a high degree of reusability, point and click impact analysis. It guides in the development cycle, provides developer-error protection, a lot of default/selectable functionality, and much more.
- For Ideo, source code for application components can be exported to ASCII text files. Developers can then use any configuration management tool they choose in order to manage version control, validation, and change.
- For mainframe components, ObjectPool provides a change management facility that allows migration of application rules between development and production environments.

PROJECT LIFECYCLE

Analysis and Design

The Human Resources Applications is headed by Allen Douthwaite. He describes their initial approach:

"We needed to develop human resource products with our target culture in mind. We needed to use technology to enable the change to occur. While being developed for a desired (not current) practice, we had to begin development immediately. In all, we've been developing applications for nearly three years. While a master plan would have been ideal, we couldn't wait three years to develop that plan, and then begin development, so, instead, we began a process of significantly changing the culture and mindset of the HR clients.

"Having identified the problem, we formed groups, drawing from three areas. These groups included users (from different layers of management and administration), business analysts, and developers (IS personnel). We also requested some technical consulting from Sapiens."

According to Douthwaite object orientation did not have to be sold. The methodology used was a RAD/JAD approach. Traditional (non-object orientation) approaches were not considered because they were too slow. Among the developers' considerations was the need to also create a shift of mindset—in management, developers, and users.

Using RAD provided high reusability. Coupled with the other features of Sapiens, they saw a significant potential for increased productivity, decreased delivery time, and decreased development effort. Managers now have more flexibility making decisions.

Reduced time in gathering requirements, faster confirmation, and a dramatic reduction in the amount of paperwork required resulted in a major benefit—a reduction of up to 75 percent.

Development

The methodology used was RAD/JAD. Users and business analysts are actively involved in the development cycle.

The Sapiens development and maintenance environment is highly reusable and modular—developers mostly deal with what is required and not how to implement it technically. Sapiens automatically takes care of technical details. The decision to use Sapiens was based on the need for fast delivery, and fast change. With that in mind, CIBC ran a pilot to verify the claims of productivity gains.

Regarding the benefits of object orientation in the development phase Douthwaite states:

"The primary benefit of using object-oriented methodology is high reusability of objects. Also, bringing the developers and users closer together led to an overall improvement in the way we work. Prototyping is faster, and screens are organized in a way that matches how people work. Because Sapiens gives you a working application from the start, we are able to involve the users throughout the development cycle."

Deployment

In effect, users continuously participate in evolving the application to meet the business needs. At the same time, they are becoming experienced with the applications, and are used as communicators/facilitators in the deployment process. For specific business areas (with a small number of users), participation in the application lifecycle substantially reduces the learning curve once the application goes into production.

Automatically produced documentation is used for user manuals/training material, and on-line cursor/field value sensitive help. This results in ease-of-use and reduced learning curve. All applications look and behave similarly, using easy-to-use and understand presentation standards encouraged by the Sapiens environment.

Maintenance

High reusability, rules encapsulated with data, central/single place of definition, inheritance, inference engine (Sapiens' positive thinking mechanism), and impact analysis tools dramatically reduce the maintenance effort by up to 90 percent compared with a traditional maintenance environment.

BENEFITS

Use of object orientation enabled technology to support the re-engineering initiative, which in itself significantly reduced the cost of the human resource function at CIBC, while providing increased functionality to the line.

Interface to employees is quicker and more direct and provides added value to CIBC as a whole. HR is now out of data collection and simple day-to-day tasks. Instead, they focus on business policies and guidelines.

There are specific benefits for the business areas, including the following.

Compensation Administration

Managers used to spend six to eight weeks just on administration using an expensive paper system. Today, line managers receive the corporate guidelines and administer all compensation activities for their unit. Performance ratings, bonus allocation, and annual merit increases all are directly entered (on-line) into our Compensation Administration system. It is rolled-up, on-line, and in real time.

Information is immediately available on a district, regional, and national level. Managers now have more flexibility in how their group dollars are allocated to employees. Managers now make increase decisions based on performance. Human Resources now can concentrate on factors such as compensation policy and design.

Job Evaluation

The total number of "official" jobs was reduced from 4,000+ to about 500. Jobs now are described consistently using CIBC's values. Pay is consistent for similar types of work. The number of job levels was reduced from 35+ to 10, while allowing for market differentiation.

Open Staffing

Job postings now are created by the manager who needs the resource, not by central HR administration. For employees, now they can see what opportunities are available within CIBC for their career stream/area of interest.

Increased Career Mobility across the Organization

Human Resources is no longer a bottleneck for employees seeking career opportunities elsewhere within the organization. The program supports CIBC's "selection from within" strategy, keeping good talent in CIBC and reducing costly external recruitment expenses. The program allows all employees confidential access via phone/fax (using IVR technology) to all potential job opportunities.

CONCLUSIONS

Allan Douthwaite shares the following observations with those contemplating a similar development effort:

> "Stress data capture at the source. Continue to reduce HR administrative costs. Only pass those responsibilities to the line where they add value to the line manager or employee. Users, business analysts, and developers working as one team produce faster and better quality results.
>
> "Investment in the new (Sapiens) approach has been more than justified. It would be impossible to achieve the same results using a traditional approach. Thanks to management commitment and RAD approach, supported by Sapiens object orientation tools, we believe that our HR operation is far more sophisticated than any of our competitors—perhaps a model for any industry segment. Speed of development and maintenance, increased functionality, and better quality can be attributed to the object orientation/RAD/Sapiens approach."
>
> "The complexity of user needs will continue to grow. Some emerging trends include more flexibility in compensation management, more flexibility in individual performance management, more flexibility in benefits selection, succession planning with open staffing, fewer job descriptions still, more generic descriptions, and fewer job levels."

Handelsregister (Commercial Register)

IBM Switzerland/Business Unit Government Solutions

THE OPPORTUNITY

The application *Handelsregister* (Commercial Register) was developed by IBM (Switzerland) as general contractor for the governmental customers Canton Solothurn and Canton Zug.

Originally a software solution was planned to be developed in 1991 for AS/400 with SYNON, a 4GL tool. An analysis was conducted with ADW in order to develop the application with the generator tool SYNON/400. The order was given for development in object-oriented programming after IBM Switzerland's Business Unit was able to prove the feasibility of C++, GUI-Master-class tree and SQL-database interface language in spring 1992.

Soon after the analysis had started the end user asked for a graphical user interface instead of a 5250-character (AS/400) oriented screen. IBM was able to show the end user how the information in the commercial register could be transferred into a graphical user interface.

THE APPLICATION

The Commercial Register application consists of four modules:

- Commercial Register *(Firmenkartei)*. This module controls and archives information regarding the registered companies in the canton. All information that has been published officially must be retrievable at any time. The information includes company name, place of registration, address, persons involved with the company, signature authorization, capital information, information about the kind of business the company is doing, and many other details.
- Business Administration *(Geschaftsfalle)*. This module provides an interface to a bookkeeping application for invoicing the appropriate amounts.
- Personal Information System *(Personen)*. This part of the application controls information about the persons registered in the different companies for their authority. This personal information system has the special requirement that every person must be known to each company as it was published. For instance, Person A is registered in company Z with his place of origin Germany and his residence in Zurich. If, at a later date the same Person A will be registered in another company Y with place of origin Germany but with residence in Basel, the person will still be registered for company A as it was published until company Z announces to the commercial register that the new residence for Person A is also in Basel.
- Code Administration *(Codeverwaltung)*. As the application is based on a relational database, much of the information—such as geographic information, currency codes, kind of company, address types, type of business case (founding, mutation, deletion, etc.)—is stored in specific code tables in the database. Code Administration was developed to manage eventual changes in these tables.

The application is designed as a "professional" application, which assumes that the employee in the Commercial Register will work the whole day with this application. The application loads all database codes into memory at startup. This takes some time at startup, but the data is already verified before the user does any additions or changes to the database.

As the user not only depends on the access rights to specific database table information but also depends on the state of registration of the company, some actions can only be initialized on a specific state of publication of the company. A mechanism was needed at the front end to control user actions. This is done with technical security objects coupled with a user profile in order to be able to enter certain changes or actions.

The application was developed with OS/2 as front-end with a DRDA (Distributed Relational Database Architecture) server. The database access is based on SQL (Static and Dynamic).

The user interface is based mainly on two types of windows. The first type of window is an OS/2 specific user interface, which shows any kind of list with different columns. Every object is able to show itself in a container, according to its specified Metainformation. The user is also able to edit the information directly in the container.

Notebook is the second type of window. All information is stored as a list in the database. In order to keep the information transparent, developers used the notebook controls of OS/2, which show the information on different pages. Figure 7.1 shows a virtual notebook page in Commercial Register.

Dialogs

The application has very few special dialogs. The user gets dialogs shown, for example, when setting up the necessary information to establish a company, or when moving information regarding different companies into another data status.

Direct Editing/Popup Menus

As user information is mostly presented in containers, the user has the opportunity to edit the information directly on the screen. According to the status and the user rights, the user can select the appropriate options from the popup menus.

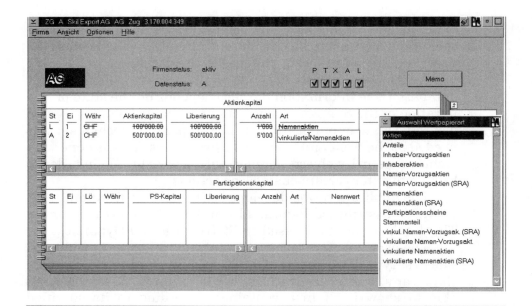

FIGURE 7.1   Commercial Register virtual notebook page.

Selection Containers/Dialog

As the user is asked in many areas of the application to select a known data item stored in the database, a special dialog called selection container is available. With this selection container the user can select a data item and this information is placed in the appropriate entry field.

Hardware and Software Used in Commercial Register

	Hardware	*Software*
Interface	PS/2 - 486 DX2	
Core Code	OS/2	OS/2 - for Front end
Database	(DRDA-Server)	PS/2, AS/400, DB/2, SQL
Development	PS/2 - 486 DX2	IBM-CSet/2 GUI_Master Application
Environment		Builder, various editors and tools

Overview of the Classes/Classtree

Commercial Register was hierarchically set up as follows:

GUI_Master-V is the Prefix of GUI_Master classes, which contain approximately 125 classes with about 41,000 lines of code. Figure 7.2 shows the GUI_Master class hierarchy.

These were the base classes for development. They include classes for the graphical user interface and some abstract useful classes for list handling, executors, and so on.

Technical classes (TGEN) consisted of 163 classes with about 25,000 lines of code and 10,000 lines of comment. These classes were developed by the team from scratch. All classes in the technical hierachy are application independent and can be reused/extended in other projects. All these classes can be completely reused. These classes were developed for areas such as:

- Easy SQL interface for static SQL programs
- Integrated technical monitoring for objects held in memory
- Integrated logging information for database access
- Logging of all SQL-Error information
- A technical security object called Security Manager controls access rights for the different functional levels of the user
- Technical mechanism for the database access
- Technical dialogs that are able to interact with the DB access
- Technical Object Manager, which replies to application requests for the different object types
- Dynamic creation of object depending on a defined object type
- Multitasking database access
- Integrated parser functionality
- Interface for script language to create document out of information held in application
- Debug tools
- Easy national language support—the dialogs and menus are dynamically set up in the user language, without having to maintain dialogs for the various user languages
- Encapsulation of the presentation manager interfaces (OS/2)
- General filter and sort dialogs/mechanism
- Direct editing/owner draw support
- Virtual notebook page support

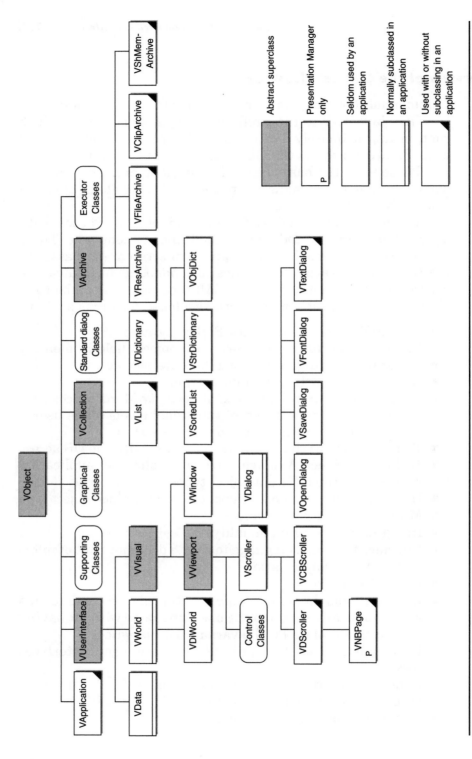

FIGURE 7.2 GUI_Master class hierarchy, VObject.

- Automatic Refresh mechanism for database objects
- Window list accessible automatically from every dialog
- Titlebar toolbox
- Dynamic bitmaps support
- General drag and drop implementation

There are eight technical general classes (application independent classes) that serve for general application functions and definitions.

- Application general classes (HGEN).
- Code Administration classes (CV). Thirty-two classes with approximately 7000 lines of code and approximately 2000 lines of comment. These classes are developed to administer the different code objects and to present the information in the appropriate selection dialogs/containers. Code administration contains eleven SQL Source files that process the necessary database updates.
- Personal administrative classes (PV). Thirty-two classes with approximately 8500 lines of code and 2000 lines of comment. These classes are for the administration of all registered personal information, such as different kind of addresses, place of origin, place of residence, date of birth, name, Christian name, and so on. Personal administration contains seven SQL Source files that perform the necessary database updates.
- Firm and business administration classes (FGEN). In this hierarchy there are 115 classes with about 30,000 lines of code and 6500 lines of comment. These classes handle the main application domain of the Commercial Register and the business administration.
- EXE-classes (EXEHR). Eight classes are set up to put the application together with the necessary logon control for the access rights of the application and its user.

Size of the System

The team developed 150 application independent classes, 200 application specific classes, and about 50 sources in C/SQL for the database interfaces.

The application contains thirty DLLs, which in the production version is almost 6 MB in size. The eleven GUI_Master DLLs are an additional 1.5 MB.

Other object orientation features used in the Commercial Register system include:

- Persistent objects. About fifty in the whole application. Each database class is named with the given prefix of its hierarchy and DB as characters 2 and 3 of the name. All these classes have the superclass TDBObj.
- The team wrote a REXX program that was able to create the C/SQL Source and its appropriate DB-Object according to the database definitions. For complex database constructs these sources had to be adapted.
- LPEX was used by most developers as the editor.
- The browser used was from GUI_Master.
- Method tracing was accomplished with a special GREP tool.
- Database linking in the application was solved at the technical level. The developer had only to define its class externally. Then the relation from the class to the database access routine could be established.
- TLIB was used as Version Control Program in the final phase of development. At the beginning the team used some IBM internal tools for check-in/check-out security.
- With some REXX utilities the team was able to create some source files for the database and its objects.

PROJECT LIFECYCLE

Analysis and Design

This is the first object orientation project completed in this IBM business unit. The reason object-oriented programming was chosen for this project was that the user wanted to have graphical user interfaces and the IT managers of the customers did not want to use C with OS/2 Presentation Manager and SQL. The team had done that in other projects that demanded very heavy code maintenance after project completion.

The choice was to develop the application with C++–OS/2 Presentation Manager and SQL, or with an object-oriented language. After some evaluation of the tools on the market, the development team was convinced that GUI_Master classtree (Volmac, Utrecht) could be a great help for the development of this application. The reasons for choosing GUI_Master as the base product were as follows:

- C++ is an international standard for development.
- GUI_Master can be bought with a source license, offering the guarantee to be independent in the future.
- Volmac employees could be hired for the development of the application. This was very essential as the other developers in the project were completely new to object-oriented programming. This guaranteed that the GUI_Master classtree would be used the right way from the beginning.
- Object-oriented programming is the only direction in order to keep maintenance/ reusability at an efficient level.

With the decisions for object-oriented programming in a new project, the classes from this project could be used in other new projects that ask for new user interfaces.

Walter Ringger led the development team for IBM Switzerland's Business Unit Government Solutions group. He cites a common problem with first efforts in object technology:

"As the analysis was already done with ADW, developers tried to change the design to the graphical 6 OOP environment. We faced some problems because the designers were not really aware of what OOP is all about.

"We started the project with a small prototype in order to learn the C++ / GUI_Master and SQL environment. After seeing positive results within four weeks of development after having conducted some education sessions for the people involved, the customers made the decision in the summer of 1992 to go with OOP. "

Development

Ringger's team used the Coad/Yourdan method in the beginning to set up the project. Two members of the team were involved in the design (database and GUI). Two members designed and developed the technical classes that had been identified at that time. Total development took eight person-years, with four to seven people involved at any given time.

Deployment

End-user education was held in the two cantons. The data entry for the existing data and cards is started the next week in Zug after having taken all personal information in the canton to the Commercial Register.

In order to use this application the users received new 486/DX2 PS/2 with 66 MHz. The users are trained with the application in a test database environment. The user help in the application was not written yet because only through user experience could it be known if any detailed help is still necessary.

Maintenance

At present there are still some small adaptations/wishes to be made for the user requirements. A new version for the program was planned to allow the automatic/electronic data transfer to the Swiss Commercial Register for the approval of the added/changed information.

At present one person is handling the maintenance.

BENEFITS

Ringger says that the big advantage of this project is that now all the technical classes can be used in the new object-oriented programming project for the taxes (Automatic Forms Control), which started the following autumn. "All the know-how has been transferred to the new project. All the developer experience is also kept for the new project as the same employees will also develop the taxes application, which was started from scratch with ANALYSE (Grady Booch)."

Chapter 9 discusses this new application, called ProFormA. Ringger lists the overall benefits of the Commercial Register as follows:

- Getting object-oriented programming experience with a real application
- The reuse of existing tested classes
- Setting up the project/development with the vision to supply other projects with a lot of general classes/procedures
- The enormous efficiency of object-oriented programming, when maintenance or serious design changes were necessary during development.

If this application had been developed with a character-oriented user interface, the user could not handle all the different screens for all the information that has to be shown to the user in the list.

CONCLUSIONS

Walter Ringger offers this observation regarding the Commercial Register project:

"We realized that project management for OOP needs special considerations, as you cannot determine all classes and reusablity from the beginning. The project progress was also very difficult to estimate, as for a long time we did not see results to show as we first developed the technical parts needed for the application domains."

"This project influenced our organization as we now have seven developers who are in OOP, six of whom are working for the new project 'TAXES'.

"The only advice I can offer is that you have to start a real project in OOP in order to see the benefit and have the drive to doing something good for a customer."

Message Text Format (MTF) Editor

8

**Naval Computer and Telecommunications
Station San Diego**

THE OPPORTUNITY

Within the Department of Defense, the term "message" refers to
a specially formatted means of information exchange that can
be broken down into two components. The first component is the
actual text of the message, which follows specific rules as
defined in JCS Pub 6-04. The text is made up of several entities
referred to as sets. Each set is made up of one or more fields of
related information about a specific message subtopic. For
example, the POC (Point of Contact) set contains information
identifying a specific point of contact, where the point of contact
is located, and how it may be contacted if additional information
is required. Each individual field within a set has specific rules
regarding the allowed values and format of the field's contents.
Additionally, there are syntactic rules regarding the inclusion or
exclusion of specific sets or fields based on the presence or
absence of other elements and or specified values.

The second message component is the communications
wrapper, which precedes and follows the message text. This
component provides message handling and routing information
to the various communications networks and automated routing
systems in place to support message communications. There are

several valid formats for the communications wrapper, each defined in a separate publication.

Prior versions of MTF Editor, developed in Pascal, provided incomplete implementations of the applicable standards. While the software had value, message generation using these versions still required access to hardcopy versions of the applicable publications to insure that the messages produced were lexically and syntactically correct. The database implementing the applicable standards was not suited to sharing common definitions and was also not easily extensible to include the entire scope of defined code lists and syntactic rules that needed to be applied.

The desired approach to address this issue was to redesign the application and underlying database, enabling a complete implementation of the applicable standards and concurrently modifying the user interface to be more in conformance with current technology standards. At that point, the scope of changes anticipated for the new release took on the nature of a secondary development effort, using prior versions of MTF Editor as functional prototypes. Because of a Department of Defense mandate, this redesign was required to be accomplished using Ada 83. All of these factors were further impacted by the need to deploy the redesigned MTF Editor in conjunction with the scheduled release of revisions to JCS Pub 6-04, constraining the development effort to a thirteen-month delivery window from requirements definition through application deployment.

THE APPLICATION

Message Text Format (MTF) Editor supports the implementation of standards for United States Message Text Format messages. These standards are defined in Joint Chiefs of Staff Publication 6-04 (JCS Pub 6-04) and implemented in Joint Interoperability of Tactical Command and Control Systems (JINTACCS) Central Database System. The USMTF program defines standard templates for the exchange of information to facilitate interoperability between tactical systems deployed in support of Army, Marine Corps, Navy, and Air Force elements.

Information contained in the publication includes detailed field, set, and message template definitions, along with rules defining the structure and makeup of sets and messages. Because of the exhaustive nature of the publication and the vast array of definitions for fields, field formats, code lists, and syntactic rules for the inclusion or exclusion of sets/fields under varying conditions, JCS Pub 6-04 is a large, multivolume publication. MTF Editor provides formatted text editing capabilities in accordance with JCS Pub 6-04 standards, automating the message generation process and eliminating the need for users to independently obtain and maintain the publication.

MTF Editor is a formatted text editor, incorporating lexical and syntactic parsing, supporting the preparation of messages within this environment. Because of the large number of publications that may be applicable to any given message, and the fact that maintaining the vast array of publications is resource intensive, a situation results where the majority of individuals attempting to generate a message do not readily have access to current publications.

MTF Editor, by implementing the standards within the application and automating the application of lexical and syntactic rules, accomplishes two major goals:

- First, MTF Editor relieves the individual of the need to reference the applicable publications in order to prepare a valid message. Before a version of MTF Editor is authorized for general use, it undergoes a certification test in order to verify conformance to JCS Pub 6-04.
- Second, because MTF Editor encapsulates an internal representation of the publications defining the format and content for message text and communications wrappers, the resource overhead associated with maintaining and disseminating revisions to the standards is greatly reduced. Revisions to the standards are implemented and certified in electronic form with the application database, eliminating the need for broad distribution of the publications and revisions in paper form.

Figure 8.1 shows the MTF Editor Message Edit Screen. The displayed message has the REF set opened for editing on line

```
   File    Edit    Block    Search   Configure   Output   Message Help
                        C:\MTFADA\MESSAGES\GENADMIN
===
RTIUZYUW RUWFSUU0800 1290800-UUUU--RUWFSGG.
ZNR UUUUU
R 090800Z MAY 95 ZYB
FM NAVCOMTELSTA SAN DIEGO CA//N833//
TO OBJECT WORLD SAN FRANCISCO//1995//
BT
UNCLAS   //N02300//
MSGID/GENADMIN/NAVCOMTELSTA SDIEGO//
SUBJ/THIS MESSAGE IS FOR DEMONSTRATION PURPOSES ONLY
/COMPUTERWORLD OBJECT APPLICATION AWARDS PROGRAM//
REF/A/DOC/COMPUTERWORLD              /DMY:010195/           /
/
AMPN/REF A IS THE OFFICIAL ENTRY FORM FOR THE COMPUTERWORLD OBJECT
APPLICATION AWARDS TO BE ANNOUNCED AT OBJECT WORLD SAN FRANCISCO ON
16 AUG 95.//
POC/L. RUSSELL/CIV/CODE N833LR/-/TEL:(619) 545-8678
/TEL:FAX (619) 545-8573//
RMKS/THIS MESSAGE IS FOR DEMONSTRATION PURPOSES ONLY.  THE PURPOSE
OF THIS MESSAGE IS TO DEMONSTRATE APPLICATION CAPABILIIES FOR
INCLUSION IN THE SUBMISSION OF THIS APPLICATION UNDER REF A.//
<M>    ORIGINATOR                                        1-30ANBS
L:  11 C:11      F1-Help    F2-Save    F6-Compress    F9-Validate    F10-Menu
```

FIGURE 8.1 MTF Editor message screen.

11, and the current selected field is field 3 of the REF set containing the value "COMPUTERWORLD."

Figure 8.2 shows the system's edit menu. The menu has familiar features: bold one-letter mnemonics for menu item selection and "hot keys."

MTF Editor was created primarily with Ada 83. Designated by the Department of Navy as a pilot project for the incorporation of software reuse, MTF Editor incorporates reuse components written in Ada 83, Pascal, and C++.

The solution was divided into three subsets:

1. The first subset addressed the HCI implementation, using the AdaSAGE library of reusable Ada components for HCI development and prototyping. The design of the AdaSAGE libraries implements five major classes of objects: Relation, Form, Keyboard Set, File Set, and Graph. The key AdaSAGE classes used by MTF Editor v4.0 include the Relation, Form, and Keyboard Set classes. The Relation class defines the structure and logical organization of stored data. The Form class defines an association between keyboard input and a message value supplied to the using software. Instances of

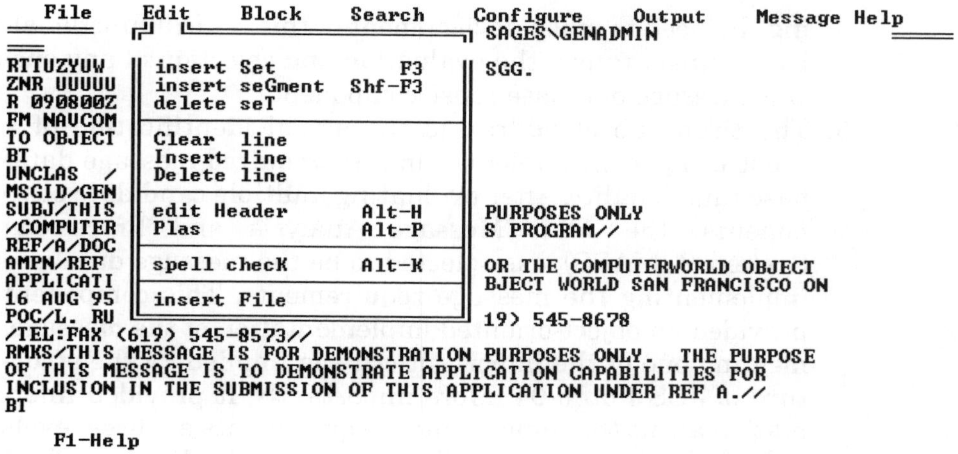

```
     File      Edit     Block     Search    Configure    Output    Message Help
          ╓──╥──╖                        ┌─ SAGES\GENADMIN
RTTUZYUW  ║ insert Set        F3  ║       SGG.
ZNR UUUUU ║ insert seGment  Shf-F3 ║
R 090800Z ║ delete seT         ║
FM NAVCOM ║                     ║
TO OBJECT ║ Clear  line        ║
BT        ║ Insert line        ║
UNCLAS  / ║ Delete line        ║
MSGID/GEN ║                     ║
SUBJ/THIS ║ edit Header   Alt-H ║       PURPOSES ONLY
/COMPUTER ║ Plas          Alt-P ║       S PROGRAM//
REF/A/DOC ║                     ║
AMPN/REF  ║ spell checK   Alt-K ║       OR THE COMPUTERWORLD OBJECT
APPLICATI ║                     ║       BJECT WORLD SAN FRANCISCO ON
16 AUG 95 ║ insert File         ║
POC/L. RU ╙─────────────────────╜       19) 545-8678
/TEL:FAX (619) 545-8573//
RMKS/THIS MESSAGE IS FOR DEMONSTRATION PURPOSES ONLY.  THE PURPOSE
OF THIS MESSAGE IS TO DEMONSTRATE APPLICATION CAPABILITIES FOR
INCLUSION IN THE SUBMISSION OF THIS APPLICATION UNDER REF A.//
BT

    F1-Help
```

FIGURE 8.2 MTF Editor menu.

these classes are defined within an object editor and then saved as persistent objects in a database of AdaSAGE objects, whose behaviors are implemented during runtime by a virtual form machine. These objects are then operated on during program execution by functions exported in the AdaSAGE libraries. From the view of the client software, each form instance is an active object that, on reaching a terminal state, returns state information for use by the client. By defining instances of the Relation, Form, and Keyboard Set classes, it was possible to rapidly develop and prototype all HCI implementations.

2. The second subset consisted of project specific code, implementing local logic and then using the AdaSAGE virtual form machine's protocol to obtain and display results from and to the user. This subset also includes a thin layer of code abstracting and encapsulating the implementation of the message database from the project code driving the AdaSAGE HCI implementation for the dynamic generation and enforcement of the message templates. This enabled development of the actual formatted text editor independent of any specific message database implementation, eliminat-

ing the need to make development of this critical functionality contingent upon the evaluation and selection of any specific message database reuse component.

3. The third subset addressed the actual identification of a reuse component implementing the required message database functionality. After evaluating multiple candidate components, the Joint Message Analysis and Processing Systems (JMAPS) was selected to be the message database implementing the message requirements. This component provided an object-oriented implementation of the message, meeting one of the important criteria implied by the structure of JCS Pub 6-04. More importantly, it provided information about the implemented requirements at three levels of logical abstraction for client software: the Message Template class, the Set class, and the Field class.

Overview of Classes

Figure 8.3 is an overview of the classes used in MTF Editor. On the left are classes implemented in Ada 83. The classes on the right are implemented using a combination of Ada 83 and C++ code.

Size of System

MTF Editor consists of over 90,000 SLOC developed in Ada 83. Of these, approximately 4000 SLOC are calls into the AdaSAGE library of reusable components, which represent an estimated 150,000 additional SLOC in Ada 83. Calls to internal project reuse libraries represent 1500 SLOC, and approximately 6000 SLOC were used to implement the Ada 83 interface to the message database, which represents an additional 175,000 SLOC in C++.

In total, the MTF Editor represents 415,000 SLOC, of which 78 percent were leveraged from libraries of reusable components or components developed for use in other projects. Of the remaining 90,000 SLOC developed by the project, 11,500 represent calls into or interfaces with internal or external reusable components.

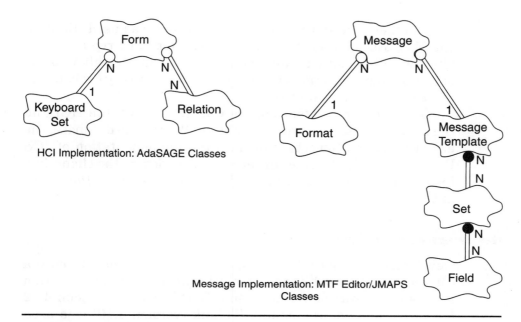

HCI Implementation: AdaSAGE Classes

Message Implementation: MTF Editor/JMAPS Classes

FIGURE 8.3 An overview of MTF Editor classes.

Using the inherent object-oriented features of Ada 83, abstractions of component objects within the MTF Editor were identified and defined in discrete Ada package specifications. Where applicable, state information associated with these objects was also encapsulated within the Ada package body, preventing direct access of state information by client functions. In the case of the message database, the implementation was abstracted and encapsulated at two levels: one at the level of the project interface, the other at the level of the reuse component.

The architecture resulting from adherence to the concepts of abstraction and encapsulation displays strong modular characteristics, with objects and externally visible behaviors defined in a single package specification and implemented in one or more closely related package bodies. This greatly enhanced the ability to delineate, assign, and track implementation responsibility for software capabilities within the project. It also proved extremely beneficial in defect isolation and resolution during integration and acceptance testing.

Another inherent feature of Ada 83 that was used throughout MTF Editor was its strong support for data typing. Combined with the static typing features of Ada 83, this allowed the detection and correction of type inconsistencies very early in the process, when fixes are easiest.

The use of persistent objects was key to both the HCI and the message database implementation. Within the database, the use of persistent objects supported the implementation of JCS Pub 6-04 standards, enabling access as needed by the client during generation, display, and manipulation of message templates in the HCI.

Hardware and Software

Development of MTF Editor v4.0 used the Meridian OpenAda compiler (version 4.1.4) on 486 platforms. Project configuration management was performed using Burton's TLib (version 4.12 for networked environments). RTLink (version 6.10) was used for linking of object modules from multiple source compilers.

	Hardware	*Software*
Interface	286	Ada
Core Code	386, 486	Ada/C++
Database	386, 486	C++
Development Environment	486	DOS / Ada, RTLink

PROJECT LIFECYCLE

There were three main objectives to be attained during the development cycle. First, the application, including a database implementing complex rules would need to be developed under a tight deadline constrained by external consideration. Second, because the human computer interface was to undergo fairly extensive revision, it would be necessary to rapidly prototype the interface in an environment facilitating rapid change. This was necessary to allow the user community an opportunity to review proposed changes and provide feedback into the development cycle early enough in the schedule to enable project response to the user community's input. Third, the level of project risk associated with developing a database system capable of implementing the full standard, coupled with the short development schedule, favored the identification and inclusion of a reusable component to satisfy this requirement.

Attaining all three objectives would provide benefits at multiple levels: to the user community, to the MTF Editor project, and to the development staff. For the user community, attaining these objectives would result in an application that greatly enhanced their ability to generate validated messages, while at the same time reducing the workload overhead by eliminating the need to acquire and maintain the various standards for message generation.

For the MTF Editor project, the anticipated benefits were threefold. A solution that addressed the need for rapid prototyping of the HCI would also enable the project to be more responsive to HCI implementation inputs from the user community. Also, if a prototyping tool could be identified whose product would directly incorporate into the deliverable product, it would be possible to use the tool and its support files to enhance configuration management over HCI modifications.

By identifying a reusable resource for implementing the database of message standards, the MTF Editor project would be able to focus the scope of the application to the actual generation, presentation, and management of the formatted templates displayed to the user for message generation. Instead of expending project resources in the development of a database that would never be directly visible to the user, these resources could be applied to the HCI representation of the database information.

It followed that a solution effectively addressing all three objectives would also reduce project overhead throughout the entire lifecycle. By increasing tool and reusable component usage, the quantity of project specific code would be decreased. This would not only decrease development and test schedules, but it would also result in a lowered number of anticipated latent defects with the delivered product.

For the development staff, the potential benefit would be a very tangible but often overlooked benefit. Because the development staff was competing with other software development agencies for the development job, identification of a solution was necessary in order to obtain the project.

Given the DoD mandate to use Ada, using Ada's inherent support for object-oriented techniques was a natural progression. However, while the syntax and structure of Ada presented a strong case for object-oriented solutions, it was not the driving factor.

The first aspect that demanded an object-oriented implementation was the simple fact that the user community viewed a message as a single object, however complex, with specific attributes based on the type (class) of message being discussed. As a result, the model that best reflected the user appreciation of the domain was to see MTF Editor as an object editor capable of processing an instance of a defined message class.

The second aspect demanding an object-oriented implementation was the desire, because of the finite time resource, to address the HCI and message database as two separate abstractions with the project-specific code being the glue to combine these abstractions into the message-editing product. This would enable the development effort to progress in two parallel efforts, one focused on implementation of the actual HCI, the other focused on implementing the message database interface, which would eventually drive the behavior of the HCI within the message editing function.

The structure of JCS Pub 6-04 was a third aspect that demanded an object-oriented approach. Because message standards are defined in an object-oriented manner, consistently associating specific attributes and behaviors with specific fields/set/messages, it became apparent that an object-oriented implementation of the publication would best map the real-world definitions to a database implementation. This became a factor in the evaluation of potential reuse components for inclusion as the message database component of MTF Editor.

The critical limitation with more conventional approaches is that, given the complexity of the domain and the time constraints, they were not going to work. Conventional waterfall lifecycles and development methodologies would not support the rapid pace of development required. Also, with rapid expansion of capabilities in the microcomputer arena, conventional approaches in similar efforts had proven ineffective in responding to emergent technologies. This could be attributed to tight coupling between project code and target platforms, poor design resulting in duplication of similar code, the actual overhead associated with conventional approaches, or any of a myriad of reasons. The bottom line was that without the use of development/maintenance tools and component reuse, the conventional approaches were too inefficient.

In addition to the Ada mandate and the time constraints, the project had to use 80286 machines for software deployment. This excluded the use of extended memory capabilities, requiring the application to use overlay technology to fit within conventional memory. Also, because of the proliferation of LAN technology, the application was constrained to run within a LAN environment, further limiting the amount of conventional memory available for use by MTF Editor.

BENEFITS

Deployed in November 1994, the principal benefit of MTF Editor is the increased level of conformance of the message database to the standards defined in JCS Pub 6-04. This increased conformance has reduced the error rate in messages prepared and validated with MTF Editor. This results in a higher level of productivity for the users. The increased conformance also has a significant impact on the principal goal of the USMTF program, enhancing the interoperability of message based tactical systems.

MTF Editor eliminates hard copy updates to the message requirements. All such information is delivered in the software package.

The ability to develop and deploy the system within the allowable time was a direct result of the use of object-oriented techniques. By applying object-oriented principles to the objectives, it was possible to identify two high-level objects with well defined behaviors, which constituted a significant portion of the overall application. Having identified these objects, it was possible to research and identify reuse libraries and components that allowed the project to meet the schedule.

The rapid development of MTF Editor is directly attributable to the use of the AdaSAGE libraries and HCI tools. These, in turn, utilize object-oriented technology to achieve the levels of abstraction and encapsulation necessary to enable the highly flexible and responsive environment supporting the prototyping and development of the HCI.

CONCLUSIONS

MTF Editor 4.0's lead software engineer, Les Russell, had a number of observations regarding this development effort:

"The two most important lessons learned from this project relate to the use of object-oriented analysis techniques in the identification of software components and potential reuse candidates. Using abstraction and encapsulation, it was possible to arrive at a highly modular software architecture which provided multiple benefits.

"Resulting modules were highly cohesive, implementing only those behaviors associated with the specific abstraction being modeled. This not only facilitated the assignment and tracking of software capabilities, it also resulted in implementations that tended to be highly reusable. Also, because the behaviors were fairly discrete and well defined, complex algorithms were frequently able to be implemented as a construct of algorithms, decreasing the number of defects.

"Because the modules within the system are highly cohesive, it was possible to readily apply the object definitions to the evaluation of potential reuse candidates. This was extremely important in reducing the resources expended in evaluation of nonreusable components. In instances where the object and its behaviors were not as well defined, it was discovered that more time was expended in evaluating reuse candidates.

"Another important lesson regards reuse, regardless of the analysis and design approach used. If an external reuse component is not reusable in black-box form, and it is not supported by the originators of the component, there is a high probability that incorporation of the component will not result in the desired productivity gains. Once project personnel begin to open up the implementation of a component, it should no longer be considered as reuse, and runs the risk of taking longer to fix than to develop from scratch. The possible exception to this would be a large reuse component encompassing a wide scope of functionality to which a well-defined and narrow scope of modifications is required. The experience of the MTF Editor project is that such modifications are best implemented by the original donor of the reuse component.

"The immediate impact of MTF Editor's success is not readily apparent. With the project staff, there is a strong commitment to a continuing development of the skills and processes that enabled their success. While there has been interest in the processes used on this project, there has not been a noticeable move toward incorporating these processes into other development efforts.

"The most important factor in undertaking a development effort like MTF Editor is the careful selection of project personnel. All MTF Editor personnel were trained Ada 83 developers, and had a solid understanding of the need for and benefits of abstraction and encapsulation. The high degree of alignment of development techniques allowed the discipline necessary to resist augmenting another package's implementation. The inclusion of personnel who are not able or willing to recognize and avoid this form of implementation contamination is, at the least, time consuming to correct, and at the worst, can undermine the project's architecture.

"A second factor to consider in undertaking this type of development effort is to give strong and careful consideration to potential reuse candidates. Identify, as early as possible, areas within the design that are candidates for a reuse component. If a viable reuse component is identified, leverage it as much as possible. However, if a reuse component is not readily identified, it is time to move on to component development. In a few cases, component development was delayed while a more exhaustive search was made for a reuse component. Depending on the size and complexity of the component, there is a critical point beyond which it becomes counterproductive to continue the search. Bounding the level of effort expended in locating a component is one of the most important aspects of effectively leveraging reusable components."

ProFormA

IBM, Switzerland/Business Unit Government Solutions

9

THE OPPORTUNITY

The application ProFormA (Professional Forms Application) was developed by IBM (Switzerland) as general contractor for the governmental customers Canton Solothurn and Canton Zug.

ProFormA is one part of a complete new tax application for the cantons Zug (ZG) and Solothurn (SO). The contract to develop an "integrated new tax solution" (INES) for these cantons covered the functionality of Tax Registration (administration of the tax subjects as people and companies), the Taxation Process, which determines the net tax income and the capital amount according to the situation of the individual tax subject, and the Tax Collection, which controls that all the tax amounts are correctly invoiced according to the factor rates on the net income and the net capital amount, which are the output from the Taxation process.

The goal of this application was to have in the future a tool that can adapt requirements generated from new tax laws into the business process of the taxation department without having to change existing software. The application ProFormA should provide the ability to design different tax forms for all the needs in tax administration, which are assigned a validity over certain taxation periods, and can be changed according to new tax regulations for a new tax period.

The two cantons SO and ZG requested IBM to develop a new tax application as their existing applications were no longer maintainable and were hardly able to be updated to conform to new tax law requirements. The software solution for the INES project was planned for development in 1992 for AS/400 with SYNON (4GL tool).

THE APPLICATION

The main benefit of the application ProFormA is that it provides a means to change forms without the need to change code in the program. ProFormA also integrates tools to dynamically compare different tax cases and to view the history of tax cases. This functionality enables the tax expert to get the required data from previous tax periods directly on the workstation without having to move to the documents archive somewhere in the building in order to perform the taxation process. It can be extended with business rules in the form of plausibility formulas and with an extensive help system.

ProFormA consists of two applications: ProFormA—Forms Design, and ProFormA—Working Mode.

ProFormA—Forms Design

This module is the tool with which the end user designs and develops the forms that will be used in the working mode of the application. The user is given all the functionality known in common spreadsheet applications such as arithmetical operators, logical operators, pictures, and so on. Additionally ProFormA provides many tax-specific formulas. Very important is the integration of external data. Because of the integration of SOM as a base for persistency, the user can employ its dispatching mechanism. So any method of an implemented class/object can be integrated with a formula within the application. For example, in order to get the name of a person, the user can specify the formula "Call(PERSON, GetName)" where "PERSON" is

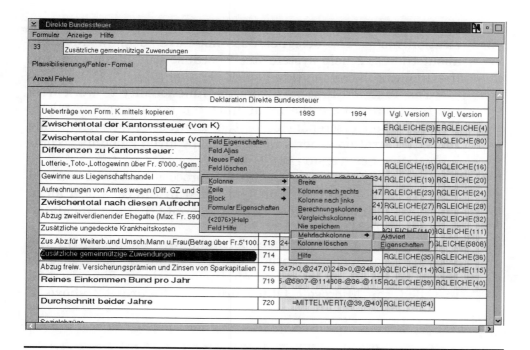

FIGURE 9.1 ProFormA forms design screen.

the class name and "GetName" is the method to be called. Figure 9.1 shows a forms design screen, Direkte Bundessteuer, a dialog that shows the form being designed. With popup manipulation, every block, row, row and cell in the form can be individually defined.

ProFormA—Working Mode

This part of the application processes the forms designed with the designer module. It knows how to process tax declarations. Bundled in a user interface with a notebook dialog, the end user can select all the necessary tax forms to process the tax declaration of each tax subject.

In the application ProFormA, a sophisticated help system is integrated that enables the forms designer to create help support for each cell, line, block, or form during the design. This functionality is given to the forms designer with a special authorization mode. The designer does not have to know anything about the OS/2 help system itself because it is integrated into the application.

The Taxation Process covers the functionality to work with the tax forms where the input from the tax subjects is taken. Depending on discrepancies of the allowed deductions/income rules, the taxation experts will correct the given amounts accordingly with a new version of the data.

All data given for a specific tax process will be calculated with the appropriate formulas specified in the cells of a form. These calculations can also include amounts that are calculated in separate subforms.

Basically all spreadsheet formulas are supported in the ProFormA application with a syntax similar to that used in Excel. This syntax was chosen because the customers had installed the Microsoft Office products. Figure 9.2 shows a

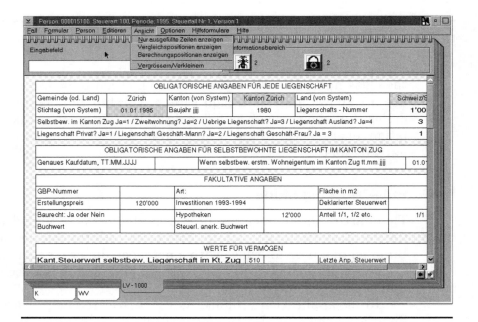

FIGURE 9.2 Real estate form, "work with forms."

"work with forms" dialog. This screen shows the Real Estate form of person xy. The "bug" button shows the number of errors in the form, and the lock button shows the number of calculated fields by formulas that were overwritten by the end user with a fixed value.

The following special requirements were made for Pro-FormA:

- Version handling of data within one tax-period. A form may undergo different versions during its processing. This may be the case when the tax subject's values are entered in the first version of a form and subsequently corrected in a second version. The ProFormA application must be able to show the data in the different versions (temporary, corrected, final, etc.).
- Change of tax form. The tax law can change from one tax period to another; for instance, new kinds of deductions could be allowed to determine the net income without having to change the application.
- Comparison of tax data between different tax periods. This functionality allows the tax experts to control the income and capital development of a tax subject without having to move physically to the archive of the tax documents to control this data.
- Dynamic row allocation. In the tax form the children of a tax subject must be shown with their names and dates of birth. For each child a separate row must be allocated in the tax form. The number of children determines the family allowance amount.
- Dynamic column allocation. In the area of real estate owned by a tax subject, each property that is located in another community/canton has to be represented in a column in order to separate the capital levy for all the properties for each community/canton as taxes are also paid in the community where real estate is located. So, for each community a separate column is created where real properties are owned by a tax subject.
- Subforms. A complete tax case consists of multiple tax forms (Main Form, Income Form, Securities, Debt Form,

etc.). Thus, final results of a Subform must be integrated in the Main Form in order to calculate the necessary tax factors.

■ Formula versus fixed amount. Formulas must be able to be overwritten; for example, a tax expert does not want to put all securities information in the securities form, but he only wants to put the final value of the securities in the appropriate field.

■ Explanation of discrepancy. The values are entered from the given figures received from the tax subject, which generates a provisional tax version. The tax expert must then make corrections on the given amount according to the tax laws. He or she must in addition give an appropriate explanation of discrepancies in the fields that show a difference. The information that a discrepancy is set in a field must be visible.

■ Error checking. All the fields entered in the tax form that are not correctly set are shown to the user visually.

■ Default values. In a tax field default predefined values can be set; for instance, the amount of deduction of a single tax subject versus the amount of deduction of a married tax subject can be preset and automatically calculated according to the information from the database of the tax subject.

■ Interface to tax register. Data from the tax register—such as complete name, children, address, confession, and date of birth—have to be filled in the tax form in the appropriate fields with defined formulas. ProFormA supports these interfaces to the tax register data pool, which is administered with the INES (AS/400 SYNON) application.

■ Interface to taxation process. The application ProFormA must be automatically informed when the tax expert has started the activities in the INES taxation process application. An interface is therefore set so that an appropriate message is generated from the AS/400 application in order that the OS/2 application receives the message identifying which tax case should be loaded with which tax forms. The ProFormA must also inform the taxation process in the AS/400 part when the work on the tax forms in the ProFormA has been completed.

- Interface to taxation collection. ProFormA also supports interfaces to the INES tax collection application part, which is also an AS/400 SYNON application part of INES. After the processing of the data in the given tax forms of a tax subject the factor rates of net income and net capital amount are delivered for processing the tax rate and invoicing the tax amount due. These interfaces can be assigned to any cell of the forms with a defined syntax in the forms designer mode.
- Different columns per form block. A tax form consists of multiple blocks of information that all have a different layout of columns and rows. Each block must be able to accommodate different designs.

The analysis and the estimation was then made with ADW in order to develop the application with the generator tool SYNON/400.

During the development of this INES application, it was decided after some time that a part of the taxation process covering a spreadsheet-like functionality should not be developed with SYNON because the user interface of character-mode screens was not adequate to allow a convenient way to work with the appropriate data. So the management decision (customer and project management) was made to evaluate a tool on the market that could be used to cover the functionality to determine the factor rates from the given income and the capital amounts. The thought was also to gain time with the development of the INES application when part of the functionality could be integrated from an existing package. After a time-consuming evaluation of an appropriate tool, one product was found to conform partially to the expectations of the customer (IT and tax) management. The main inhibitor was that this evaluated tax forms tool was running on a completely different hardware and operating system (Dataflex), which meant that special conversion programs would have to be developed for the integration of that tool. At that time (autumn 1993) the object technology development team that was working on the Handelsregister application was able to show an attractive user interface to the end users, which convinced them that only a graphical user interface should be used for the taxation process in an advanced, modern INES solution.

The object technology development team was also able to convince the IBM and customer management that a lot of benefits could be taken when the tax forms application in the INES project would be solved with object technology.

It was decided at the beginning of October 1993 that the tax forms application was to be developed with object technology, although a tough time schedule was given—the development should be finished in spring 1995. However, the ability to use an experienced object technology development team for this complex application was giving the customer and IBM management confidence for this decision. So the development of the ISOV-ProFormA (Professional Forms Application) was started with an object-oriented analysis in October 1993.

Overview of the Classes/Classtree

The application was hierarchically set up as follows:

GUI_Master Version 3.0 -   "V" is the Prefix of
                            GUI_Master-classes

138 classes with about 37,000 lines of code and 3100 methods

GUI_Master Classtree is a product of CAP Volmac in Utrecht/Netherlands. It consists of a graphical classtree with an application builder. This classtree can be used for OS/2, Windows, and NT.

This classtree was the base product for our development in object technology. The classtree is developed especially for the graphical user interface and some abstract general classes (e.g., list handling, executors, etc.). Please see Chapter 7 for more information on GUI_Class Master.

Technical Classes (TGEN)
(General technical application independent classes)

218 classes with about 49,000 lines of code and 4000 methods.

These classes were originally developed by the ISOV-Handelsregister developers at IBM Switzerland. With the development of ProFormA the technical classtree was enhanced with all the technical requirements from the spreadsheet functionality; 120 of the technical classes are reused in ProFormA and 50 were implemented by this project. All the technical classes are application independent and therefore candidates to be reused by any future application.

Technical SOM (System Object Model)-Based Classes

80 classes with about 18,000 lines of code and 1400 methods.

All of the classes shown in Figure 9.3 were introduced by ProFormA. They implement a dynamic data request broker, which manages the objects held in memory and will, depending on request, retrieve the appropriate objects from a database and instantiate them dynamically. This implementation makes the persistent classes completely independent of the data store chosen by the application environment.

One big advantage of using SOM as the vehicle to implement the data request broker was that we could save a lot of SQC code (static SQL source code) that would have to be written using the mechanisms used in the ISOV-Handelsregister project. With the implemented architecture, developers could save more than 30,000 lines of SQC source code that otherwise would have to be produced and maintained.

General Forms Handling Classes (IGEN)

170 classes with about 36,000 lines of code and 2600 methods.

All of these are independent of the problem domain taxes and are therefore reusable in any application needing forms-handling capabilities. They can be categorized into three different parts. First, the metainformation (model), which provides the definition of a form; second, the view tree used to represent the information; and third, the data pool, which serves as a container to hold the data entered in the working mode. Included in

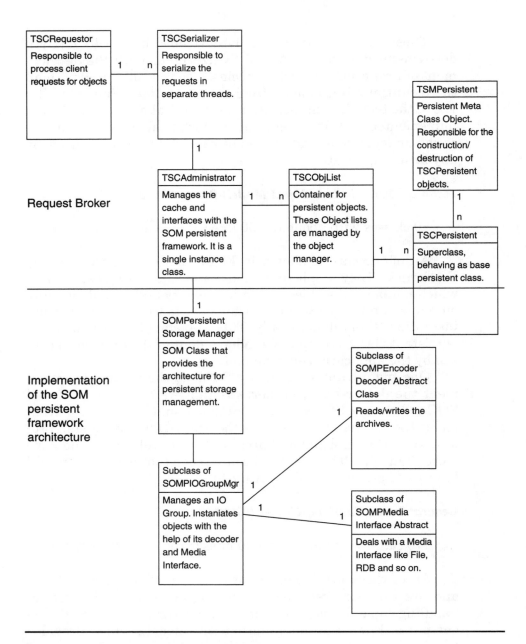

FIGURE 9.3 Technical SOM (System-Object-Model) based classes.

this section are also the classes that build the executable to design the forms. Figures 9.4, 9.5, and 9.6 show these three trees (whole/part structure).

All persistent objects are subclasses of TSCPersistent, all other objects are subclasses of the GUI_Master class VObject. The designer application exclusively deals with the meta and view trees; the working mode concentrates on view and data-pool.

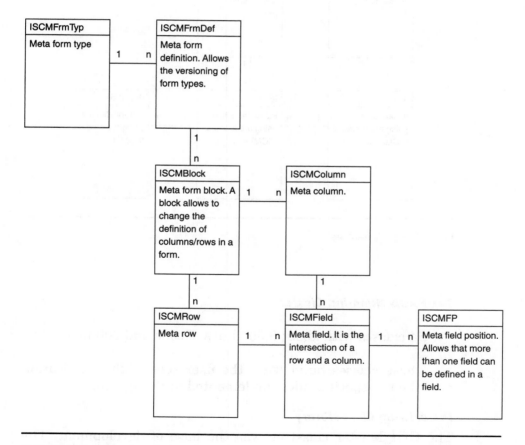

FIGURE 9.4 Meta-tree.

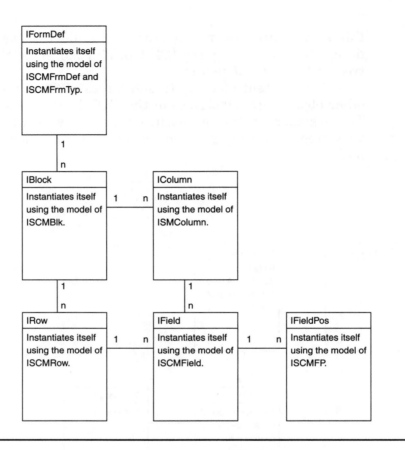

FIGURE 9.5 View-tree.

Tax Forms Handling Classes

64 classes with about 8,000 lines of code and 600 methods.

These classes build what the user sees of the application plus the tax-specific rules implemented in the system.

Pre-existing Class Library

The GUI_Master classtree was the base of development. The application makes use of TGEN-classtree, which was developed

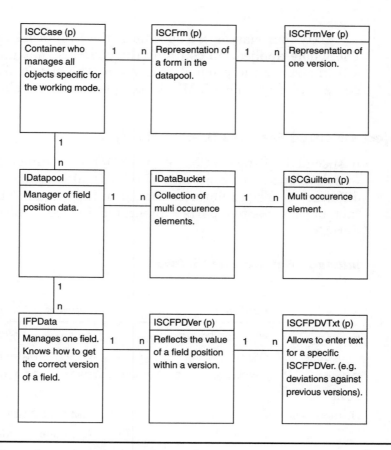

FIGURE 9.6 Datapool (p means persistent).

with the ISOV-Handelsregister application, as well as the SOM-Classtree development toolkit.

Size of the System

ProFormA consists of 670 classes that have 11,700 methods implemented with 148,000 lines of code; 436 of these classes are application independent and are therefore candidates to be reused in every application; 170 classes are reusable for other projects needing forms handling capabilities.

Sixty-four classes are specific to the ProFormA application. The whole application contains thirty DLLs that are almost 6 MB in size for the production version. The eleven GUI_Master DLLs are additional 1.5 MB for the production version.

Object-Oriented Features Used in the System

A special implementation of the SOM persistence framework was developed for ProFormA. With GUI_Master 3.0 and SOM 2, different base class libraries coexist in the system. There are no "not object-oriented parts" integrated in the application Pro-FormA.

Interfaces Hardware and Software

	Hardware	Software
Interface	PS/2–486 DX2/Pentium	PC-Support/400
Core Code	OS/2	OS/2 / SOM–for Front end
Database	(DRDA-Server) PS/2, AS/400	DB2/ 2, DB2/400, DDCS,
SOM		
Development		IBM-CSet/2 GUI_Master
		Application Builder,
		Various editors and tools, SOM
		Toolkit development toolkit

Inheritance:

VObject -> . . . . IBGen -> . . . . IHdr -> . . . . IRow/IColumn

The row IRow has VObject as the superclass and inherits all its behavior. Every element of a form is derived from the class IBGen, which provides all elements (row, column, block, field, and so on) with the capabilities common to all elements. IRow is also an IHdr class that contains the capabilities that are common between a row IRow and a column IColumn. In fact, the only difference between a row and a column is that one lies horizontally and the other vertically on the display.

A formula can be defined for every element. So the method "evaluate" is defined as a virtual method in IBGen. Formulas on rows or columns are special, so this method is overridden in IHdr. These formulas are special, as they determine the number of occurrences of a row. Otherwise this element uses the same parsing and formula-resolving mechanism. The evaluation determines additionally to the base behavior the number of IHdr occurrences that should be generated.

The project team implemented the SOM persistent framework in order to provide the persistence. Every persistent object is a subclass of TSCPersistent and has therefore the capability to be stored/restored by the framework. The objects are not aware where they will be stored/restored. This must be defined with a special configuration application. At run time TSCAdministrator reads this information to determine which IO group manager must be used for a class. The team implemented three different IO group managers with their corresponding encoder/decoder and media interface classes: one to store to a file (provided by SOM, but overridden because of performance reasons), one to store to relational databases, and one special to call remote procedures that write archives on an AS/400 (via Dataqueue).

The SQL IO Group manager implementation provides a framework to the user (developer) with the advantage that he or she does not have to code one special SQL statement, because every request is generated dynamically using a data definition object. This implementation allows the developer to write his or her own code for storing to a file. Whenever the developer wants to change to a relational database system, he or she just has to take the configuration application and enter the appropriate data definitions (data link).

Dynamic Class/Method Generation

All SOM classes are generated dynamically. ProFormA also makes extensive use of the provided interface repository, that allows the retrieval information about the signature of methods and attributes at run time.

Hardware and Software

Hardware

PS/2 486/DX2 with minimum 50 MHz

32 MB storage

400 MB file

Software

IBM C/Set++	LPEX-Editor
IBM Toolkit 2.0	GUI_Master Application Builder
SOM Toolkit	GUI_Master Browser

Analyzing Tools

EXTRA part of C/Set ++

SOM-Tools part of SOM developers toolkit

Storage Management

TLIB was used as Version Control Program during the development.

Code Generation

SOM Compiler generates C++ skeletons for SOM-classes

GUI_Master generates C++ skeletons of new classes

PROJECT LIFECYCLE

Analysis and Design

Daniel Scholz (project manager) and Thomas Buehrer (systems designer), both of IBM Switzerland, describe the analysis and design phase:

"ProFormA is the second Object Technology project of our business unit. As we had a good experience with the ISOV-Handelsregister application we had an object-oriented experienced development team. We started the

ISOV-Handelsregister object technology development in Autumn 1992.

"In the INES project an ADW analysis had already been done by a software house with the intention to realize the application in a 5250 environment. Then the decision was made to realize the application with object technology, we decided to make a complete OOA and OOD, and took the existing ADW analysis as information material only. We chose Rational Rose as our A&D tool, which is based on the Booch methodology.

"At the beginning we also started to write a system design paper, which was continually updated, and in early 1994 was presented to the customer and IBM management. We also decided for this project to use SOM for the persistent classes. We were convinced that SOM reached a level to be really practical use for production applications.

"At the beginning two team members started the analysis of ProFormA and the other team members who were foreseen as developers were involved in a weekly analysis and design meeting, while they were still developing the ISOV-Handelsregister application. During that phase user representatives of the customers were involved for detailed information requests.

"All developers were also educated about the special tax requirements at the tax locations of the two cantons. So we ensured that all developers knew about the business domain of the application.

"The design was also led by the two members of the team who did the analysis, but also during this phase the other members of our object technology team were regularly involved. In February 1994 we developed a basic functional application for the Forms Designer part. After one month we were able to show the customer a base version. From then on we presented with the 'roundtrip' approach every two weeks a new version with the defined new functionality to the end user. This process lasted until Summer 1994.

"An evaluation was done to buy a separate product for the 'Forms Mechanism' in the INES project in order to keep the tough time schedule for the whole INES project and to reduce the development effort. At that time it was not foreseen to use object technology for this application area as our object technology team was still fighting in ISOV-Handelsregister development to succeed.

"The evaluation showed that one product could be bought on the market which conformed to the functional specifications of the INES project. This product was not running on a compatible system environment other than Dataflex. One customer was willing to integrate that product into the INES project.

"Our object technology development team was then able to convince the management of IBM and the customers to develop this highly complex application part with our established object technology environment. The following reasons led to the decision that this application should be realized in object technology."

- The development team of ISOV-Handelsregister could be kept together and continue to work with a follow-on project. New object technology team members could be educated and integrated in a team with practical/experienced object technology developers.
- Future maintenance tasks for ISOV-Handelsregister and the tax forms application could be handled with the same development team.
- The technical classes that were developed in the ISOV-Handelsregister could be reused in the follow-on project Tax-Forms.
- The development environment that was set up for the ISOV-Handelsregister development could be used also for the tax forms application. The environment was C++, GUI_Master Classtree from CAP Volmac.
- The setup of the tax forms development team could be smoothly arranged with the deployment of the developers from the ISOV-Handelsregister development team.

Methodology Employed

"Before we started the analysis and design of ProFormA we ordered the booklet *An Evaluation of Object Oriented Analysis and Design* (Author: Cribbs, Moon, Roe, SIGS Books, 1992). According to this document we were convinced to use the Booch method as we also had the tool Rational Rose available on the market.

"After having bought this tool we performed the analysis and design according to the Booch method. "

Development

Development was started with two people who began to build a basic ProFormA application that showed the user what the product would look like and to serve as the basis for the roundtrip development process. One of these developers was responsible for the ProFormA designer module and the other was responsible for the ProFormAWork module.

One person developed the whole SOM persistence interface and object management, whose functionality is based on the object management approach used in the ISOV-Handelsregister application. For the SQL interface a different approach from the first project was developed. In ProFormA all SQL statements are dynamically created at execution time. In ISOV-Handelsregister all persistent classes had its own static SQL source files for reading, adding, and updating.

One person developed the interface classes to include the AS/400 data queue mechanism to optimize the cooperative process from AS/400 to OS/2 application part. In addition that person was responsible for supplying the interface mechanism to get appropriate information from the Tax Register part of INES, such as personal information of the tax subjects.

One person developed the database administration. In addition he developed a "Help" system that can be generated by the user with a special startup parameter. It is also based on SOM objects.

Two persons (new to object technology) developed special requirements given by development leaders. They were also responsible for interfacing to the customer's forms designer specialist in order to verify that their needs were covered with the functionality of the ProFormA application. At the end they were also responsible for the testing of ProFormA.

The elapsed development time was twenty months (10/93–5/95), and consumed sixty person-months.

Deployment

For all end users new PS/2 with minimum requirement DX/2 with 66 MHz and 24 MB were installed at the customer side.

The pilot users were trained because they had to design all the tax forms applicable for their canton. Thus, they got heavily involved in order to get to know the functionality of ProFormA. The customer was in charge of end user training.

At the beginning end users expected something like a spreadsheet, but with time they realized that they will get the functionality of an application far beyond normal spreadsheet applications.

Maintenance

At present one person is assigned to ProFormA for further testing, one person for maintenance, and one person for new requirements. Technical classes responsible for maintaining ISOV-Handelsregister are conducted.

BENEFITS

Scholz and Buehrer cite numerous benefits of object-oriented development in ProFormA, including the big advantage of reusing existing classes from another project.

"Roundtrip design allowed us to involve the customer continuously. This had a great influence on customer acceptance and reduced the number of design change requests. We are convinced that no other methodology could have efficiently handled an application of such complexity. Compared with our first project (which was approximately the same size) we used forty person-months less to complete the application. That means 40 percent increase of productivity."

CONCLUSIONS

Scholz offers these final observations:

"Project Management is a big issue in object-oriented development. Teamwork is vital. Roundtrip OOA->OOD->OOP —>..works great, but one problem remains: How and when do you do the estimates?"

10

Medical Examiner System

Palm Beach County ISS

THE OPPORTUNITY

The Office of the Medical Examiner is under the Public Safety Department in Palm Beach County, Florida. The Medical Examiner is responsible for determining manner and cause of death when the death happens under unusual circumstances. The output of the Medical Examiner's work can have both legal and public health implications.

In Palm Beach County, all tracking of the Medical Examiner cases had been a manual process. Due to the reporting requirements, and to assist personnel in their daily activities, it was determined by the Public Safety Director that a computerized system should be sought.

Information must be made available to the various law enforcement agencies in a timely and accurate manner, and to health and safety agencies to determine if deaths may be avoided by initiating legislation regarding public safety.

The Public Safety Director wanted a system that would expedite the flow of information between investigators, technicians, and other medical personnel, and allow diversity of reporting capabilities.

THE APPLICATION

The Medical Examiner System tracks those deaths that must be investigated by the Medical Examiner's Office, from the initial report to the Medical Examiner's Office, through investigation and determination of causes and manner of death, and finally, the release of the body to the funeral home.

Details regarding a death are retained in the system, including vehicles involved in the death, scenes, toxicology results, specimen tracking, parties involved with the deceased, and other evidence.

In order to provide the required flexibility in reporting, a relational database was chosen. Although conventional process-driven approaches could have worked, the object-oriented approach allowed the reuse of objects from other applications. This approach also produces systems that more closely emulate the customer's work flow.

The application consists of 59 windows with approximately 300 underlying objects to support the functionality. Following are sample screens (Figures 10.1 to 10.5) from the Medical Examiner System.

This menu is displayed after the security login windows. It is built by comparing the user's security to functions in the security tables. Those functions that the user is allowed to see are then displayed.

This window displays information about a case. The menu or toolbar across the top may be used for various actions to perform on the displayed data. The twelve buttons are used to open windows to maintain the data described on the button. Buttons were chosen for these actions in order to show information (the number of records), as well as initiate actions. Notice the bar below the data that displays "changed by" information. This is a user object that contains its own function for maintaining this information throughout all tables that utilize these columns.

This window shows a typical help screen within the Medical Examiner System.

This window is displayed from the Technologist Maintenance Option. It displays specimen information grouped by date

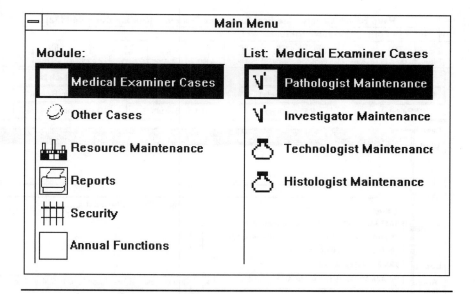

FIGURE 10.1   Main menu for Medical Examiner System.

received. It updates the date received from the toxicology laboratory. Batches may be entered as received by double clicking on the received date. This causes those not yet received to be updated with that date.

This window displays information in special print formats, such as labels. It also prints graphics such as anatomical diagrams for use during an autopsy.

Object-Oriented Functionality

The ME System is Palm Beach County ISS's fourth client/server, object-oriented application, all developed with PowerBuilder. Three of these were developed based on PowerCerv's PowerTool template object-oriented library. Developers use a template application as the foundation for new applications. This template consists of security modules and a system development module to assist in the building of the new application.

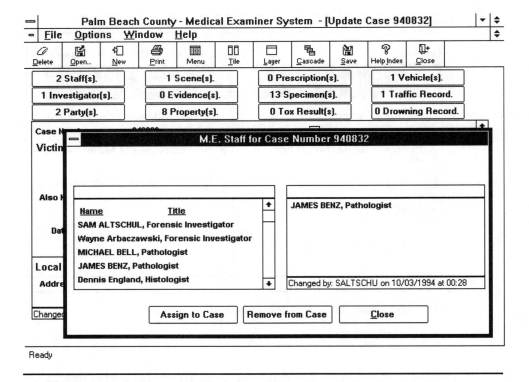

FIGURE 10.2 Investigator Maintenance Option.

There are usually three levels of inheritance in the windows. These main ancestors are from PowerCerv's PowerTool. In Palm Beach's applications, they sometimes add their own ancestor, which increases the level of inheritance to four. This does not seem to cause a noticeable increase in overhead.

In PowerBuilder, encapsulation is accomplished through the data object's independence from the code in the window. Developers have been able to use the same window for several user functions and swap the data objects. They use constraints in the Oracle database for relationships and unique

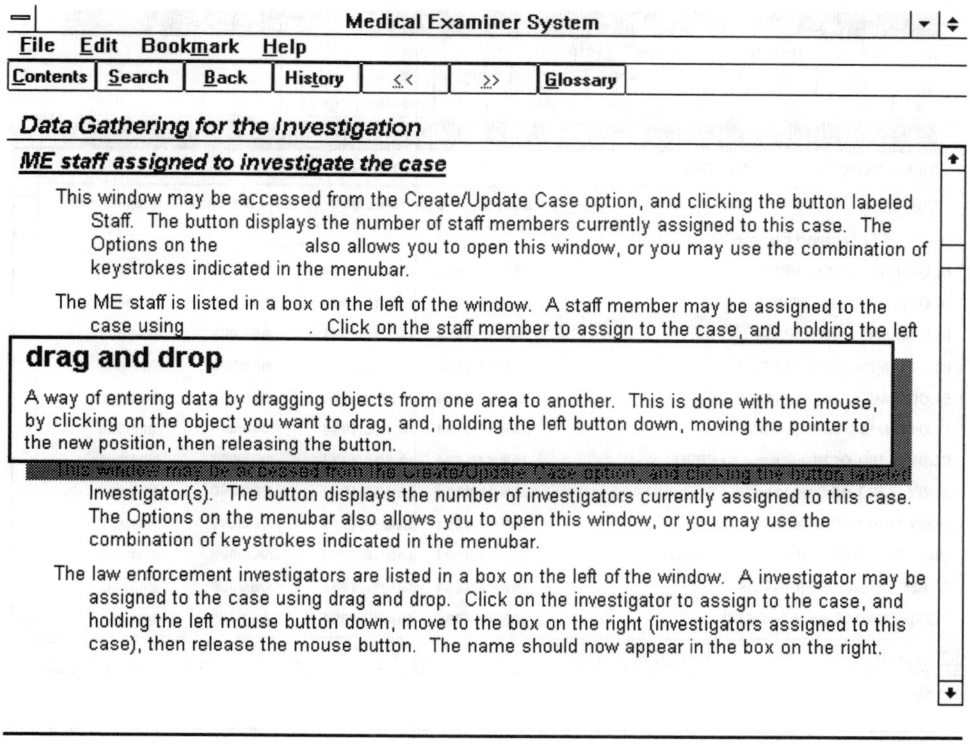

```
━┃                         Medical Examiner System                    ┃▼┃↕
  File  Edit  Bookmark  Help
┃Contents┃ Search ┃ Back ┃ History ┃  ‹‹  ┃   ››  ┃ Glossary ┃
```

Data Gathering for the Investigation

<u>*ME staff assigned to investigate the case*</u>

This window may be accessed from the Create/Update Case option, and clicking the button labeled Staff. The button displays the number of staff members currently assigned to this case. The Options on the   also allows you to open this window, or you may use the combination of keystrokes indicated in the menubar.

The ME staff is listed in a box on the left of the window. A staff member may be assigned to the case using   . Click on the staff member to assign to the case, and holding the left

drag and drop

A way of entering data by dragging objects from one area to another. This is done with the mouse, by clicking on the object you want to drag, and, holding the left button down, moving the pointer to the new position, then releasing the button.

Investigator(s). The button displays the number of investigators currently assigned to this case. The Options on the menubar also allows you to open this window, or you may use the combination of keystrokes indicated in the menubar.

The law enforcement investigators are listed in a box on the left of the window. A investigator may be assigned to the case using drag and drop. Click on the investigator to assign to the case, and holding the left mouse button down, move to the box on the right (investigators assigned to this case), then release the mouse button. The name should now appear in the box on the right.

FIGURE 10.3   Typical help screen.

columns, but have not used triggers or stored procedures in this project.

Use of polymorphism can be seen in the menu bar. The same menu item triggers the save event, but the event on the window may have a different script. The same menu bar is associated with different windows throughout the application.

There are approximately thirty main windows and dialogue boxes in the system. Some of these windows are used in different functions within the application.

The template libraries consist of approximately 160 objects.

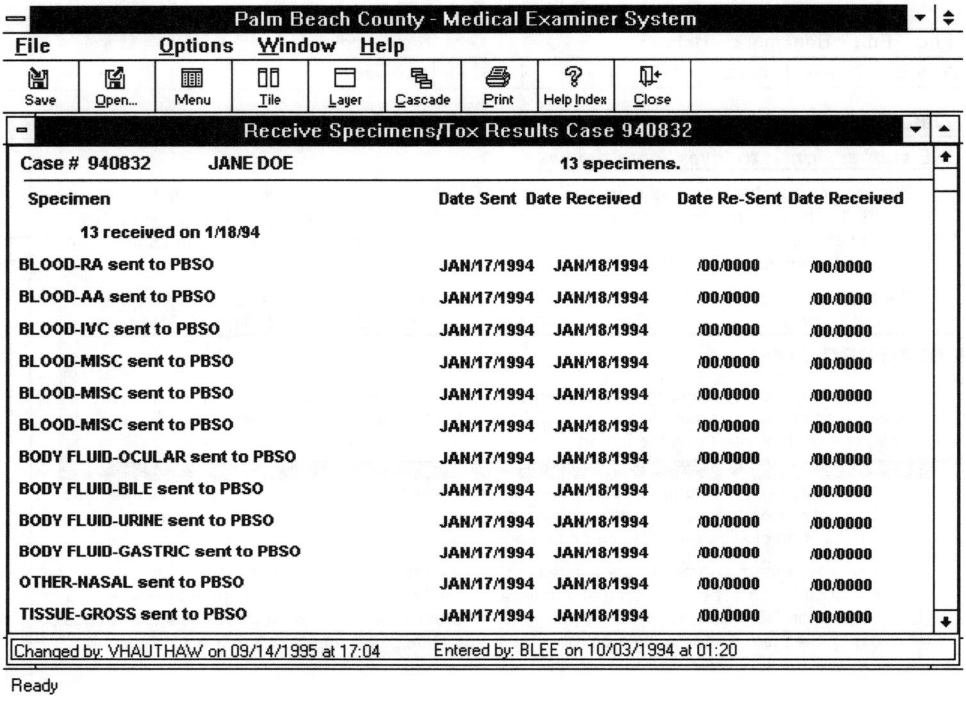

FIGURE 10.4 Receive Specimens/Tox Results.

Hardware and Software Used

	Hardware	Software
Interface	486	Windows 3.1, SQL*Net, PowerBuilder LAN WorkPlace PowerCerv's PowerTool
Core Code	SPARC 1000	SunSolaris 2x
Database	SPARC 1000	Oracle 7
Development Environment	IBM-SPARC 10 PS/ValuePoint	Win 3.1, PowerBuilder

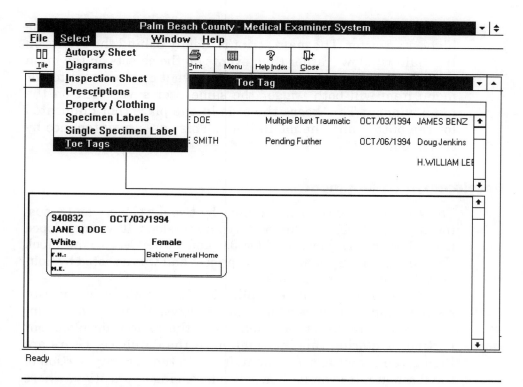

FIGURE 10.5 Toe Tag Window.

The NAV template application from PowerCerv was used as a foundation for the ME system. It uses several tables to control the application, display the main menu, open windows, and place data objects on the windows. This allows a window to be used in several user modules. For example, the same actual windows may be opened to update transportation records, drug records, or other tables that require basic add-change-delete functionality.

Palm Beach ISS's mainframe programming environment has a strong adherence to functionally cohesive programming. They appreciate the ease of maintenance inherent in this style, and have made an early attempt to remain functionally cohesive in the event-driven, nonprocedural style of programming.

To accomplish this, they defined generic user events in the highest ancestor. The main script is ideally behind the events on the main window (rather than events on the objects on the main window). This means that the clicked event on a save button or menu item will both trigger the same user save event on the main window. This keeps the code in one place (not duplicated for the button and the menu item). This eases maintenance by consistency in the code.

Development Environment

The system was designed and built by two developers and a customer group during weekly prototyping sessions. It was developed using PowerSoft's PowerBuilder 3.0 and PowerCerv's PowerTool. Valerie Hauthaway managed the project and was assisted by Software Engineer Sam Stadlock.

PowerCerv's template application is a combination of user security and system development windows. Menu options, windows, and data objects are defined in the system development portion by storing this information in the database. Users are then given access to these menu items in the Security portion of the template. It is actually a self-referencing application, where the menu is built by reading a table in the database, and windows are opened based on the window name column value. Data objects are placed on the window based on the data object column value. This allows the same window to be used in several places, with a different data object attached. No library management tools were used, and, due to the nature of the template application, the developers worked closely to avoid conflicts in the design.

Storage Management

During development, the application was stored on a Novell LAN. The development database is an Oracle database on a SUN Sparc 10. Although not currently using library management facilities, developers expect to use LBMS for library management in the future.

The template application's function and security tables are shared by all applications running on the same server. The reason they are shared is due to the fact that the template SQL cannot be coded to point to a specific tablespace and still remain a pure template to start the next application.

Developers changed the template to include an application id in these tables and made these template tables public synonyms. This allowed all applications written with the template on a single server to share these function tables.

The PowerBuilder DataWindow Painter generates SQL. In the future, developers hope to use CASE tools to generate triggers, procedures, or PowerBuilder scripts.

A problem came up during the first PowerBuilder application they developed, according to ME system developer Valerie Hauthaway.

"We connected to the database as the owner during development, and the SQL generated was not prefixed with the schema name in the select statement. When we tested the application by connecting to Oracle as a user, none of the tables were found. Oracle looked for a schema name in the SQL, and since there was not one, the user's schema was used to look for the tables. The tables could not be found because the user was not the owner. We learned from that experience to sign on as a user (not owner) when building the application. This forces PowerBuilder to generate the schema name in the SQL."

PROJECT LIFECYCLE

Analysis and Design

In some past applications, Knowledgeware's ADW was used for analysis. However, it was designed to build COBOL, CICS applications. During the analysis of this system, LBMS's System Engineer was being tested for possible purchase. They took the methodology as far as the entity relationship diagram, the foundation of the database. Design of the system was done during the JAD sessions during actual system development.

Interviews were conducted with the personnel at the Medical Examiner's Office to identify and define processes, task scenarios, and entities.

The object-oriented methodology did not have as much of an impact on the user as did the fact that the application would be client/server, and run in Windows environment. Since there was no existing system, these options were all acceptable to the customer.

Development

Design and development of the ME system began in December 1993 and was completed in April 1994. Weekly prototyping sessions (JADs) were held with the customers. Iterations of the system were shown each week, and changes were made based on the customer's input. The result of the joint application design was a system that satisfied the customer's needs and flowed in a manner consistent to their work flow. It also reduced the training needed after deployment of the system.

Approximately 350 programming staff hours were required to complete the system.

Deployment

Customers who were new to Windows attended an introductory Windows class. Customers who were involved in the design of the system needed very little training and served as trainers for their staff.

A LAN and ten new PCs were installed. The customer connects to an offsite SUN SPARC 1000 through a router. A notebook PC may be used in the future to enter data from the field.

Some of the considerations for user acceptance addressed during prototyping were ease of use, the system's ability to assist the user in expediting the flow of case information, and flexible reporting capabilities.

According to Hauthaway, the benefits of object-oriented development were seen in the ease of use of the system. This includes the consistency of user interface, as well as a mapping of user tasks to the system functions.

Maintenance

With this application, and their other client/server application, maintenance issues are still being formulated. Currently the developers maintain these systems.

Since the application runs on the customer's PC (client), one of the special considerations in maintaining client/server applications is version control. Customers are on their own LAN, so currently the developers load the most recent version to their LAN. When the customer logs into the application, a function checks the version of the application against a version number in a table in the database. If the version is not the most recent, a batfile executes to download the new version from the LAN.

BENEFITS

Since the application is new, benefits are predicted to be some or all of the following.

- Ability to provide statistical reporting to various public health offices and the public.
- Ability to internally manage flow of paperwork surrounding a case more efficiently.
- Faster handling of a case by automating the processes, including labels and diagrams. This may result in less overtime for the staff.
- Ability to monitor the efficiency of the providers of external services.

CONCLUSIONS

Ms Hauthaway cites some of the issues that are important in her organization, and that she would advise others to look for in order to develop more and larger applications in this environment:

- Network management tools for distributed environment
- Security procedures for databases in a distributed environment
- Library management for applications in a distributed environment
- Building skills in object-oriented, GUI application development, and in SQL, and PL/SQL, and in client/server methods
- Establishing test procedures and incremental version test procedures
- Establishing a good template library for reusability in future applications
- Standardizing the method of navigation within new applications
- Standardizing the underlying architecture of the windows
- Establishing and enforcing coding standards

The customer response to these applications has been very positive. They are looking forward to using ad hoc query SQL-based tools to access their databases and create their own reports and inquiries.

The successful implementation of this and similar applications developed using object-oriented methods in a distributed environment have motivated our management to proceed with proposed object-oriented projects.

Hauthaway describes the current direction of her department:

"Our direction in 1995 is focused on three-tier technology. We have developed applications using PowerBuilder for the frontend GUI, and OEC toolkit, C, and COBOL for the middle tier. In the frontend, a single nonvisual user object with an unbounded two-dimensional array was designed to call the functions in the middle tier and populate the windows.

"This function is placed in the ancestor of all windows that need to call the middle tier. This function was designed jointly by the manager of development, Phil Davidson, Richard Chuilli, a system integrator, and myself.

"It took all of our ideas about object-oriented principles, and a strong focus on efficiency, before the design was completed, but by using the object-oriented methods, we saved countless days of hard-coding the retrievals.

"We have also developed an application for the Division of Consumer Affairs in Palm Beach County that is being offered for resale to other governmental agencies. There has been a lot of interest in the application. "

Object Technology and Enterprise Applications

OVERVIEW OF SECTION IV

Enterprise applications are big software systems that are used throughout a company. They determine the payroll of everyone working for the company. They balance and consolidate the accounts each night to determine the current status of the bank. They monitor the inventory. They are big applications and they are critical to the success of the organization.

It's one thing to use a new technology on smaller, departmental applications. It's another thing to decide that the new technology should be used to create applications that must be created and done right if the organization is to continue to prosper.

There isn't any unique technology involved in enterprise applications. All of the elements we have considered in other contexts apply here. The applications need to be done on time and within a budget. They are often distributed applications; in many cases they span the world. They often integrate existing legacy applications to accomplish their tasks. They frequently involve the use of large databases and they often operate in heterogeneous environments. Tools used to develop enterprise applications need to scale up.

As you look at some of the applications that have received awards in the enterprise application category, you'll notice that some of them have been developed in tools that have combined AI techniques with object-oriented techniques. As a generalization, AI techniques add the kind of power and flexibility that is often vital for very complex applications.

ARTIFICIAL INTELLIGENCE AND OBJECT TECHNOLOGY

People talk about object technology as if they could easily define it. In fact, object technology is very difficult to define because it involves a basic paradigm shift in computing and it is involved in almost all aspects of computing. There are object-oriented operating systems, object-oriented middleware products, object-oriented languages, object-oriented methodologies, object-oriented CASE tools, object-oriented 4GL tools, and object-oriented databases. People talk about using objects to develop basic definitions of numbers and strings and they talk about encapsulating large COBOL applications as objects. Clearly this technology encompasses a wide variety of different techniques.

Most of the popular accounts of object technology that appeared in the mid-to-late eighties tended to stress the object-oriented language/interface tradition. Object techniques, according to this explanation, were first used in the Simula language and then were further developed by Kay, Goldberg, Robson, and others at Xerox PARC. The first well-known object-oriented language was Smalltalk, which was initially used at Xerox PARC to develop graphical user interfaces.

A secondary branch of the object-oriented language/interface tradition, which we might call the object-based tradition, used a subset of the object-oriented language and object-oriented interface techniques to create systems that combined object orientation and procedural features to solve specific types of practical problems. The Apple Macintosh (developed in Object Pascal by Larry Tesler and others who left Xerox PARC and went to work for Apple) was one offshoot of the Xerox PARC efforts. Various windowing interfaces for workstations were another result.

At some point, according to the mainstream object orientation tradition, application developers realized that modularity, in addition to facilitating interface development, made it possible to reuse code, develop applications faster, and reduce maintenance problems. Brad Cox probably did the most to promote this point of view with his popular book, *Object-Oriented Programming: An Evolutionary Approach.* In the mid-eighties Bell Labs introduced C++ and Objective C and Eiffel soon followed. Later Apple and then Borland made object-oriented versions of Pascal and the C++ available. Next Inc. used Objective C to create the NextStep operating system to show what lay beyond the Macintosh. Microsoft's introduction of Windows 3.0 finally brought everyone's attention to graphical operating systems, and by 1990 the object orientation revolution was in full swing.

A less well-known account of the development of object technology starts with Marvin Minsky's work on frames and goes through early object-oriented enhancements to Lisp, like Mixins and LOOPS to early expert system tools like IntelliCorp's KEE. (KEE, Version 1, released in 1984, was a pure object-oriented development tool written in Lisp. It was probably the first commercial object-oriented development tool.) Later versions of KEE added more AI and non-object orientation features in an effort to make the tool more commercially acceptable for the eighties (see Figure IV.1).

The earliest accounts of expert systems stressed rules and inferencing, but by the mid-eighties, all of the major expert system-building products had incorporated frames. These early expert system tools used frames in two different ways: (1) to create interfaces and (2) to structure and store knowledge. In addition to their other problems, by the mid-eighties, expert system vendors were trying to explain and sell products that supported inferencing, logic and constraint programming, frame and object-oriented programming, and client/server techniques. Only the best programming groups could begin to grasp all of the new technologies, let alone figure out how to integrate them successfully.

Two things that particularly hindered the early expert system tool vendors were (1) a lack of standardization regarding how to represent rules and frames, and (2) a lack of a standard-

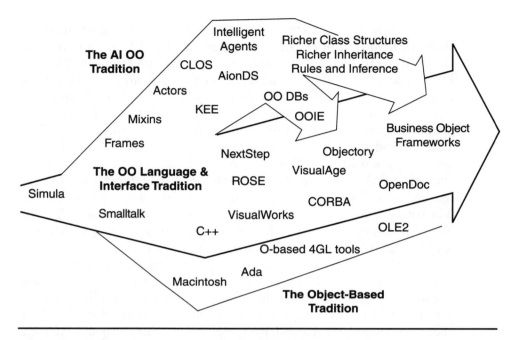

FIGURE IV.1 Different traditions leading to today's object technology.

ized methodology for developing expert systems. The best effort to develop a standardized methodology was undertaken by the European Community (ESPRIT) and resulted in KADS. The first version of KADS, which came out in the mid-eighties, stressed designing systems to solve specific types of decision-making tasks and stressed rules and inferencing. KADS 2, which came out toward the end of the eighties, was enhanced to incorporate object techniques.

During the same period, Lisp was standardized as Common Lisp and then proceeded to evolve into CLOS (Common Lisp Object System), which has played a minor but consistent role in the object-oriented language market. Expert system tools and languages, in turn, led to the development of the first object-oriented databases (i.e., G-Base, a semantic database that has evolved into Matisse) designed to facilitate the storage of knowledge objects.

In the nineties, as object-oriented development became more strongly associated with object-oriented languages, the object-oriented database vendors shifted their emphasis and modified their products to work with C++ or Smalltalk. This is interesting, since neither of those object-oriented languages supports persistent instances, while most of the expert system tools have relied on persistent instances since the mid-eighties. Thus, although the AI-derived branch of object technology initially received less attention, recent accounts are beginning to pay more attention to it and a synthesis between the two object traditions is now well underway. In the late eighties and at the beginning of the nineties, object orientation conferences were mostly focused on object-oriented languages and databases. In 1994, most of the shows were focused on object-oriented 4GL client/server tools and object-oriented CASE tools and all the shows have a good sprinkling of object-oriented products developed by former expert system vendors. Moreover, most recent accounts of the object-oriented market have at least mentioned expert system tools as one way to approach object-oriented development.

To illustrate how AI vendors are selling at the high end of each object-oriented niche, consider Figure 2.3 in Chapter 2. It provides an analysis of object-oriented application development tools. The figure emphasizes that tools with inferencing and rules are especially good for logic-intensive, enterprise-wide object-oriented applications. It also emphasizes that few of the current tools support true distributed development or the Object Management Group's Common Object Request Broker Architecture (CORBA). It does not emphasize the difference between objects and frames, which we will consider in a moment.

Developers and companies have been cautious in their adoption of object technology. Most companies began by acquiring object-based products. (Object-based products provide some object components, but lack the full complement of features that most people associate with object-oriented products. Most object-based products, for example, don't support class hierarchies that developers can access or subclasses.) In the past two years, as they have learned more about object technology, many companies have upgraded to true object-oriented products. The advanced object-oriented products will probably remain a small part of the overall object-oriented 4GL niche, however, because most of the products are written in their own internal languages. The object-oriented client/server tools tend to be written in Smalltalk or C++ and make it possible for companies to move classes developed in one tool to other tools or to use them with object-oriented languages. The development of an object orientation repository might make the advanced object-oriented tools more popular, but this remains to be seen. In the meantime, the emphasis on open systems is definitely limiting the market for most of the advanced object-oriented products.

THE OBJECT-ORIENTED LANGUAGE TRADITION VERSUS THE OBJECT-ORIENTED AI TRADITION

Smalltalk and C++ object models have been consistently simpler than the frame-based models. The hierarchies of classes are only used to facilitate the generation of instances and the instances are transient. Multiple inheritance mechanisms are so limited that most object-oriented developers avoid using them. Great stress has been placed on encapsulation.

By contrast, frames were originally conceived of as a way to structure knowledge. Thus, frames at any level may be accessed for information. It's common, for example, for an AI system to begin with a lower-level frame (i.e., an instance), find that it lacks sufficient information, and then move to a higher-level frame and reason on an abstract level.

Assume we are trying to find out some things about a bird. Unfortunately, the class Bird doesn't contain any information about what birds breathe. Knowing that a bird class is a child of the animal class, however, leads us to examine what we know about animals. By examining the attributes and values associated with the animal class, we determine that animals breathe air, and thus, we can infer that birds also breathe air. The fact that frame systems keep useful knowledge at many levels in their systems has led to more complex inheritance mechanisms and to programming techniques that allow developers to direct messages to frames at various levels in a hierarchy. The original frame systems lacked methods and relied on demons and rules and an inference engine that could operate across all the frames in the systems. Demons were linked to specific target frames. Thus, the use of rules and demons violated encapsulation. (Some early expert system tool vendors tried to encapsulate rules within specific frames and found the process too confusing and inefficient and abandoned it.)

In the late eighties, as companies began to become interested in object technology, most of the major expert system tool vendors added some kind of methods to their frame systems, making them more like objects in Smalltalk, but rules continued to remain outside the frames. By creating a dual way of handling procedural information, the expert system vendors made their products more complex and developers were faced with still another option: when to use methods and message passing and when to rely on rules and inferencing. In addition to these considerations, the high-end AI-derived products support greater dynamics and more complex polymorphism than languages and tools based on Smalltalk. Thus, for example, some AI tools can dynamically create new classes and modify methods while they are running.

In spite of the emphasis that Smalltalk and C++ vendors have put on encapsulation, it has never been considered a defining characteristic of object orientation. Peter Wegner, in his popular discrimination between object-oriented languages and object-based languages, omits encapsulation and includes CLOS among the object-oriented languages. In effect, frames are considered a type of object, and methods can either be encapsulated, or in the environment, as they are in CLOS. At this point, most object-oriented theorists ignore frames and simply stress that AI-derived tools, like CLOS, are simply more complex than most other object-oriented products.

Most corporate object-oriented developers started out in C++ or Smalltalk and are a bit overwhelmed by the complexities of the more sophisticated AI-derived object-oriented tools. As more complex object-oriented applications are developed, however, the more sophisticated object-oriented developers are increasingly looking to AI techniques to help them model problems that are more complex than those commonly discussed in introductory C++ courses. AI developers introduced rules and inferencing, after all, to modularize complex chains of procedural logic. Many object-oriented developers begin by assuming that they are modularizing procedural code when they break a conventional application into methods and associate different methods with different objects. They are modularizing it, of course, but as they move from applications that primarily involve manipulating data to those involving large amounts of knowledge and complex decisions, they find that even methods can get complex. CLOS offers developers the option of using methods with associated preconditions and postconditions to handle more complex situations. At some point, however, it becomes easier to conceptualize the logic as rules and let an inference engine handle the search. In fact, some would argue that it is only when a developer uses both objects and production rules that he or she has really modularized an application in the most systematic manner.

One of the more interesting developments in object orientation and CASE is the number of object-oriented CASE vendors who are incorporating some kind of inferencing and rules to allow developers to incorporate "business rules" in applications. The best example of this trend is Object Management Workbench (OMW), an object-oriented CASE product with business rules and an interpreted development environment that is sold by IntelliCorp and James Martin Associates. OMW sits on top of IntelliCorp's ProKappa product. In effect, the power of the AI environment is hidden from the user, who develops object models using standard object diagramming conventions. Production rules are changed into business rules and specified independent of the object model. The power of the AI environment is apparent to users because they can execute diagrams at any time and edit diagrams and while they are being executed. To the developer, however, this is simply a nice feature and does not raise the implementation issues that are raised when one considers trying to field an application developed in some of the advanced object-oriented client/server development tools.

In the early nineties, as interest in new expert system-building tools declined and companies became enthusiastic about objects, expert system tool vendors began to reposition themselves. There have been at least five responses:

- Expert system tools repositioned as flexible interface development tools (e.g., Neuron Data's Smart Elements)
- Expert system tools repositioned as object-oriented 4GL development tools (e.g., Inference's ART*Enterprise)
- Expert system tools repositioned as a foundation for object-oriented CASE tools (e.g., IntelliCorp's Kappa)
- Expert system tools repositioned as domain specific object-oriented development environments (e.g., Gensym's G2 and ReThink)
- Expert system tools used as the basis for a CORBA environment (e.g., ExperSoft's Xshell)

It's a little early to say which of these strategies will be most successful, but in each area, some vendors are taking advantage of AI and object-oriented techniques to create interesting products. One way to gage the success of the AI vendors' efforts to reposition themselves as object-oriented vendors is to consider how products with both object-oriented and AI characteristics have done in the annual contests sponsored by OMG and Computerworld at the last three Object World shows in San Francisco. Each year there have been five winners, and each year one of the five winners was developed in an expert system-building tool (i.e., KEE and Kappa PC).

As companies move from smaller object-oriented applications to more sophisticated systems, we expect that developers who have used expert system (ES) building tools in the eighties will prevail on their companies to use object-oriented AI tools for tasks involving complex logic.

APPLICATIONS

Two of the applications in this section illustrate how large, complex problems can be solved with tools that combine both objects and inferencing techniques.

Boeing Defense and Space Group's PreAmp (Design Automation Pre-Competitive Advanced Manufacturing Process)
Winner, Category 5, 1995

This application supports concurrent engineering of printed circuit assemblies (PCAs) for the electronics industry. The development of this system was supported by NIST and the group responsible for the overall development effort included Boeing, DEC, HP Hughes, Lockheed, Rockwell, Versant, IntelliCorp, and others.

Conventional approaches had been attempted and they had failed to produce acceptable applications.

The finished application involved hundreds of classes and thousands of instances. Five separate databases were needed. The application was developed with IntelliCorp's Kappa PC, an object-oriented application development tool that includes AI capabilities. Thus, in addition to object-oriented technology, this application was able to incorporate inferencing and rules for complex decision making tasks. Kappa has a proprietary internal language but generates C and C++ code for the final application. The development of this application required some 60,000 hours of effort. The resulting application, though not as fast as some users would like, is able to accomplish the task in a satisfactory manner.

The developers claim that object orientation allowed them to model the problem realistically. In addition, the interpreted development environment allowed them to modify the system to test alternatives. The resulting system can be modified quickly and ease of maintenance is probably the most important overall benefit. Aside from the fact that without taking a combined AI and object orientation approach, it probably wouldn't have been possible to analyze the problem and design the application in the first place.

Boeing Defense and Space Group's Analysis and Requirements Traceability (DART)
Winner, Category 4, 1994

DART is an application that keeps track of requirements on very complex projects. The system was developed using Kappa

PC, a tool that combines object-oriented and AI capabilities. Conventional approaches had been attempted and failed because they couldn't handle the extreme variability of document styles and formats. By combining object orientation and knowledge-based approaches, Boeing was able to create this application in Kappa PC. The incremental prototyping available in Kappa made this problem easier to approach. The final solution runs on a PC and integrates Microsoft Excel and Microsoft Word. Here again, the developers especially praised the ease with which they could revise and maintain the application.

PreAmp (Pre-competitive Advanced Manufacturing Processes)

Boeing Defense and Space Group, Design Automation

THE OPPORTUNITY

The PreAmp (Pre-competitive Advanced Manufacturing Processes) Program is a three-year research program that began in July 1992. The goal of the program is to enable concurrent engineering of printed circuit assemblies for the electronics industry. The program is using the Standard for the Exchange of Product model data (STEP) to accomplish information sharing for concurrent engineering. The purpose of the program is to improve the printed circuit assemblies (PCA) development process in ways that reduce development time and costs while improving quality.

Typically, PCA designers develop their designs in a vacuum, unaware of the capabilities of their manufacturing facilities. This allows designers to create designs that are either not manufacturable (cannot be made within cost) or not producible (cannot reproduce many of them within cost). PreAmp provides a database that defines the capabilities of the manufacturing facility. It provides a producibility advisor to compare the PCA design against the limitations of the factory. This allows designers to resolve their manufacturing problems before they ever reach the manufacturing facility. The savings of discovering and correcting manufacturing problems in the design cycle, before they ever get to manufacturing, is typically in the range of 20 to 30 percent of manufacturing costs.

Additionally, customer requirements for PCAs have traditionally been stored in document form. No automated facility or process existed to test the PCA product to determine if it indeed fulfilled the design requirements. PreAmp provides a facility to define requirements and to test the design against these requirements.

In addition to these features, PreAmp provides a rule definition and execution facility for its end users to define their own rules. This facility allows users to examine any component of the PCA or factory and define their own comparisons. For example, a rule could be written to determine the tallest component on the PCA and compare it with the smallest clearance factory equipment to potentially identify a conflict. This ability has allowed the present users of PreAmp to define rules for design for test, design for producibility, design for cost, and design for manufacturability. These areas were previously untestable with existing EDA (Electronics Design Automation) systems.

THE APPLICATION

PreAmp is a UNIX-based PCA design framework. It provides PCA designers with a user interface to access each of the tools required for their job. The system aids the user in accessing the required data and programs. The software allows a user to access applications that design a PCA and subsequently perform analyses on the PCA to determine its manufacturability, testability, and producibility. These analyses are performed before the PCA product is ever sent to the manufacturing facility. The further upstream problems can be found in a PCA product, the higher the cost savings.

The National Institute of Standards and Technology's (NIST) Advanced Technology Program supports PreAmp with a grant. PDES, Inc. and PreAmp member companies provide matching funds. The PreAmp team includes SCRA, Boeing, Digital Equipment Corporation, Hewlett Packard, Hughes Aircraft, Lockheed Martin, Mentor Graphics, Rockwell, and Versant. Arthur D. Little, Battelle, D. Appleton Company, STEP Tools, Inc., International TechneGroup Inc., and IntelliCorp also participate in the program.

The primary objectives of the PreAmp program are to define and demonstrate the technology that enables intelligent information sharing for concurrent engineering automation in PCA product design, product manufacturing, and manufacturing process design, manufacturing knowledge capture and application, and shared database access.

The PreAmp program will enable shared information environments across organizational boundaries. Sharing information electronically supports just-in-time production and the early discovery and resolution of design and manufacturing issues. It reduces non-value-added activities and it provides timely information on product or process changes.

The PreAmp program has four phases:

Phase I.   Requirements and architecture definition
Phase II.   Software prototyping
Phase III. Pilot Project 1, verify functionality and quality of software
Phase IV.   Pilot Project 2, determine system performance and estimate cost savings

The PreAmp program developed object-oriented software for the electronics design automation (EDA) arena. Five object-oriented databases (PCA Product, Manufacturing Factory, Design Rules, Design Issues, and PCA Processes) have been integrated with existing and PreAmp-developed EDA software. PreAmp developed a system user interface, a database translator (to utilize legacy PCA data), a manufacturing resource editor (to define manufacturing capabilities), a producibility advisor (to determine producibility problems with the PCA design), a rules definition and execution facility (for users to define and run rules of their definition in areas such as design for test (DFT), design for manufacturing (DFM), etc.), and a generative process planner (for considering part routing during assembly before actual production). The system user interface is constraint driven to aid users in following the required sequence of events to design a PCA product. Figure 11.1 shows the PreAmp architecture.

The PreAmp architecture integrates vendor computer-aided design, manufacturing, and test tools with the PreAmp database and PreAmp developed tools. The System User Interface provides access to CAx and PreAmp developed tools. A data access mechanism filters information flowing to and from the database.

The core of system is the PreAmp database. This STEP represented database management system consists of schemas for products, issues, design rule checks, rules, processes, and factory data. The product schema is the STEP printed circuit assembly product representation application protocol of AP210.

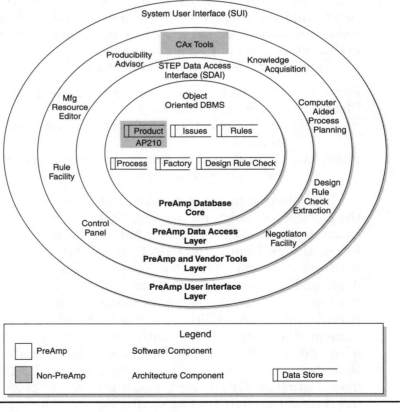

FIGURE 11.1   PreAmp architecture.

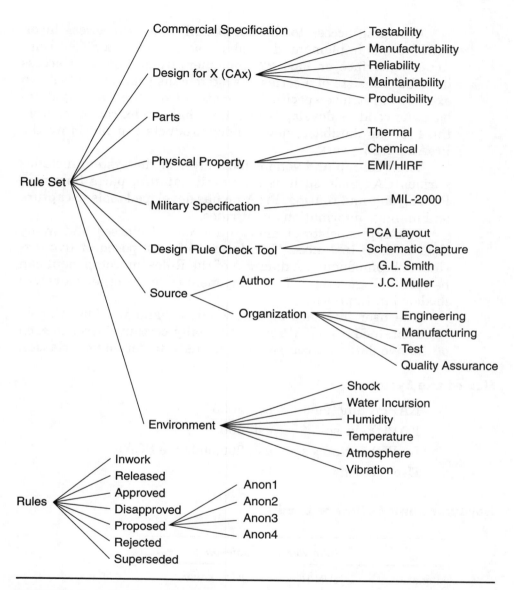

FIGURE 11.2 Example rule sets and hierarchy.

Providing access to the database is the data access layer. PreAmp has implemented database access using a STEP Data Access Interface or Part 22 implementation. The data access interface consists of a series of system calls that a CAx tool can execute to retrieve specific information from the PreAmp database. As vendors develop translators that can extract data from the PreAmp database, new vendor products can plug into the PreAmp framework.

The PreAmp and vendor tools layer of the system includes various CAx tools such as schematic capture, parts librarian, PCA layout, and routing. PreAmp has developed tools to capture and manage information about rules.

PreAmp consists of many hundreds of classes and many thousands of instances. The database is composed of five distinct subcomponents. A diagram of the Rules subcomponent can be seen in Figure 11.2. This component (like the other four) was modeled in Express.

The user interface menus, windows, and window widgets were obtained from KAPPA. Additionally, certain classes in each of the five database components are used to derive new classes.

Size of the System

KAPPA functions	est. 2000
KAPPA classes	est. 500
KAPPA instances	est. 200,000 (ave PCA)
User screens	50+

Hardware and Software Used

	Hardware	Software
Interface	SUN/HP	UNIX, KAPPA
Core Code	SUN/HP	UNIX, KAPPA, C, C++
Database	SUN/HP	UNIX, KAPPA, C, C++
Development Environment	SUN/HP	UNIX, KAPPA, C, C++

Notable features of PreAmp include:

- Function programming provided by the rules definition facility
- Rule based programming using KAPPA
- Repository via a Part 22 file storage mechanism
- Language code and complied code generated by the rules facility
- Utilization of a Standard Data Access Interface (SDAI)
- Online standards schema glossary
- Factory configuration capture tool based on STEP

PROJECT LIFECYCLE

Analysis and Design

Problems with designers understanding manufacturing have been around since the first products were created. Each of the members of the PreAmp team has similar problems in his or her manufacturing facility. The PreAmp team developed the initial requirements, with additional requirements coming from users.

Involved in the project were the PreAmp team, the manufacturing team, the design team, potential users, and developers.

The methodology employed was "semi ad-hoc." Extensive data modeling activity was used to define manufacturing resource, design rules, issues, processes, and PCA product databases.

The database content and size required the use of object-oriented technology. Additionally, the need for multiple applications that were developed by different individuals (at different companies) to share the same look and feel required the use of object orientation practices.

Conventional approaches had already been attempted. They failed due to the extreme variability of manufacturing and producibility. This approach of using object-oriented technology and knowledge-based technology proved to be extremely flexible and versatile.

A significant constraint identified during this phase was the need to integrate with existing commercial off-the-shelf electronics design automation software. The system had to run on platforms that supported the COTS software. Translators were developed to accept data from legacy EDA systems and load the PreAmp repository.

Boeing Defense and Space Group's Design Automation department has six people trained in object orientation concepts out of twenty people in the group. They have used object orientation for over five years under different operating systems and languages. Greg Smith has been using object orientation for eight years.

PreAmp is being very well accepted and used at member companies due to its extensive use of international product standards.

Smith mentions the usual benefits of object orientation in this phase, ease of extensibility and incorporation of changes. But he also mentions one drawback: object orientation requires a lot more up front work than traditional approaches.

Development

During the development phase the team sought to define extensive requirements and to create complete models of all the database components. They then used incremental prototyping to develop application around the database.

Development has taken approximately three years (begun July 1992). It has required five full-time and five part-time development people at 1000 hours per year for a total of approximately 45,000 person-hours.

The development software was chosen because it had been used on other successful object orientation projects. However, it had to be sold to other developers on the team.

For the project to be successful, an enormous amount of software had to be written in a short period of time. Object-oriented methodology allowed for rapid replication of application interfaces.

The benefits of object orientation in the development phase were rapid development, minimum bugs found in the system, and no surprises.

Deployment

The system required higher power machines than were currently available (in some areas) due to the concurrent use of PreAmp and COTS software. Additional resources are required to handle the extensive data translations, data loading, and data analyses.

Figure 11.3 shows the PreAmp PCA development process. The user interface enforces constraints to direct the user along the preferred path.

Users access the system user interface that constrains their activities to only those appropriate to the state of the design. Figure 11.4 shows the main panel of the user interface.

The user interface provides point-and-click access to all EDA applications (legacy systems, commercial off-the-shelf software, and PreAmp-developed tools). Figure 11.5 shows a typical screen within PreAmp, the Rule Definition Facility Main Rule Panel.

At any time during the design process users can elect to analyze their designs based on producibility, manufacturability, or testability. The manufacturing facility has previously been defined and subsequently allows the users to access this data. The user can also execute previously defined rules to test design or customer constraints. The software was integrated into existing user workstations.

A formal training course was developed by the PreAmp team at various companies, aimed at training future trainers. Some users were able to walk through a small test case with the developer. Many users were able to train themselves, after a short introduction, by following the context sensitive menus. One user developed fifty rules in eight weeks without formal training on the system.

Maintenance

Maintenance currently requires one person full time. Users have requested database extensions. The developer provides the code maintenance; users aid in data maintenance.

Because the system is being used by numerous large firms, all changes to the system need to be generic (e.g., not specific to

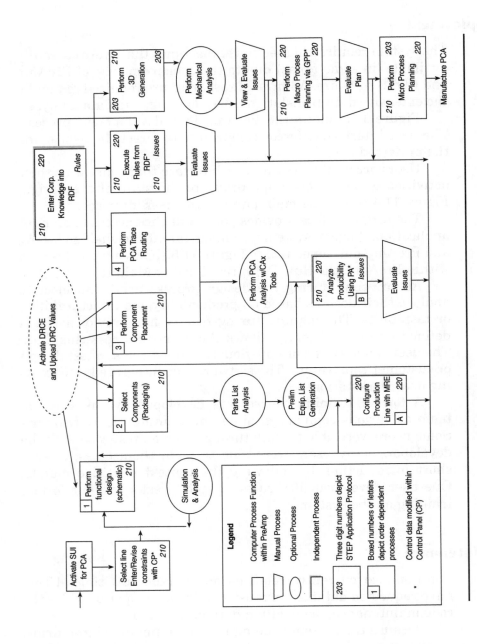

FIGURE 11.3 PreAmp development process.

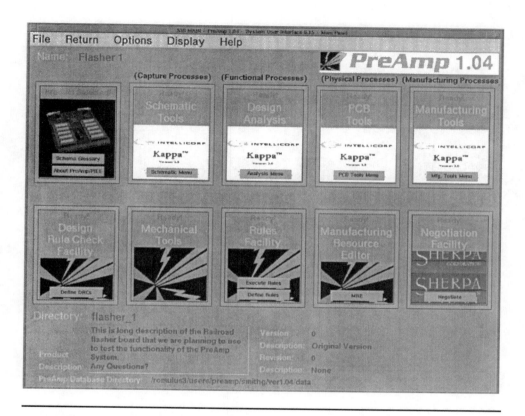

FIGURE 11.4 SUI main panel (after product selection).

any one body of users). As a single set of user interface objects was developed and shared by all developers, a common look and feel has propagated to all components of the system. The object-oriented environment simplified the incorporation of user specified changes.

BENEFITS

The most tangible benefit of PreAmp is the elimination of manufacturing, producibility, and testability problems before they reach the manufacturing facility.

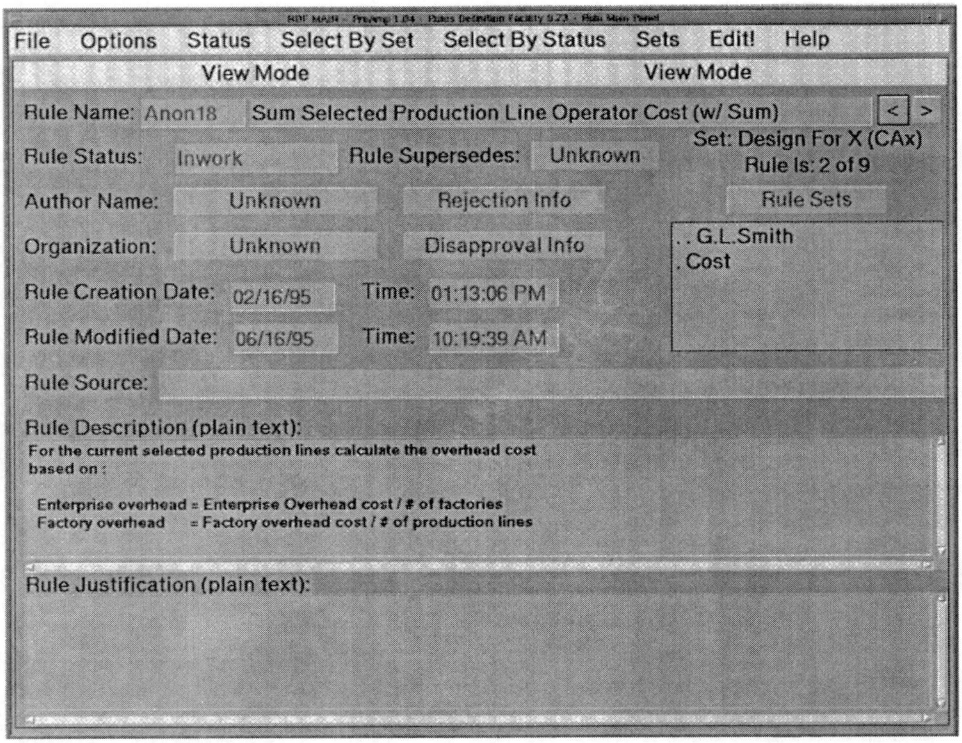

FIGURE 11.5 Rule Definition Facility Main Rule Panel.

The industry-led PreAmp program involves precompetitive, generic technology development. It is developing technologies that will improve the competitiveness of the U.S. electronics industry. An important part of every phase of the program is technology transfer. The program will demonstrate the technology through member company implementations and vendor commercialization. In addition, the PreAmp team provides research findings to other organizations, such as standards bodies and related research programs.

PreAmp delivers different benefits to each of the organizations (engineering, manufacturing, quality assurance, etc.) that are using the system. The manufacturing facilities are seeing fewer unmanufacturable designs. Designers are creating better designs that are more producible and testable. No quantification of these factors is available at this time. (Most of the large companies using PreAmp would not give out this information because it is competition-sensitive.)

Based on findings of the PreAmp team (documented in the Pilot Project 2 report), an average design iteration using PreAmp was less than one hour and the initial cycle time was from one to three hours. This is a significant reduction as a direct result of the data-sharing capabilities of PreAmp. In comparison, a typical design iteration without using PreAmp requires days for evaluating an engineering change order (ECO).

Based on findings of the PreAmp Payback Analysis Document, preliminary results indicate that the PreAmp Software System will have its greatest impact on three cost drivers: exchanging PCA data between design and manufacturing, reducing PCA design rework, and saving time in PCA manufacturing testing scenarios. It was determined that, in these areas, an implementation of PreAmp would result in savings in excess of 1 million dollars after two years. In addition, companies utilizing PreAmp can reduce PCA development costs initially by 14 percent and with a potential savings greater than 20 percent with a fully commercialized PreAmp software product and approved AP210 Electronic PCA ISO 10303 standard.

Benefits of the system attributable to object orientation include: simplification of maintenance and ease of incorporation of user requested changes. Representation of the data closely resembles real life, allowing simpler understanding of the objects and their relationships. A single set of user interface objects was developed and shared by all developers; a common look and feel has propagated to all components of the system.

Other individuals contributing to this project include: Gerry Graves (SCRA), James Muller (Lockheed Martin), Charles Gilman (STEP Tools, Inc.), Mike Keenan (Boeing), Lynwood Hines (SCRA), Adam Owsley (SCRA), Michelle Shammon (DEC), Jeff Brodsky (Hughes), Craig Lanning (Northrop Grumman), Ken Buchanan (ADL), and Dawn Snow (SCRA).

CONCLUSIONS

Greg Smith had the following observations regarding PreAmp:

- Providing a generic Standard Data Access Interface allowed all of the PreAmp applications the same access to the object-oriented database. This streamlined the development process; however, it slowed down the execution of the system.
- We have been using object-oriented technology for some time. This project only reinforced the organizational stand on using object-oriented technology whenever feasible. Because of the success of projects such as PreAmp, object-oriented technology is now migrating to the main line business systems within Boeing.

He advises:

- Create a strong set of requirements!
- Allow users to critique any or all parts of the analysis, design, and implementation. User feedback at all phases of system development is essential!

Analysis and Requirements Traceability (DART)

Boeing Defense and Space Group

THE OPPORTUNITY

When Boeing is contracted to build a product, an airplane for instance, the requirements for the entire project are contained in a large RFP (request for proposal). When Boeing subcontracts parts of the project, it must create a mini-RFP (called a Statement of Work) for each subcontract. To create the statement of work (SOW) Boeing authors extract those paragraphs from the RFP appropriate to the specific subcontract. This is essentially an editing job: cutting, pasting, and renumbering. Before DART, the job was done manually with standard word processing tools.

Subcontracts management required the automation of this process. The generation of requirement allocation matrices to aid in requirements traceability was also required. System engineering required the consistent extraction of contract requirements for tracking and contract verification. System engineering also required the creation of requirement information sheets, a summary of all activity on a single requirement. Finance required the comparison of government and nongovernment contracts to determine dual coverage. DART can perform all of these functions.

THE APPLICATION

DART automatically identifies paragraph text, paragraph titles, and paragraph numbers. Concurrently, the system builds a table of associated military standards, document references, paragraph references, and other user-requested information. All information extracted from the document is referenced to the applicable paragraphs. The generated documents and matrices are created in Microsoft Word for Windows and Excel respectively. A knowledge-based system (KAPPA-PC from IntelliCorp) is used as the knowledge broker and configuration control manager. Extensive use of the Microsoft Windows Dynamic Data Exchange (DDE) facility provides communications between Word, Excel, and KAPPA. The system is currently being used by several Boeing programs.

During the critical period of proposal development, requirements have been identified for a tool that tailors a document to fit specific conditions, provides traceability by mapping the changes to the original document, provides for real-time modification of the conditions for document tailoring, and performs this operation in an accurate and timely manner.

For a proof-of-concept demonstration, DART was applied to the process of generating a subcontract SOW from a prime customer SOW. The subcontract SOW must include all tasks from the customer's SOW that will be levied on the subcontractor. These tasks may be applied directly or may be tailored to fit specific conditions. It is also important that the requirements being identified in the subcontractor SOW be traceable back to the customer's SOW to demonstrate compliance and to facilitate any contractual changes. A correlation matrix is used to establish the relationship between the customer SOW and the subcontract SOW and identify key document entities.

As inputs to the system are received from various customers, the system has the added requirement of accepting documents in different electronic formats and from numerous host systems. Yet, the documents produced must be consistent throughout. The documents must also reflect the requirements established by the preferred process.

Rapid prototyping was selected as the most cost-effective system development method. In order for the system to be funded, it had to demonstrate a relatively high return on investment with a minimal startup cost. Off-the-shelf software was chosen for word processing and decision support functions to reduce development and maintenance costs.

Additionally these tools were currently used and accepted by the end users. The initial work on DART began in July 1991.

Document Generation

Although the system was initially prototyped for subcontract SOWs, any document that is organized by numbered paragraphs with optional titles can be analyzed by the system.

Based on this generalization, the primary objective of the system is then to generate a revised (destination) document and report (correlation matrix) from an input (source) document. The destination document will consist of all the text from the source document (though some text may be hidden). Users can specify changes to the structure of the destination document by modifying a source to destination paragraph map or outline.

DART's secondary objective is to extract information from the source document and present the information to the user in a predetermined report format. In one scenario the report is implemented via a spreadsheet where rows define document paragraph properties and user-tailorable columns contain references extracted from that particular paragraph.

This is called a correlation matrix. DART can extract any set of characters that match a predefined pattern.

The User Interface

The user interface for the system was built using KAPPA PC, an expert systems development environment. KAPPA PC also provides configuration control and configuration management for the system. When the system is initiated, a help screen is displayed to the user. The help screen guides the user to the next preferred process step.

When a step is completed, the next preferred process help screen is displayed. The help screens can be discontinued at any time by upgrading the user level from novice to advanced. Depending on the experience of the user and current process step of the program, the user may or may not heed the information provided. Figure 12.1 shows the startup user interface.

After login and selection of a particular program, the current user and program are displayed in the title bar. Each user and program have unique identifiers and are defined to the system as objects, their characteristics detailed in slots of the objects.

All program activities, documents, reports, and options are stored in a folder. The system creates and maintains folders automatically when a program is created and selected. When a program is selected, the user is provided with a complete transcript of activities previously executed on that program including activity date, time, author, and author comment. Each of

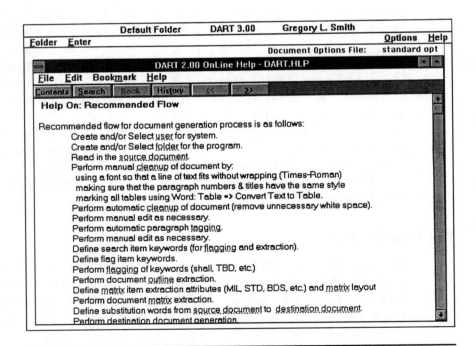

FIGURE 12.1 Startup user interface.

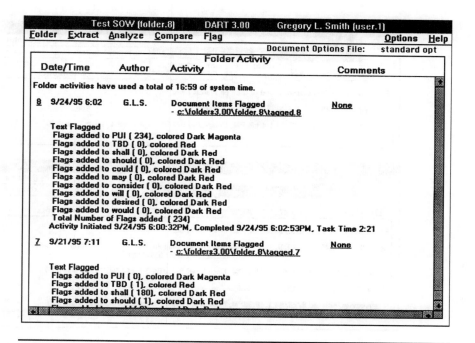

FIGURE 12.2 An in-progress program has been selected.

these activities is defined to the system as an activity instance in the activity class. Figure 12.2 shows the user interface after an in-progress program has been selected.

The user makes selections from pulldown menus to activate system functions. To encourage users to follow the preferred process, menu paths that are outside the preferred process are displayed in ghost font and cannot be selected. As the user selects these context sensitive menus and executes program activities, menu selections are updated to support the next step in the preferred process. Additionally, menu bar selections change from process to process to allow only appropriate tasks to be executed. Figure 12.3 shows menu selections before and after entering a source document into DART.

Each selection on the menu bar represents an instance object in the lifecycle class.

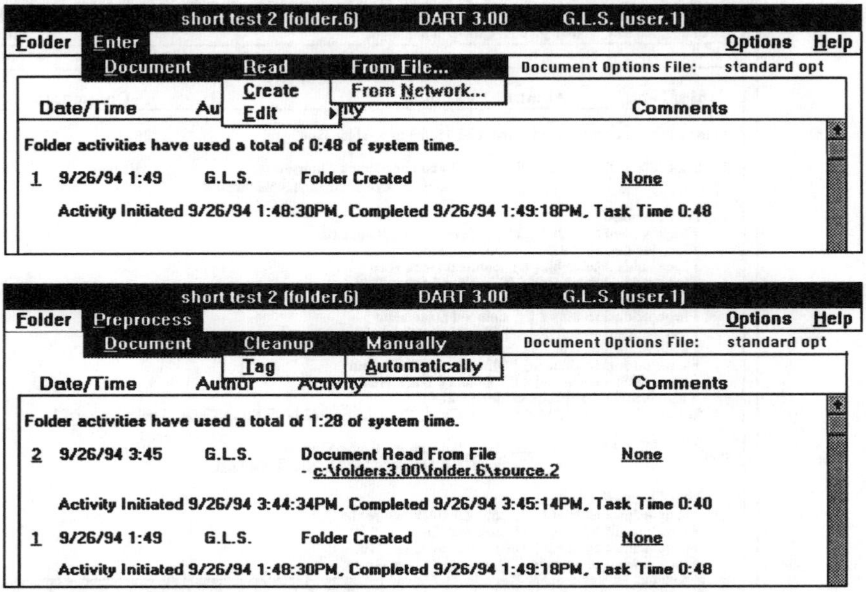

FIGURE 12.3 Menu selection (top) before and (bottom) after entering a source document.

After a source document is entered into the system, the following activities can be performed on it:

1. **Document cleanup.** Removal of superfluous white space; removal of mid-paragraph carriage returns; recombining of hyphenated words; spell checking.
2. **Document analysis.** Identify document meta-knowledge such as paragraph extents, numbers, and titles; tag these attributes with Word bookmarks; users can manually tailor paragraph number identification.
3. **Document flagging.** Specific text can be flagged in order to provide additional traceability from source document to destination document.
4. **Document translation script (outline).** All paragraphs are mapped to an Excel spreadsheet. The user then modifies destination paragraph numbers and titles, eliminates unneeded paragraphs, and adds additional paragraphs if needed.

5. **Destination document generation.** DART opens the source document and automatically cuts and pastes paragraphs to the destination document. Figure 12.4 shows a section of a destination document. Note the apparent duplicate paragraph numbers and titles. The first number refers to the source document, the second number refers to the destination document.

6. **Document information extraction.** DART opens the source document and copies previously defined information to an Excel spreadsheet. This information can include (but is not limited to): document references, data item definitions (DIDs), customer data requirement lists (CDRLs), supplier data requirement lists (SDRLs), paragraph numbers, paragraph titles, and requirement text.

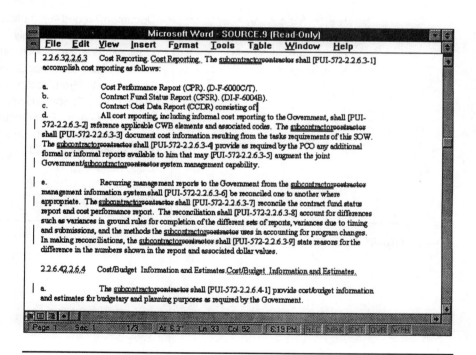

FIGURE 12.4 Destination document.

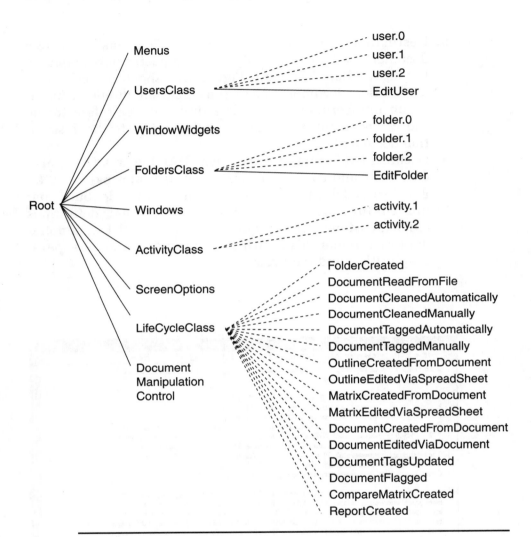

FIGURE 12.5 Diagram of system classes.

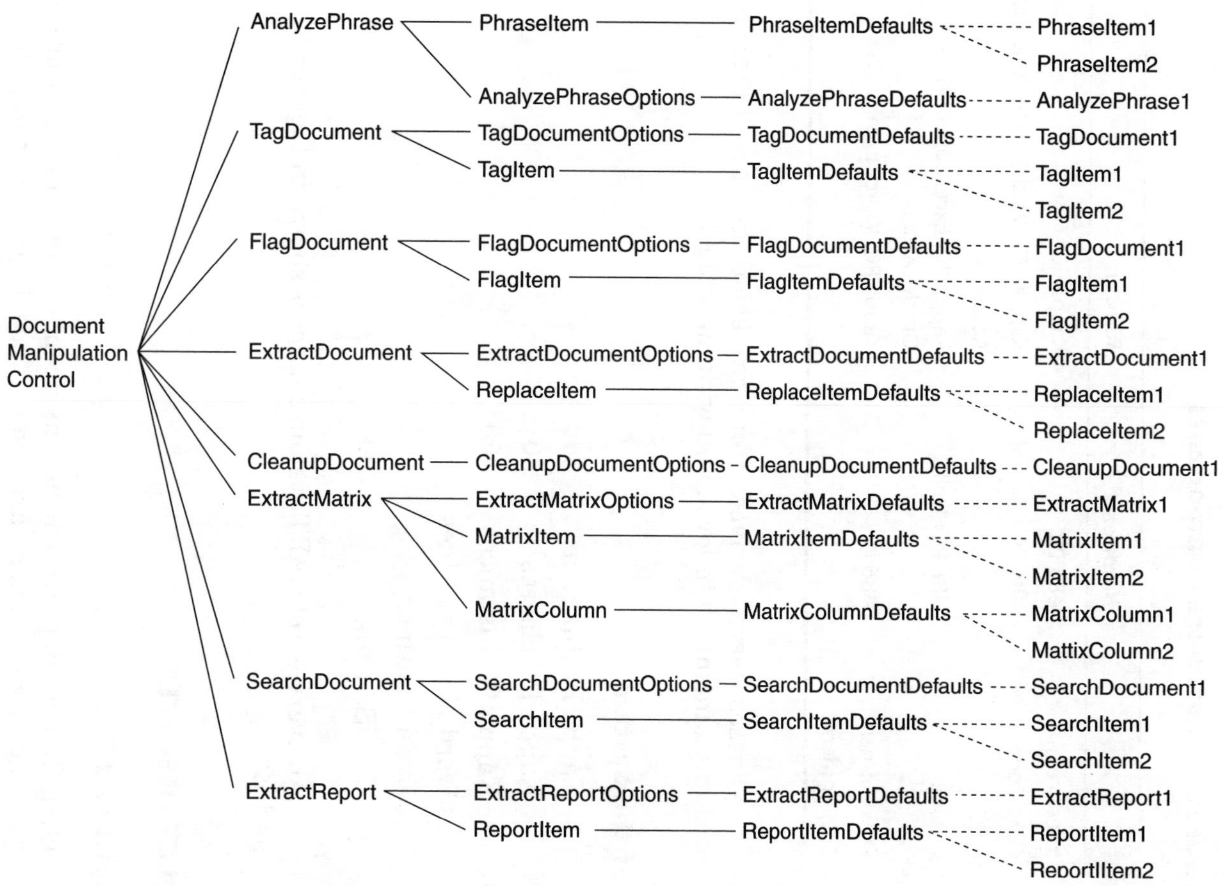

FIGURE 12.6 Diagram of system classes—document manipulation control.

Hardware and Software Components

	Hardware	Software
Interface	486 PC	Kappa PC
Core Code	486 PC	Kappa PC, Word & Excel Macros, Access
Database	486 PC/ UNIX	Kappa PC, Excel Spreadsheets, Oracle, Access
Development Environment	486 PC	Kappa PC, Word, Excel, Access

Classes were derived from pre-existing class libraries, including menus, windows, and window widgets.

Size of the System

Kappa PC function	300
Kappa PC classes	80
Kappa PC instances	350
Word Macro routines	50
Excel Routines	20
User Screens	20

An overview of DART system classes is shown in Figures 12.5 and 12.6.

PROJECT LIFECYCLE

Analysis and Design

Greg Smith's department has six people trained in object orientation concepts. There are twenty people in the group. They have used object orientation for more than five years under different O/S and languages. The system developer has been using object orientation for eight years.

The problem was identified by upper management and Continuous Quality Improvement (CQI) team. CQI team developed initial requirements. Additional requirements came from users. There was no need to "sell" an object-oriented approach since object orientation has a successful track record at Boeing. Also, several other non-object orientation approaches were attempted and are currently available, but those systems lacked the power and extensibility of the object-oriented approach. They failed due to the extreme variability of document style and format. This approach using object-oriented technology and knowledge-based technology proved to be extremely flexible and versatile.

Analysis and design was conducted by the developers, CQI, and the end users. There were no A&D tools used. The methodology employed was "semi ad-hoc." Data modeling activity was used to gather required objects and relationships.

Smith cites the ease of extensibility and incorporation of changes as a major benefit during the A&D phase, but notes that the object-oriented approach required more up-front work than traditional approaches.

Development

Development of DART took approximately three and a half years, with one person working less than half time on the project for a total of approximately 2000 person hours.

At the outset the users didn't know all of the requirements and didn't know what actually could be done so an approach of incremental prototyping was employed.

Kappa PC was used for this project because it had been used at Boeing with great success.

Benefits of object orientation during development include rapid turnaround of user changes (minutes or hours depending on the complexity), minimum bugs were found in the system, and there were no other surprises.

DART allows the user to enable/disable constraints to identify paragraph extents, paragraph titles, paragraph numbers, in addition to specifying specific information to extract. Although Kappa PC provides a rules capability that would support this capability, it was not utilized as the constraints had to be applied within the Word application. Executing rules across a DDE link would have been inefficient.

Deployment

In some areas more powerful equipment was required to accommodate the concurrent use of Word, Excel, and DART.

There were three training modes:

1. Boeing's training center developed a formal training course and made it available to users on an as-needed basis.
2. The developer was available for a one-on-one walkthrough of a simple test case, on an as-needed basis.
3. In most cases, the software was loaded on users' machines with no instruction given, except to point out the context sensitive menus and help notes that recommend the next step upon completion of a current step. Many users were able to train themselves.

In general user acceptance was high. Of course, some complained that the system wasn't fast enough. And some of the users were Mac devotees who were reluctant to deal with the IBM PC-compatible world.

Maintenance

The object-oriented environment simplified system maintenance. Each user creates documents that are dramatically different from each other, so many system options had to be made available. This was the cause of most required maintenance.

BENEFITS

According to Smith, the three major benefits of DART are contract verification, requirements extraction, and document comparison. Each of these items has a different benefit to each of the organizations (subcontracts management, finance, system engineering, materials, etc.) using the system.

The main benefits attributed to object orientation are the simplification of maintenance and the ease of incorporation of user requested changes. This is due in part to the representation of data, which closely resembles real life (high level of data abstraction), allowing quicker understanding of the objects and their relationships.

DART has achieved over 30 percent reduction in document preparation time depending on the complexity of the document. Formerly, authors had to type the requirements into the document. With DART, the source document is read into the system electronically and the author's tasks are reduced to decision making and requirement tailoring when necessary. One program cited an excess of forty hours to manually generate a correlation matrix; DART generated the identical matrix in less than four hours. The manually generated matrix had several typing errors (paragraph numbers, paragraph titles, etc.); the DART-generated matrix had no errors.

Other Boeing staff contributing to this project included Roy March, Mike Wong, Bill Henry, Chuck Williamson, Jo Scott, and the members of the cross-functional quality improvement team.

Section **V**

Object Technology, Legacy Systems, and Non-Object-Oriented Tools

OVERVIEW OF SECTION V

Many new technologies are more or less incompatible with the technologies that came before them. Thus, for example, the move from early COBOL applications that were directly linked to hierarchical databases to relational databases required that databases be entirely reconceptualized and developed anew. The transition was so demanding that most companies have never moved the data stored in older databases and have simply used relational databases for new application development efforts.

One of the important attributes of object technology is its ability to encapsulate legacy applications and incorporate them within an object design.

In a similar way, object technology can be used with non-object-oriented tools. In many cases companies use object-oriented analysis and design techniques and then use conventional tools to actually code the applications. Remember that object technology is more fundamental than object-oriented languages or object-oriented databases. Object technology is a way of conceptualizing software development. Thus, I can design an object-oriented system and then implement it in C or COBOL. Because object technology is so pervasive, it's common to see applications that mix object-oriented and non-object-oriented approaches. Thus, for example, many object-oriented systems use object technology for interfaces and conventional code for the application logic. Or, they use object-oriented for the interface and application logic portions of the application and then link to relational databases to access data. Indeed, the ability of object technology to mix with conventional applications and tools assures that companies can transition to object-oriented systems in an incremental and systematic way. And that, in turn, is one of the most attractive features of object technology.

Let's briefly consider how we might integrate an object-oriented application and a conventional application. Figure V.1 illustrates how an object-oriented application can link with a legacy application. We often talk about encapsulating the legacy application. Typically, we simply mean that we create an object that represents the legacy application and that henceforth all communications between the other objects and the legacy application occur via the legacy interface object. Thus, if any object in the new system needs information generated by the legacy system, it sends a message to the legacy application interface objects. The message includes any parameters that the legacy application will need. The interface object stores the information received, then sends its own message or actually triggers the legacy application via a procedure call, launches the application, and provides it with the information it needs to run. The results are passed back to the interface object and then sent, via a message, back to the object that requested the run. Thus, although the legacy application is not an object, it is effectively encapsulated and it functions like an object, since it is only contacted and only contacts others via messages.

If the legacy application is large and has a modular structure, developers may subdivide the legacy application and create interface objects for each module of the legacy application. In this case, each module communicates with every other module via objects. If the developers do this, they can then decide to replace any one module with objects and thus begin to migrate the legacy application in an incremental and systematic manner.

In a similar way, objects can be used to encapsulate databases. A database interface object can be created for each data-

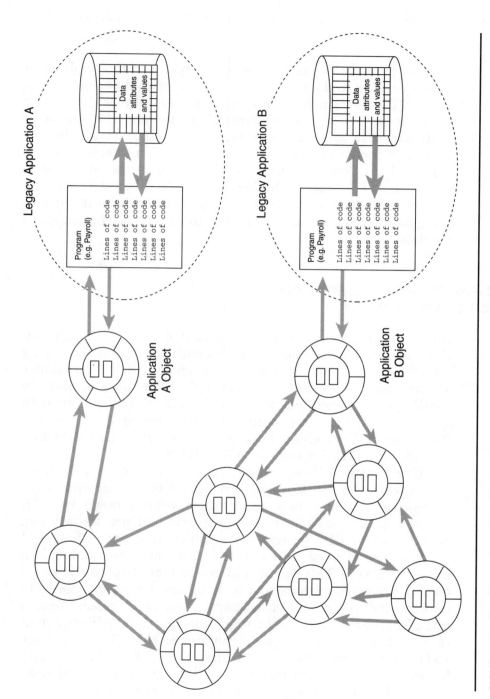

FIGURE V.1 An object-oriented application that includes two legacy applications.

base an application needs to access. Objects in the application send messages to the database interface object that then generates SQL to obtain information from the database and then passes it back to the object requesting the data. If a system is modularized in this manner, then later, if the developer decides to change the location of the database or even to change databases, all the developer needs to do is change the code associated with one database interface object. The other objects in the system can continue to send messages to that object without being concerned with the location of the database that supplies the data.

RE-ENGINEERING BUSINESS PROCESSES AND OBJECT TECHNOLOGY

One of the themes that occurs in several of the winning applications, and especially those that deal with enterprise and legacy systems, is business process re-engineering (BPR). Companies are rethinking how they do things and, in the process, they are creating new applications that combine legacy applications with a variety of techniques, including object-oriented techniques. We'll consider how object technology is being used in BPR in a moment, but first, let's consider BPR itself.

BPR means different things to different people. Like most hot topics, everyone is prepared to give it his or her own twist. To assure that everyone understands what I mean by BPR before I go any further, this first article will provide a broad overview of the BPR process and establish a basic vocabulary.

The goal of most BPR efforts is a major improvement in a business process. This can result from increased speed, increased quality, improved responsiveness to customer requests, more efficient procedures, or decreased costs. Typically it results from a mix of all these things. In its original formulation, BPR aimed at radical change; processes were redesigned from the ground up. Today, most companies are willing to try to achieve major improvements, but are unwilling to take the substantial risks that really radical change always entails. On the other hand, most companies expect a BPR project to involve more change than traditional incremental change efforts usually involve. Thus, most BPR efforts aim at major changes while being mindful of existing constraints.

To achieve major changes in business processes, companies must still be willing to take some risks. Companies must reconsider what products and services they want to sell, how they relate to customers and suppliers, how they use information systems, and how people within the company perform their work. In each of these areas, old assumptions must be set aside and new approaches considered.

One important characteristic of BPR is its reliance on information technology. In the 1980s there were a number of studies indicating that companies were spending vast sums of money acquiring computer hardware and software without any significant gains in productivity. Several studies suggested that this was because information systems were simply being tacked onto existing business functions. Companies weren't reorganizing themselves to take advantage of the things that information systems could do. To justify large investments in information systems, companies need to make major changes in their processes and procedures to change the ways things are done to take advantage of the latest information technologies.

BPR also relies on changes in way employees work. To use the latest computer systems in the most effective way, companies often need to reconceptualize jobs and how people work. In some cases, several jobs are combined into one job and the individual doing that job is supported by new software systems. In other situations, workers are grouped into teams that work together and take responsibility for entire processes. In all cases, companies need to reconsider what information employees need and what responsibility they should be given. In general, the new designs call for delegating more decision-making power to the employees who interact with the customer.

BPR also places a heavy emphasis on the customer. It reexamines assumptions about what product characteristics and services the customer actually wants, and reconsiders all of the interfaces between the customer and the company to be sure that the company is providing the customer with the maximum possible value.

BPR is process focused. It requires that companies begin by reconceptualizing how they are organized. Most companies are organized into hierarchies based on functional departments. This organizational structure grew up with the industrial revolution and emphasizes breaking each task into smaller tasks until each can be done by a highly specialized employee. Adam Smith is often credited with emphasizing this approach at the beginning of the industrial revolution. Smith, in the *Wealth of Nations,* demonstrated how several pinmakers, each specializing in doing only part of the job, could make thousands of pins a day while each individual, working alone, could only make a few complete pins in a day. In the last hundred years, the growing emphasis on functional, hierarchical organizations and job specialization has gradually become dysfunctional. What has worked well for several generations no longer works today.

In hierarchical organization, departments often try to maximize their own efficiency, even though what works well within a department is often detrimental to the overall processes that create and deliver products and services to customers. Departmental managers often spend most of their time trying to protect their own turf and things most often go wrong when they are handed from one department to another. Moreover, as a result of departmental distinctions and job specializations, there's hardly ever a way for a customer to find out who is doing what to a specific order. Salespeople will explain that the order has been passed to manufacturing. Someone in manufacturing will explain that he is waiting for paperwork from accounting, and so on.

During the course of the last twenty years, organizational theorists from a number of different disciplines have concluded that it's more efficient to conceptualize business organizations in terms of processes rather than departments. A business process, as used in BPR, refers to a stream of activity that begins with a customer's request and ends by producing a product or service that the customer wants. In effect, a process cuts across a traditional organizational chart in a horizontal manner (see Figure V.2). To successfully sell widgets, a company must somehow coordinate activities of a number of different departments, including purchasing, sales and marketing, manufacturing, inventory, and shipping. Each department is organized in a

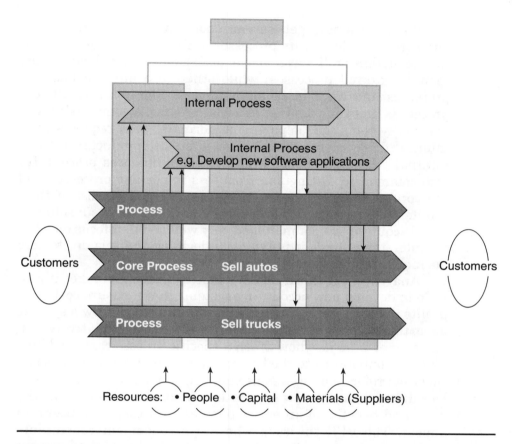

FIGURE V.2 Business processes cut across traditional departmental hierarchies. External processes consume resources and respond to and deliver value to customers.

vertical fashion and only handles a portion of the overall process. Traditionally, various departments have passed paper to each other to stimulate and document actions. Thus, sales passes sales orders to manufacturing and to accounting. Manufacturing or shipping tells accounting when it has produced the widgets and shipped them to the customer and requests that accounting check to see that the company gets paid, and so on. For historical reasons, lots of paper is passed more than once. Most processes aren't very efficient, in large part because no one has the responsibility for managing the process as a whole.

When a company gets serious about analyzing a company (or enterprise) to identify its processes, it finds that some processes fit the definition I gave above and have external customers (hence, external processes) while others are internal business processes and have internal customers. The order fulfillment process is an example of an external process. A company's information systems (IS) department normally gets requests from internal departments and delivers systems (products) to these internal customers, hence it's an internal business process. It's also common to distinguish from less important processes and the core processes that actually earn companies most of their profits. When a corporation decides to divest itself of subsidiaries it has acquired but not managed very well and to refocus on what it understands best, it is typically deciding to focus on its core business processes.

Analyzing organizations in terms of processes makes it possible to develop new accounting systems that measure costs and profits in more useful ways. It's hard to talk about how a specific department contributes to corporate success. It's relatively easier to determine just how much a specific process costs and how much it contributes to the bottom line. To emphasize this, some theorists refer to processes as value streams. Books on activity-based accounting, a new approach to accounting that tracks the costs and benefits of an entire business process, have begun to appear. The BPR theorists who are management consultants tend to put great emphasis on analyzing processes, determining what they cost and then carefully planning changes and recalculating the costs to prove that changes will result in significant improvements in corporate productivity.

Although most BPR theorists analyze processes the way I have, many companies that are undertaking re-engineering projects are limiting their efforts to a portion of a complete process. There's nothing wrong, of course, with starting small and improving a subprocess before moving on to a larger process. It always makes sense to test methodologies and tools on a smaller project before trying a larger project. If a company sticks with smaller projects, however, and avoids really large BPR projects, it's unlikely to make the major improvements that ultimately justify BPR efforts. Unfortunately, even if they are only focusing on a few procedures within a much larger process, many writers and analysts still tend to say they are doing process redesign. This, in turn, leads to a lot of confusion about what really constitutes BPR and makes some reviewers question whether BPR is really resulting in the types of changes its advocates have argued it would achieve. It would be nice if everyone could agree on a term for subprocesses and use that term to avoid confusing others about what actually constitutes a business process. All I can do here is to use the terms consistently and warn readers when other authors use their terms in different ways.

THE BPR LIFECYCLE

Figure V.3 provides an overview of the major phases in any BPR effort. We have divided the BPR lifecycle into five broad phases and a separate ongoing management activity. We are not proposing a detailed BPR methodology. Different companies have succeeded by doing different things and there is no one right way to organize BPR efforts. To organize our overview, however, I have conceptualized a generic BPR effort. Let's briefly consider each of the phases described in Figure V.3.

BPR Management

In most large companies, the overall management of BPR projects is vested in a senior manager who is a member of the corporate executive committee. In addition, there are usually managers for the different processes being redesigned and their are team leaders and BPR teams that report to the process managers. As a general rule, higher level executives must participate in the initial analysis of the firm and set BPR goals for the organization. Thereafter, they must monitor and support the various BPR efforts to assure they succeed. If serious resistance arises, this senior group must be prepared to intervene.

The day-to-day work of re-engineering is usually delegated to process managers and to BPR team managers. They also play a significant role in communicating and helping the corporate culture adjust to the changes that any BPR effort will initiate.

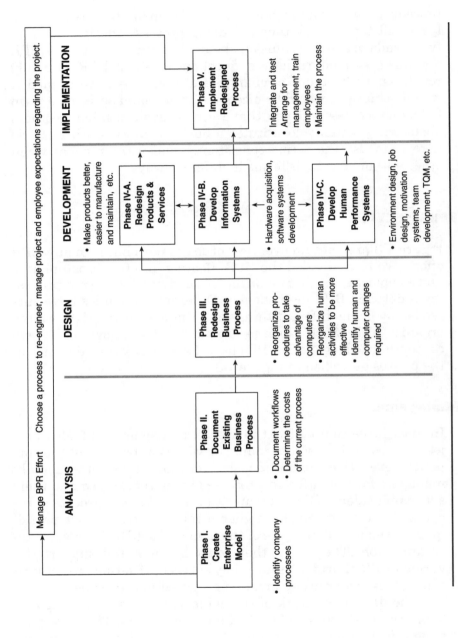

FIGURE V.3 An overview of the major phases in business process re-engineering project.

They also have direct or indirect responsibilities for analyzing and redesigning selected processes and for developing and implementing the actual BPR changes the company decides to undertake.

Phase I. Enterprise Modeling

The first phase in any serious BPR effort is to reconceptualize the company in terms of its processes. Organizations that are serious about BPR usually change their management structures and appoint a manager to manage each specific process. This manager is then responsible for increasing the efficiency and profitability of the entire process.

In an ideal BPR effort, the entire company is analyzed and divided into processes and the costs and value of each process are estimated, in at least a rough way. Then, the most important process, or at least a process that was particularly inefficient, is selected for detailed study and re-engineering. In fact, many organizations take a more informal approach to BPR and don't begin with an enterprise-wide analysis. Many companies don't even begin by analyzing an entire process, but identify a subprocess and begin their re-engineering work there. Obviously there's nothing wrong with these halfway approaches to BPR, but they don't tend to result in the really significant improvements that some companies have obtained when they have taken a more comprehensive and more risky approach. By omitting a comprehensive reconceptualization of the company, organizations end up selecting a process with poorly defined boundaries. It can also mean that managers of departments and other processes that will be affected by the change are insufficiently committed to the effort. If BPR is to result in a major or radical change in the way the company does business, it will necessarily be a very political process and top management should begin by assuring that the entire senior management team is completely committed to the change process.

Phase II. Business Process Analysis

However one identifies a process to redesign, the next phase involves the examination of that process to determine how the process currently works. Whether one begins by examining the entire corporation or simply selects a process with a clearly identifiable product and customer, the key to defining a process is to define a sharp boundary and then trace every activity, form, phone call, and decision involved in the process. Discrete internal processes, such as the personnel process that hires new employees and the IS process that generates new software applications, may be ignored, but every recurring event that contributes to producing the product and any surrounding services provided to the customer should be included in the analysis space. In addition, a complete analysis of the existing process usually defines the resources used by each activity, the cost of each activity, and the quality control or measurement points that are currently used to manage the process (see Figure V.4).

In Figure V.4 we show how activities that take place in various departments contribute to the overall process by which some hypothetical company produces widgets for customers. Obviously this diagram simplifies the process, omitting departments and lots of activities. Typically, when one examines a process, one finds lots of duplication and lots of inefficient procedures. This is especially common when information is being passed back and forth between departments. At the same time, customers are often surveyed to determine how the products and services produced by the process could be improved and other company processes are usually examined to gain some insight into how efficient others have been able to make the process.

The existing process is normally documented by means of workflow diagrams. In some cases, process flowcharts are done on paper, but in most cases they are developed by means of a software diagramming tool. Different tools and methodologies use different kinds of symbols to represent activities, flows, measurement points, and so on. Some analysts are businesspeople who know little of software and use notations popular in business schools (e.g., PERT). Human performance analysts, for example, are interested in tracking things like motivational feedback. Operations researchers are interested in tracking the specific activities of employees and IS analysts are usually interested in determining when information must be saved or decisions must be made. The current changes taking place in

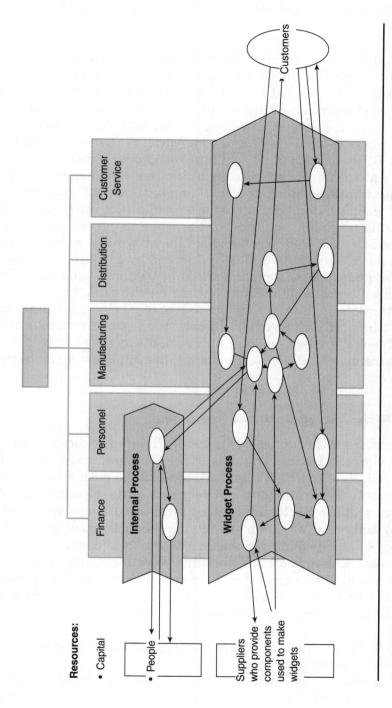

FIGURE V.4 An analysis of a process must identify every individual, activity, decision, service, form, or information flow involved in providing a product or service to a customer.

computing have resulted in considerable competition between conventional IS diagramming techniques and object-oriented notational systems. In addition, many software tools that are designed to document work procedures are also able to analyze costs, document measurement points, and run simulations of the process. Thus, there is a wide variety of different notations that BPR analysts must evaluate and choose from.

As a generalization, companies that seek incremental or minor improvements put a lot of emphasis on analyzing the current process. Companies that seek radical improvements often only do a cursory analysis of the existing process, since they intend to start from scratch when they begin the redesign effort and don't want to be unduly influenced by current assumptions or practices. Most companies take a balanced approach. They spend a reasonable amount of time on the analysis of the current process to assure they are aware of all the constraints that can't be easily changed. Then they turn to the redesign phase and seek to make as many improvements as they can within the constraints they discovered during the analysis of the current process.

Phase III. Redesigning Business Processes

The third major phase of most BPR efforts focuses on the redesign of a business process. If the company is seeking a radical redesign, the BPR team will often begin with a blank sheet of paper and brainstorm entirely new ways of organizing the process. If the BPR team is attempting a more modest redesign, they will usually begin by reviewing the analysis of the existing process and looking for specific ways they could modify the process. Both approaches work and we will consider both.

In addition to general methodologies for approaching redesign efforts, BPR teams need to know what their options are. As a generalization, a team can do any of the following:

- Redesign the overall process (e.g., eliminate redundancies, increase customer contact)
- Redesign the product or the service (e.g., to better satisfy the customer, or to make it easier to manufacture or service)

- Redesign the information systems that support the process (e.g., automating some things and providing better support for employees in other cases)
- Redesign the human performance systems (e.g., changing to work teams, empowering employees, redesigning jobs, and providing new feedback and incentives)

A good methodology ought to provide the BPR team with guidelines for deciding which changes would give them the best results in a specific situation. No methodology can help, however, if no one on the team even knows about a specific option.

Phase IV-A. Redesigning Products and Services
Phase IV-B. Developing New Information Systems
Phase IV-C. Developing Human Performance Systems

The fourth phase in most BPR efforts involves the actual changes that must be made to improve a process. Many BPR books ignore this phase, as well as the implementation phases, preferring to focus only on management, analysis, and redesign issues.

In addition to developing the systems necessary to implement core business processes, the actual processes involved in developing systems may themselves need be redesigned. Indeed, many companies have launched BPR efforts to redesign a core process and identified information systems, for example, that would need to be developed to implement the new process design. Then, to their dismay, they have found that their IS groups were incapable of creating the new systems they needed within the time allowed. At that point, many companies have instituted re-engineering projects to improve their IS groups. This is the point at which companies often introduce object technology. In effect, to re-engineer the software development group and the corporate infrastructure, the company decides to introduce object-oriented products and train the programmers in object techniques. The assumption is that object-oriented products and techniques will lead to new ways of doing software development and in increases in productivity.

Phase V. Implementing a Redesigned Process

The final major phase of any BPR project occurs when all of the changes are in place and the company actually implements the redesigned process and then maintains the process. If companies are successful in making themselves into more flexible, learning-oriented organizations that continually adjust to the market, then the development, implementation, and maintenance of corporate processes will evolve into an ongoing process.

OBJECT-ORIENTED BPR SOFTWARE TOOLS AND METHODOLOGIES

Having considered the entire BPR lifecycle, let's briefly turn to the problems involved in choosing BPR software tools and methodologies. Figure V.5 provides an overview of the BPR development process that we described earlier. In this instance, we have used our overview to help classify the different types of tools and methodologies one finds in the current BPR market. Some BPR tools use conventional methodologies or procedural programming approaches, but others rely on object-oriented techniques.

Object-Oriented BPR Methodologies

Several object-oriented methodologists have urged companies considering BPR efforts to take a comprehensive object-oriented approach to the entire BPR process. Ivar Jacobson, David Taylor, and Robert Shelton have each written books or given tutorials urging an object-oriented approach to BPR. Similarly, Anderson Consulting, Gemini Consulting, and other consulting groups have offered systematic object-oriented approaches to BPR. Some companies are experimenting with these approaches. More often, companies are using these approaches when they want to re-engineer their software development process itself. Most of the object-oriented BPR methodologies come with tools to help implement the approach.

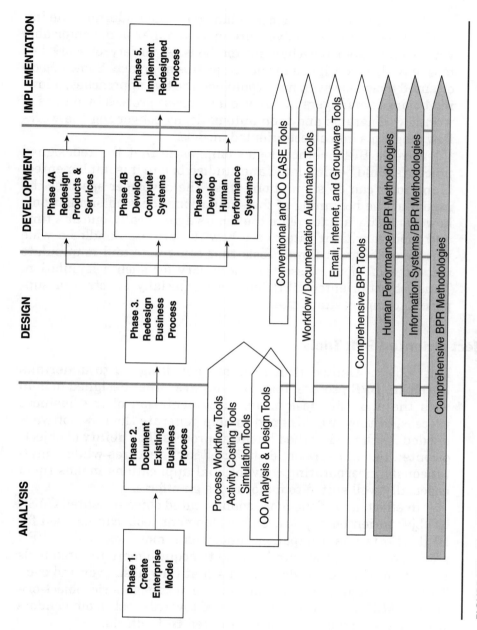

FIGURE V.5 The BPR process and the various methodologies and software tools that support the process.

In most cases, the business managers who undertake the initial business process analysis are more familiar and comfortable with step-by-step flowcharting methods. A variety of workflow tools have been designed to encourage this approach. Some object-oriented tools, however, have combined the two approaches, allowing business managers to analyze a business process by means of workflow diagrams and then automatically converting the workflow diagrams into object-oriented models.

Several BPR methodologies emphasize that the redesigned process should be simulated and studied before it is implemented. Many tools can do simulations when the developer specifies the inputs at the beginning of the simulation. For good simulations, however, you want to create the inputs dynamically, one at a time and then vary their rate to see how the process handles a wide variety of different flows. Tools that can create and manipulate instances of input classes are necessary for such a simulation. Thus, object-oriented BPR tools are especially effective in supporting complex simulations.

Object-Oriented BPR Tools

Most object-oriented BPR tools are not designed to undertake the entire BPR process. Instead, they are either designed to help with the analysis, design, and documentation of the business process, or they are designed to help generate the new software needed for the redesigned business process. The ability of object-oriented tools to support distributed architectures while simultaneously incorporating conventional applications makes them especially well suited to major redesign efforts.

In effect, any of the more sophisticated object-oriented CASE or object-oriented application development tools can be used for BPR efforts. As companies undertake more extensive BPR efforts, of course, they are inclined to acquire more tailored tools to avoid having to recode elements that they need over and over. Thus, although some companies are using generic object-oriented CASE tools, others are inclined towards tools from vendors who have specialized in object-oriented BPR efforts.

We expect that companies will continue to re-engineer themselves throughout the remainder of this decade. At the same time, companies will continue to adopt object technology and re-engineer their software development processes to be more efficient and productive. Thus, we expect that object-oriented technology and BPR techniques will continue to grow together and reinforce each other.

APPLICATIONS

Several applications described in this book take advantage of object technology to integrate legacy applications and existing databases with new object-oriented applications. Some of them also rely on BPR concepts. In this section we will describe four applications that were winners or finalists in the Object World object technology and legacy application category.

IBM Credit Corporation's Financial Marketing Workbench (FMW) Winner, Category 2, 1995

This application is a good example of how an object-oriented application can integrate with legacy applications. IBM developed an object-oriented application that gathers information from customers who want to obtain leases from IBM Credit. Then, depending on the lease situation, the object-oriented application launches and uses any of thirteen large legacy applications, running in MVS and using DB/2 databases, to process the request.

The object-oriented application was begun in C++, but the developers subsequently switched to Smalltalk V. The Smalltalk version ran fast enough and was much easier to develop. Hence, the first claim the developers made was that this approach to developing a large, critical client/server application made them much more productive. WindowBuilder Pro was used for GUI development. The developers used responsibility-driven design and CRC cards to help in the development.

The object-oriented application was developed as part of a major IBM re-engineering effort. The resulting application reduced staff by 45 percent while simultaneously increasing bookings by 146 percent. The success of this large, critical application convinced IBM Credit IS managers that object technology was appropriate for serious, enterprise application efforts.

Obviously this application would have been impressive in several categories and provides one of the best examples of an application that results in significant cost savings. Skeptics could argue for a long time, however, about the relative roles of BPR analysis vs. object-oriented development in attaining the cost savings associated with this application. Suffice to say that IBM did both: They rethought the business problem in a fundamental way and they rethought the software development process and created a new and much more effective process.

Canadian Tire's Automotive Kiosk
Finalist, Category 1, 1994

This system is another example of an object-oriented system that provides an interface to legacy applications. The application lets customers use a touch-screen in a kiosk to describe their vehicle and thereby determine what parts they need. The system supports bilingual screens and accesses an AS/400 database. In effect, this application redesigned the company's customer service interface, making it much easier for customers to determine what they needed.

A Visual Basic version had been in prototype for two years when Canadian Tire, with the help of outside consultants, decided to use Enfin's Smalltalk. An object model was developed in a hybrid object-oriented methodology that combined techniques from Rumbaugh and Jacobson. The actual prototype was then developed in eight days. The developers claim that the application was quickly developed taking advantage of the ease of use provided by Smalltalk as well as the integration capabilities of object technology.

Caterpillar's Forging Steel Planning and Problem Resolution
Winner, Category 2, 1994

This application was developed in an effort to re-engineer the management, procurement, and use of steel in the Caterpillar forge shop. At the same time, this application was undertaken to explore the use of object technology as a way of improving the software development process. This project relied on the responsibility-driven design approach to prototyping. The object-oriented application itself was developed in Smalltalk V. The GUI was developed in WindowBuilder. The system relied on legacy data in an IMS application. The links between the object-oriented system and the IMS data on the mainframe were hand-coded. The object-oriented frontend reduced the department's mainframe costs by some $50,000 per year.

This is another nice application that could have won in several categories and displays several common recurring themes: ease of development, use of legacy systems, and cost savings.

Financial Marketing Workbench

IBM Credit Corp.

13

THE OPPORTUNITY

In the spring of 1993, IBM Credit Marketing came to the IS department with a proposal to build a deal tracking application to solve three business problems:

1. The Financial Marketing reps were facing a major shift in the marketplace to high-volume, low-cost client/server products. They needed a system to track the financing opportunities from identification to closure in order to handle the increasing volumes of transactions they were involved in.
2. Marketing needed a communication vehicle for sharing information about financing deals between financing reps and their administrative support as IBM consolidated field administration into geographic centers.
3. Many legacy mainframe systems were in place to perform the various marketing tasks, but rekeying of data was required in many instances and the field force was looking to automate the interaction with these systems as much as possible.

IS was already working on leveraging the power and ease-of-use of OS/2's Graphical User Interface to provide a frontend to the lease pricing system. These newly identified marketing requirements caused the IS department to take a new, broader approach to the financial marketing process, though much of the object-oriented analysis of the marketing subject area was still applicable to the new problem domain.

THE APPLICATION

The IBM Credit Corp. Financial Marketing Workbench (FMW) is a financing deal tracking application developed by the IBM Credit Information Systems department in partnership with the marketing organization. The application, written in Smalltalk, acts as a frontend to thirteen legacy mainframe applications as it organizes financing opportunities and automates the associated administrative tasks.

The purpose of FMW is to streamline the marketing and customer service process for leasing, from the initial identification of the opportunity to the booking of a lease in the billing and accounting system. IBM Credit Marketing Reps—Financial Marketing Advisors (FMAs)—and their administrative support use the FMW tool to perform tasks such as:

■ Forecasting financing volumes
■ Gathering customer information
■ Applying for credit
■ Obtaining financing rates
■ Preparing, printing, and faxing proposals and contracts
■ Accepting signed contracts

In the past, each of these activities was accomplished using a separate mainframe application. While each of the legacy systems provides powerful function, oftentimes the user had to rekey data as the deal progressed through the process. FMW ties the process together, avoids the rekeying, automates the process, and provides a communication vehicle within the marketing community.

FMW is able to operate either connected to a mainframe host or standalone on a notebook PC. Since a large portion of the user community was mobile, it was critical that they be able to access and update deal information on the road, and then "synch up" when they were back in the office or able to dial in via modem.

Figure 13.1 shows the list of pending deals for a particular Financial Marketing Advisor. This serves as the end user's "home base." Note that a deal regarding Sam's Bail Bonds is one of the pending deals.

Figure 13.2 shows the first page after Sam's Bail Bonds was opened from the previous screen. The user executes various deal-specific functions.

Object-oriented design techniques and a pure object-oriented programming language were selected for this development effort in order to rapidly develop a solution to the customer's immediate need while building a modular, extensible, and reusable framework for future development.

FMW is a watershed application for IBM Credit. FMW proved that client/server, object-oriented development is a viable approach to large-scale mission critical development in their organization. In 1994, as a direct result of the success of object-oriented development in FMW, IBM Credit formally changed its IS strategy to include object-oriented client/server frontends customized to specific user processes.

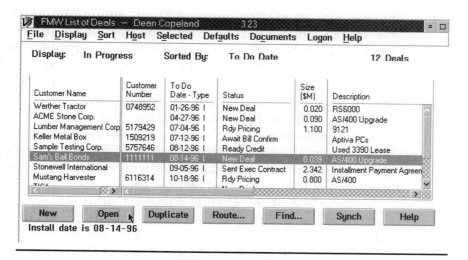

FIGURE 13.1 FMW list of deals.

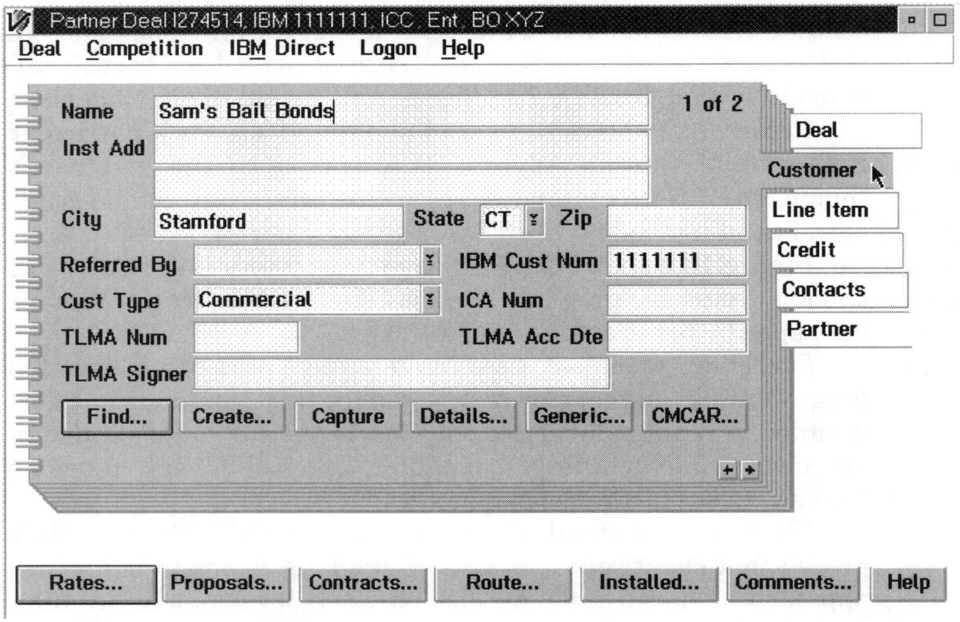

```
┌─────────────────────────────────────────────────────────────────────────┐
│ ▨ Partner Deal I274514, IBM 1111111, ICC, Ent, BO XYZ            □  □     │
│ Deal   Competition   IBM Direct   Logon   Help                           │
├─────────────────────────────────────────────────────────────────────────┤
│   Name    Sam's Bail Bonds│                      1 of 2                   │
│   Inst Add                                              ┌──────────┐      │
│                                                        │   Deal    │      │
│   City    Stamford          State  CT │ Zip           │ Customer ↖ │     │
│   Referred By            │  IBM Cust Num  1111111      │ Line Item │      │
│   Cust Type  Commercial  │  ICA Num                    │ Credit    │      │
│   TLMA Num           TLMA Acc Dte                      │ Contacts  │      │
│   TLMA Signer                                          │ Partner   │      │
│   [ Find... ] [ Create... ] [ Capture ] [ Details... ] [ Generic... ] [ CMCAR... ]│
│                                                              ← →          │
├─────────────────────────────────────────────────────────────────────────┤
│ [ Rates... ] [ Proposals... ] [ Contracts... ] [ Route... ] [ Installed... ] [ Comments... ] [ Help ]│
└─────────────────────────────────────────────────────────────────────────┘
```

FIGURE 13.2 FMW partner deal—Sam's Bail Bonds.

FMW is a key component in IBM Credit's re-engineering of the financial marketing process. Since rolling out FMW, this process has reduced administrative headcount 45 percent, and centralized much of the administrative workload, while booking 146 percent more contracts, and contributing to improvement in already high customer satisfaction by 2 percent, and improvement in Return on Average Equity by 4 percent.

FMW could not have been developed and deployed in the required time/cost without the use of object-oriented techniques. Cycle time, quality, the ability to inexpensively integrate legacy systems, and the extensibility are a direct result of the rigorous application of object-oriented techniques.

Using FMW, IBM Credit Financial Marketing reps and administrators work from a window containing their list of deals. This window acts as a central control panel that organizes their work in customer financing and allows them to work with deals. They can sort, search, filter and print their list of deals as well as "zoom in" to see the open "to do's" for each deal. Other functions include the ability to fax documents to customers, specify communications options and various user preferences.

When the user opens up a deal, the information is organized into an easy-to-use notebook-style interface. Depending upon the type of financing deal, some of the pages of the notebook vary, but the same concepts apply. Pages are dedicated to information about the deal as a whole, customer information, credit information, contacts for the deal, and so on. In addition to data entry and display fields, each page contains pushbuttons for the user to access secondary dialogs and to interact with host systems. As the user "works the deal," he or she tabs through the notebook, using the pushbuttons and secondary dialogs to find and capture information. This style of user interface is particularly appropriate for the financial marketing process, which has a common set of process building blocks, but the order of execution can vary from one deal to the next.

FMW enables geographically dispersed sales teams to collaborate on leasing transactions. As the deal progresses, FMW automatically moves the deal along to the next logical phase and keeps a running history of what happened and when. This is particularly helpful as deals are routed from person to person or when someone has to answer an inquiry or work a deal when the primary owner is unavailable.

Built into FMW is the knowledge of how to navigate the various host screens and which data elements to capture into the deal notebook. FMW is "smart enough" to manage multiple emulator sessions for the user, navigating in and out of the host applications with minimal user intervention.

Hardware and Software Used

	Hardware	*Software*
Interface	486 PS/2, ThinkPad	OS/2 PM, Smalltalk
Core Code	486 PS/2, ThinkPad (client)	OS/2, Smalltalk, C++,
	9021 MOD 900 Mainframe (server)	CICS OS/2, MVS, CICS, EHLLAPI

	Hardware	*Software*
Database	486 PS/2, ThinkPad (client), 9021 MOD 900 Mainframe (server)	DB2/2 on OS/2 (client) DB2 on MVS (server)
Development Environment	486, 16Meg RAM Token Ring LAN	Smalltalk V/PM, WindowBuilder Pro, PVCS, PL/I, VisPro REXX

FMW was developed using Digitalk Smalltalk, Objectshare Systems WindowBuilder Pro, IBM DB2/2 and CICS OS/2 on the OS/2 operating system, and IBM PL/I, CICS, and DB2 on the MVS operating system.

PROJECT LIFECYCLE

Analysis and Design

Both application development and user management were in agreement that an iterative approach should be taken with early production use. In June 1993, early prototyping generated both excitement among the users and management approval to proceed with a production pilot by September, 1993.

The development team consisted of six developers and one Financial Marketing Advisor who provided user requirements. The combination of a small, focused development team and a dedicated domain expert proved successful in meeting an aggressive target date with function rich enough to gain user acceptance.

Contract programmers with expertise in object-oriented analysis, design, and programming were used in a mentoring role to provide guidance in this, the first major object-oriented project undertaken by IBM Credit.

The team was educated by taking a combination of classroom training, self-study, and online tutorials. Extensive reading on client/server and object-oriented techniques provided a broad and balanced basis for development. Key authors included Booch, Orfali and Harkey, and Budd. The team also made use of the IBM "Red Books," covering practical object-oriented examples and techniques.

It was critical that the application be developed very quickly, while providing the flexibility to change as the business process and priorities change in support of IBM Credit's re-engineering. As with most organizations undergoing significant changes in their marketplace, the ability to react quickly to new markets, customer requirements, and competition is the number one priority. In developing this application, the team was trying to develop not only a solution to the specific problem at hand, but a framework that could expand in scope and be reused in other parts of the organization.

Development

Using object-oriented tools and techniques, a framework was developed that proved extensible and robust. As the application has been extended, there have been many new requirements for new views, but the core underlying business object model has remained largely unchanged. Entities such as Deal Customer and Transaction, for example, are common to all types of leasing activity, though different types of deals use these common objects in different ways. The object-oriented design process allowed these objects to be identified early in the development cycle and then be reused as the scope expanded.

Development Environment

The team needed tools and techniques to handle the complexity of the graphical user interface environment. Early experience with coding graphical screens in C++ made it clear that power tools were needed, or the project would never get off the ground.

Various code generators and object-oriented tools were considered. The code generators provided a quick start, but fell short of providing rich function once the shell of an interface had been generated. Other object-oriented tools had drawbacks of high initial cost, runtime fees, poor performance, and immature development environments and class libraries.

Digitalk Smalltalk/V for OS/2 was chosen as the development language along with WindowBuilder Pro for GUI layout.

IBM DB2/2 is used to store the data locally on the user's workstation while DB2 on MVS serves as the master database providing nationwide connectivity between users, data backup, and management decision support reporting.

Smalltalk proved to be an extremely productive environment for development:

■ During development, code changes can be made on the fly without stopping to recompile the module. Smalltalk handles virtually all of the memory management. In C++, bad pointers would cause frequent crashes. Smalltalk usually displays a graceful "Does not understand" or "Runtime Error" message, and the application continues running.

■ The built-in Class Hierarchy Browser and rich class library allowed developers to focus on the problem domain rather than the implementation details. The team was able to make effective use of the mature Smalltalk class hierarchy, particularly the collection and user interface classes that provide much of the needed behavior right out of the box.

Historically, a major drawback of Smalltalk has been its runtime performance. Advances in hardware and improvements in the Smalltalk implementation internals have combined to minimize this concern. The huge improvements in developer productivity offset the slight degradation in runtime performance as compared to C and C++.

The FMW development environment spans from PCs to mainframes. Programmers developing client code work in Smalltalk, C, and REXX on individual workstations, accessing shared disks on Local Area Network servers. The server code is developed in PL/I on MVS.

Code distribution is accomplished using both VM on mainframes and NetView DM/2 over a LAN. Using VM, remote users are able to "pull" FMW upgrades down to their workstations without technical assistance. Using NetView DM/2, the technical support group is able to "push" upgrades onto LAN-connected user workstations during off-hours without any user involvement.

Interaction with Legacy Applications

PC-host communications fall into two main categories: (1) communications between the FMW client and the FMW central deal tracking server, and (2) communications between the FMW clients and the thirteen legacy applications.

A step-by-step approach was taken to PC-host communications. Communication between the PC and the various host systems was initially developed using EHLLAPI (LU2). This provided the ability to get up and running quickly before architected interfaces were developed.

Communication with the central deal tracking server is accomplished using a dedicated host emulator session that serves as a communication pipeline between the PC and a blank CICS screen. Streams of data are written to and read from this screen to save deals to the host, allow deals to be routed between users, and so on. The team is currently converting the EHLLAPI-based communication to CICS OS/2 (using LU 6.2 protocol) to provide greater reliability and real-time performance.

Also, EHLLAPI is used in a "screen scraping" mode to interact with thirteen different legacy mainframe applications on six different mainframe computers. FMW is the glue that ties all of these applications together in a single frontend. These mainframe applications perform financing functions such as:

- Customer information retrieval
- Credit applications and approvals
- Financing rates
- Proposal and contract preparation
- Used equipment inventory/availability

FMW leverages the power and capacity of these legacy mainframe systems while presenting the user with an easy-to-use, integrated user interface.

The strategy is to move to a three-tiered client-server model, allowing flexibility in function and data placement. The plan is to replace each "screen scraping" interface with architected, program-to-program communication links. Already, certain interactions with the credit and pricing applications have been converted to program-to-program style server calls resulting in improved performance and reliability.

The design methods used included:

- Data-driven and use-case analysis. To "discover" the basic objects in the problem domain.
- Responsibility-based design using CRC cards. Brainstorming sessions were held with developers personifying the class instances and role-playing the objects to decide which objects should have knowledge and/or responsibility for certain behaviors and attributes.
- Event flow diagrams. Early on, many interactions were traced out before coding, resulting in a cleaner implementation.
- Division of responsibilities. Early on, the classes were split into View Objects, Business Objects, and Communications Objects. This clean separation of function allowed the classes to be developed and then "snapped together" seamlessly.

A key benefit of the object-oriented approach is that the code maps closely to the terms and concepts of the financial marketing subject area. As new requirements come in, users and programmers are much closer to "speaking the same language" than with a more traditional procedural approach.

Following object orientation principles, the classes that communicate between the FMW clients and the mainframe server encapsulate all of the functions associated with communications. Thus, the view and business object classes are insulated from communication protocols and the details of interaction with legacy applications. This has had the benefit of facilitating the migration from LU2 "screen scraping" communications to LU6.2 communications as well as containing the impact of host screen changes to legacy applications.

The object-oriented approach also proved beneficial when the team was challenged with extending the support to new types of financing deals. Initially, the system tracked financing of new equipment through the direct IBM marketing channel. This was able to be cleanly extended to support the sale and financing of used equipment as well as IBM Credit's telesales and remarketer channels without major redesign.

This extensibility has allowed IBM Credit to adopt FMW as the strategic marketing support tool for all of our leasing channels, eliminating redundant application development efforts. It is having the positive side benefit of providing all IBM Credit reps the capability to immediately adopt process improvements developed in other channels.

Reuse

The FMW classes were built with an eye toward reuse. On several occasions, the FMW class library has been reused and extended within IBM Credit. One application needed to "screen scrape" one of the legacy systems that FMW already interacted with. After minor changes to generalize the interface, the classes were able to be shared between the development groups. In another case, the code delivery and installation mechanism the FMW developers created was reused by another development group in its entirety.

By far the largest and most successful example of reuse was the Retail Sale of Used Equipment project. Reusing the FMW user interface design, object model, and communications approach, this project was able to quickly build a full-function application to support the sale of used computer equipment that had been returned at end of lease.

A single programmer was able to accomplish the work of a team of four resulting in a 75 percent savings in development resource. We anticipate significant savings in maintenance and user training as well.

Technical Challenges

- Interfacing with DB2/2, EHLLAPI, and CICS/OS2. Since Smalltalk did not provide classes which supported direct communication to DB2/2, EHLLAPI, or CICS OS/2, Smalltalk wrappers and C DLLs were written by the team to encapsulate their interaction.
- Geographically distributed user community. The users are spread across the United States. All users have mainframe

connectivity, but a Wide Area Network (WAN) infrastructure is not yet completely in place. This made distributed systems management particularly challenging. The code distribution problem was solved by using existing mainframe VM mini-disks to store the code and automating the download and installation process in Smalltalk. The tracking of user version numbers was accomplished by having the client code report its version number to the mainframe server each time it connects.

Deployment

Seventeen users in three cities were targeted with the initial release. The plan was to pilot the application for three months and then roll it out across the United States over a six-month period. As it turns out, demand for the application drove an aggressive rollout that included new PC hardware to over 100 users by February 1994 (four months ahead of schedule). Subsequent releases added to the base functionality and expanded the scope with the benefit of actual end-user experience with the application. This iterative approach allowed the users to gain the benefit of the application earlier and kept the development effort focused on functions that the users needed most.

Statistics

Number of users: 180

Number of new deals per month: 1,500

Number of active deals: 9,100

Processed over $1 billion of financing opportunities in the last year (Estimated to more than double this year).

Number of dialogs: 97

Number of Smalltalk classes: 356

Average number of class methods per class: 2.5

Average number of instance methods per class: 19

Number of source lines of code on the PC: 45,448 (Including Smalltalk, C and REXX)

Number of source lines of code on the host: 19,890 (PL/I)

BENEFITS

FMW is a key component in IBM Credit's re-engineering of the financial marketing process. Since rolling out FMW, this process has reduced administrative headcount 45 percent, and centralized much of the administrative workload, while booking 146 percent more contracts, improving already high customer satisfaction 2 percent, and improving Return on Average Equity 4 percent.

As discussed above, FMW could not have been developed and deployed in the required time/cost without the use of object-oriented techniques. Cycle time, quality, the ability to inexpensively integrate legacy systems, and extensibility are a direct result of the rigorous application of object-oriented techniques.

CONCLUSIONS

- Include a domain expert as a member of the project team; he or she can be critical to the success of the project. In the case of this project, a respected financial marketing representative provided a very practical vision to guide the development effort. During the rollout, he had the credibility to sell the concept to gain acceptance in the user community.
- Keep the team small. Four to five developers, including an object-oriented expert/mentor, was a good-sized team. Within this team, however, a broad range of expertise is required.
- Work closely with the group that provides distributed computing services. The logistics of rolling out hardware, education, and support are every bit as important as the application itself.
- Keep development cycle short. Initially, releases were every two to four weeks. This stretched to six to eight weeks as the application matured. Short cycles keep the risk low, while keeping the developers in constant touch with the users of the system.
- Plan to spend a certain amount of time reworking the code. Once developed, new opportunities to improve the structure of classes (and eliminate code) become evident.

- Put as much function as possible into the business objects, rather than the user interface objects. There is a natural tendency to put function in the view that really should be the responsibility of a business object. This is a key item to watch during code walk-throughs.
- Centralize worldwide backroom infrastructure (consolidate legacy applications).
- Centralize host data warehouse with distributed access.
- Customize object-oriented client/server frontends to specific user processes.
- Enhance distributed systems management, develop broader and deeper function, and integrate with other marketing support tools.

14

Automotive Kiosk (Electronic Parts Look Up)

Canadian Tire Corporation, Limited

THE OPPORTUNITY

Canadian Tire Corporation, Limited, headquartered in Toronto, is a major international purveyor of leisure goods, sporting goods, hardware and houseware products, tires, and auto parts.

Canadian Tire has always been known as a "dispenser of product" in its retail operations. A customer usually knows in advance what he or she needs, and more often than not the product is in stock. If Canadian Tire could enhance its service by dispensing information as well, empowering the customer, it would help maintain a competitive edge.

The premise in satisfying consumer needs in the auto parts business is to provide the customer with the correct part for the vehicle. This process requires that an electronic application database be made available, or that application books or charts be accessible on the retail sales floor. The electronic database requires that the customer interact with an automotive parts specialist via a computer program that is designed for parts professionals in the automotive industry. As for the data books or charts, they are unwieldy, out of date, and are not uniform in how customers can look up the different parts for their vehicles.

Canadian Tire has had, since 1962, its own proprietary auto parts database for the identification of auto parts to vehicles. This system was designed to be used by parts professionals only, through a keyboard and an awkward vehicle identification coding system.

Providing a consumer friendly electronic parts look-up system that utilizes and extends CT's legacy system would improve customer service and increase sales and margins, therefore increasing their competitive advantage. The solution was also needed within a very aggressive timeframe for a dealer convention.

THE APPLICATION

Canadian Tire's Automotive Kiosk is a client/server application utilizing object technology and a Graphical User Interface via a touch screen. The client portion of the system was developed under OS/2 using Enfin Smalltalk.

An AS/400 at the store provides the application with inventory information that is part of a legacy IMS system begun in 1962. Advanced program-to-program Communication (APPC) programs on the AS/400 were done in RPG. The accumulation of this much data over time has become a competitive marketing advantage, however, the lag time for Information Services (IS) to deliver what marketing needed was prohibitive.

As a result, the Automotive Kiosk project was launched by the corporate automotive marketing area as opposed to the IS department. Its original purpose was to aid dealer franchises in increasing customer service. The Kiosk was designed to replace a cumbersome text-based keyboard driven look-up system that was originally meant to be used only by auto parts professionals.

Using an intuitive touchscreen approach, CT now has given its customers access to a database that spans several million locations (part numbers) that are serviced through the 70,000 SKUs carried by Canadian Tire's Automotive Division. The do-it-yourself customer can access the proper part and related products by responding to a series of screens with the touch of his or her finger. The Kiosk provides pricing information, regular and promotion price savings, and product location within the store. The customer can also print out the list of products that are related to his or her vehicle and retain it for future use.

Cross-merchandising is a key factor in that the system automatically provides the customer with all the necessary parts information to perform a proper repair to their vehicle. For example, a customer looks up spark plugs. In addition to plugs, the system will provide the following, which are necessary when performing a tune-up on a vehicle:

Distributor cap	Air filter
Rotor	PCV valves
Ignition wires	Oil filter
Gas filter	Tune-up kit

FIGURE 14.1 Choose a system (the customer chooses Ignition Parts).

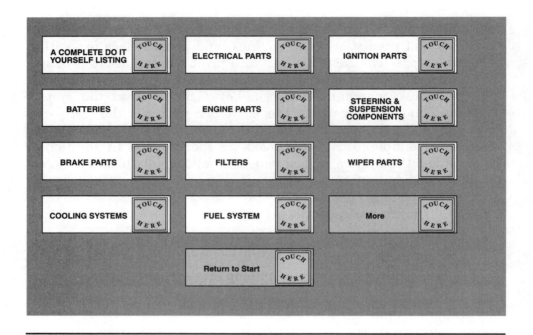

FIGURE 14.2   What Ignition Parts? (the customer chooses Spark Plugs).

When a Canadian Tire customer visits the Automotive Kiosk, the system asks a series of questions (vehicle year, make, model, engine, and product) to choose the right parts for the job. Once the customer selects the parts, the system uses APPC to capture the actual inventory information from the AS/400 located in the store.

Figures 14.1 through 14.4 show typical screen in a brief Automotive Kiosk customer interaction.

IBM's Database Manager located on the PC provides the system with the data it needs in order to alert the customer to any additional parts required to do the repairs. Once the customer has all the information he or she needs, the application will also provide a printed shopping list. If the part is not in stock, the customer is directed to someone in the Parts Centre. From the print menu screen the customer also has the option to specify additional parts that may be unrelated to the original job.

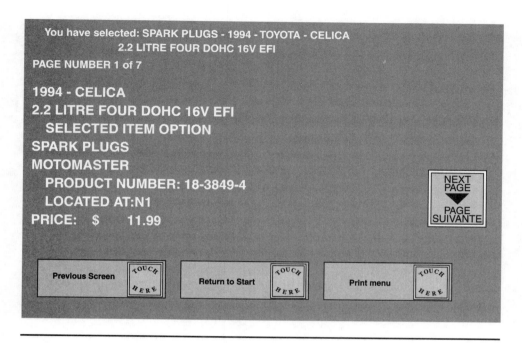

FIGURE 14.3 Here's the part number, location, and price.

The system also records the customer transaction, which then provides demographics of vehicle ownership. With this information, Canadian Tire can then build retail modules to optimize store square footage. Parts that do not move quickly can be placed in in-store warehouses instead of taking up valuable space in the store.

By Canadian law, the Kiosk must accommodate bilingual issues, and so three screen versions were necessary—English, French, and Bilingual.

Size of the System

The loadable application was 2MB. The system was written in Enfin Smalltalk, therefore most object-oriented features were used in development.

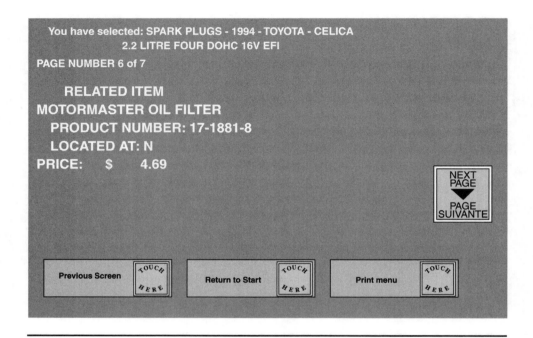

FIGURE 14.4 Here's something else you might need.

There are no persistent objects within the actual program, which is data driven. The application is event and data driven. For each step or event that the program executes, the layout and information presented depends upon the previous request.

The development environment used was Enfin/3 for OS/2. Enfin is a Smalltalk-based application development environment that provides all the classes to do GUIs as well as support access to a wide variety of databases.

Object-oriented features used in this tool include graphical developer interface, interpreted internal language, graphical browsers (Enfin provides browsers, but they are character-based), and automatic method tracing. Although Enfin does provide automatic links to a variety of databases, this feature was not used for performance reasons.

Development version control was not necessary, since only one developer worked on the application at any one time. There are several runtime versions, however, that are necessary to accommodate the bilingual environment. Runtime version control is managed through a configuration file. The compiled code generated is p-code and Enfin .exe files

PROJECT LIFECYCLE

Analysis and Design

Richard Goulet of Canadian Tire's IS department led the development effort. According to Goulet:

> "Speed of development as well as flexibility of design required an object-oriented approach. We needed a prototype for a dealer's convention that was in six weeks from the time of the project's beginning. The application also needed to access live data on the store's AS/400, and the object-oriented tool we were using supported this as well.
>
> "Conventional approaches wouldn't have solved the problem because the prototype was quite complex, and was needed within a very short timeframe. Utilizing an object-oriented development environment enabled us to complete the project within that time."

Canadian Tire had no prior history with object orientation. There had been non-object orientation approaches considered. Originally the system was to be developed in Visual Basic, and had been in prototype mode for two years.

Erwin was used for the A&D tool, with a JAD methodology. Database layouts were provided to Mark Winter & Associates by Canadian Tire.

Rapid prototyping and an iterative development cycle produced the initial prototype in eight days.

Development

The Automotive Kiosk application was developed by Mark Winter & Associates using an object-oriented methodology that is a hybrid of Rumbaugh (OMT) and Jacobson.

Elapsed time   4 months
Person hours   790 hours

The development software was recommended by Mark Winter & Associates. The tool requirements were that it must be object oriented, and provide support to various databases—that is, connectivity to AS/400 (via APPC)—and Database Manager.

The iterative and rapid development cycle enabled the developers to deliver a fully functional application within the allotted time Flexibility inherent in the object-oriented development environment also facilitated changes as the system evolved.

Deployment

Canadian Tire's hardware vendor will set up each new system with all the software necessary to operate the application, so the stores receive the systems from Corporate already loaded. The only issues the franchises need to handle are those involving communication, that is, whether they have a LAN in place, or are using twin-ax to connect to the AS/400.

Canadian Tire initially deployed the Kiosk in two of their concept stores, one located in London, the other near Montreal.

The new equipment required consisted of IBM Value Points and Mitsubishi monitors with touchscreen.

A video is provided to the dealers to handle training and maintenance issues. The tape covers topics such as how to replace printer paper and how to coach customers through the system. By nature a touchscreen application interfacing to the general public must be very intuitive. They just follow the screen prompts, which say "Touch Here."

Maintenance

The data-driven architecture of the application is very stable. The system has been running in fourteen locations between two pilot stores for one year, and no problems, errors, or system crashes have occurred. Maintenance has really been in the form of enhancements, which are still ongoing as the system evolves further with CT's business.

Many stores do not have a LAN environment that would facilitate the distribution of new releases.

Maintenance and upgrades are completed in a fraction of the time compared to traditional 4 GLs.

BENEFITS

The major benefit derived from the application has been one of improved customer service. The customer is now in control of the part look-up process. Customers are spared the embarrassment of not knowing specific vehicle details—for example, engine size or number of cylinders. There is faster execution of the purchase.

Since the Kiosk's implementation CT has found additional benefits.

Increased Store Staff Productivity

- 40 percent increase is estimated after twelve months of operation
- Customer knows what he or she needs and if a product is on the floor, the customer gets it. If the product is in the on-site warehouse, the parts professional no longer has to work with the customer to identify the proper part for his vehicle. The parts professional needs only to get the part that has been identified on the printout.

Staff Training

A retail environment makes use of part-time help, especially high school students who do not know or necessarily understand the auto parts business and could not work with a customer to identify all the parts necessary to properly perform a repair. Through the cross-merchandising feature, the store staff easily learn about related products and their applications.

Cost Effectiveness

- System updates are automatic and implemented behind the scenes

- Data updates can be made daily, whereas in today's environment electronic catalogues are updated every five weeks, and retail floor-bound catalogues are updated every two years
- Cost of unit is 30 percent of a part-time staff's annual salary

Statistics Gathering

Demographics of vehicle ownership facilitates optimization of retail square footage.

When asked what contribution object orientation made to the success of the project, Goulet returns to rapid development: "The speed with which the application was developed and is continuing to evolve to meet our dynamic business requirements impacts both customer service and the cost effectiveness benefits."

CONCLUSIONS

The technology and expertise actually does exist that enables us to successfully challenge our current information system. Knowing that, we shall continue to do so.

The project has affected my group more than Corporate IS, since my area really is in the user community and we did outsource the application development. Although it began as a "Skunkworks" project, it is now a fully funded and successful corporate venture. With the success of the Kiosk, it is possible that our IS department may now more seriously consider object technology viable for providing solutions to our business issues quickly and cost effectively.

To others contemplating a similar development effort Goulet advises, "Definitely go for it. With the right coaching the benefits are well worth it."

15

Forging Steel Planning and Problem Resolution System (FSPPRS)

Caterpillar, Inc.

THE OPPORTUNITY

Caterpillar, Inc. is one of the largest purchasers of steel in the United States. Whenever possible Caterpillar tries to combine its steel needs with those of its suppliers to ensure the desired quality levels are maintained, and to maximize volume purchase discounts.

The steel procurement section was using a mainframe COBOL/IMS application to manage steel forging supplier inventories. In addition to having many rigid 3270 character-based screens, the application depended upon a previous generation materials control system (MCS) for data. Due to the small user base for MCS, support costs were high. Caterpillar deemed the old system too expensive and not flexible to the company's changing business requirements. An added factor in the opportunity was that the steel procurement section had installed IBM PS/2 PCs with OS/2 on a LAN, for unrelated reasons. The users much preferred the new point-and-click interfaces to the 3270 emulation they'd been used to.

In 1992 Caterpillar recognized the potential of object orientation and began to look for prototype candidates. The Forging Steel system was selected for the following object orientation/

Smalltalk benefits: iterative development process, GUI event type of focus, potential for reuse, ability to maintain and modify through encapsulation, and potential productivity gains.

THE APPLICATION

The Forging Steel Planning and Problem Resolution System is the tool used by the Steel Procurements Section of Central Purchasing Department to manage the procurement and usage of steel by the forge shop suppliers. The system assures that forge shop suppliers have the required steel to produce over 3000 forging part numbers for domestic production facilities.

The system includes a requirements planning module and an exception reporting module. The requirements planning module compares demand for the steel required to produce forging piece parts against the steel on hand and on order in forge shop supplier inventories to determine a suggested procurement plan. This plan is used by the steel procurement analysts to issue purchase orders to steel mills for direct shipment to the forge shop. The exception reporting is provided through an interactive graphical user interface that is used by the steel procurement analysts for problem resolution. The application is very data intensive; however, shortages, surpluses, and other error conditions are easily identified and resolved using point-and-click through GUI windows.

Figure 15.1 shows the flow of steel and steel related information through Caterpillar. Figure 15.1a represents physical plants, equipment, and materials. Figure 15.1b shows the same flow of information through FSPPRS.

The Forging Steel system is an OS/2 client/server application developed using object-oriented analysis and design techniques, and Smalltalk/V was used as the development tool. The system uses the IBM host mainframe, an IBM PS/2 model 77 OS/2 LAN server, and IBM PS/2 OS/2 clients.

Early each morning following the completion of the daily corporate requirements run (legacy systems on the mainframe), the data related to forgings is automatically downloaded to the OS/2 LAN server using NDM/NDM-PC. Once the data is down-

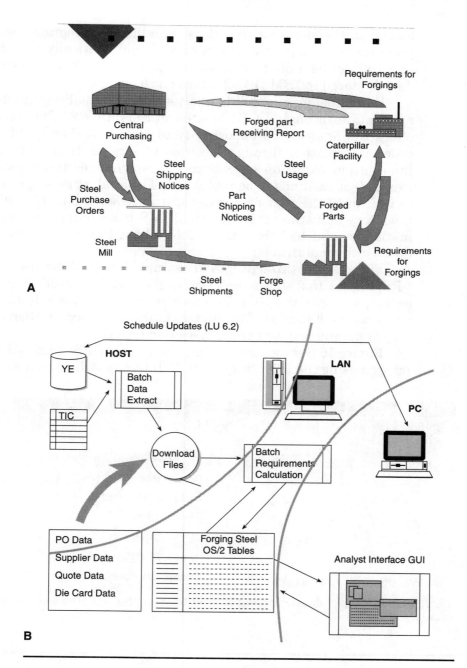

FIGURE 15.1 Forging steel information flow.

loaded to the server, a "headless" Smalltalk/V program (batch program with no graphical interface) is automatically initiated to calculate the daily forging steel requirements. The persistent data is stored in IBM DB2/2 tables on the server.

Each steel procurements analyst accesses the Forging Steel application through a GUI written in Smalltalk/V. The system offers the analyst the opportunity to change on-hand and on-order information through a series of screens that filter the information based on exceptions. These changes immediately cause steel positions to be replanned. The analyst no longer has to wait until the next day or replan run to see the results of an inventory adjustment. In addition, IMS transactions are automatically launched from the PC to adjust the legacy systems data on the mainframe.

Figures 15.2 through 15.4 are sample screens from the FSP-PRS. Figure 15.2 shows the Forging Steel Main Screen. It is the entry point into the GUI. The user inputs selection criteria by pressing the Exception Parameters button. The screen then displays exceptions based on the selection criteria.

Figure 15.3 shows the system's help screen. FSPPRS is documented using the IPF utility. Each GUI screen is displayed with a

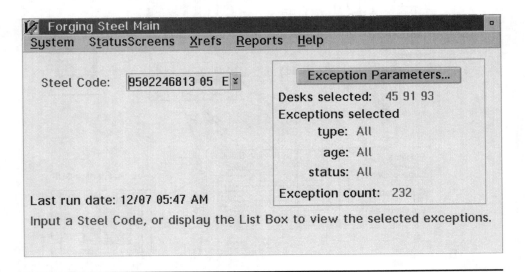

FIGURE 15.2 Forging Steel main screen.

Bit Map image. Text is then displayed to document that screen. Hyper-text is included to switch to related areas of information.

Figure 15.4 shows the Purchase Order grief screen. This screen is used to resolve PO grief found in the system. Selecting an item on this screen will open a dialog used to correct the grief situation.

Pre-Existing Class Libraries

FSPPRS uses many classes from pre-existing class libraries, including:

Batch—Daily Forging Steel Requirements

This part of the application primarily uses the class library that comes with Smalltalk/V to create all the business classes. However, it used a prewritten set of data access classes (db/C) to create a persistence framework for preparing to store the objects/data in DB2/2 DBM tables. These classes included an API (EsData-BaseManager) provided by Digitalk to connect to DB2/2 DBM.

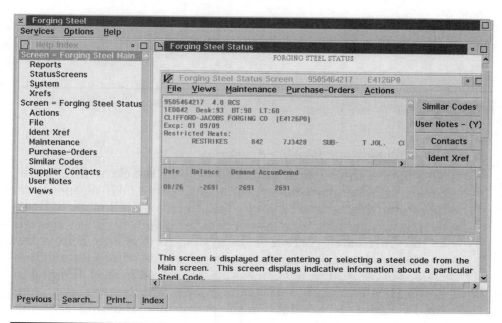

FIGURE 15.3 Forging Steel Help screen.

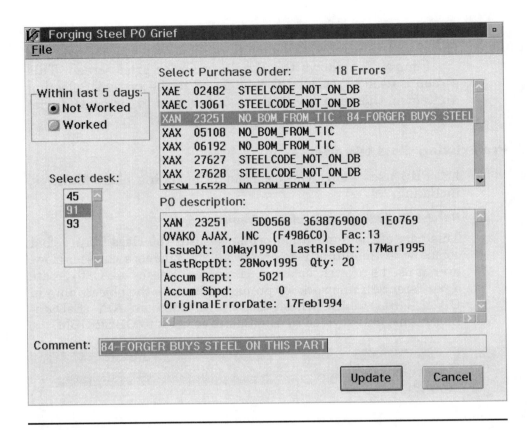

FIGURE 15.4 Purchase Order grief.

GUI—Planning and Problem Resolution

This part of the application primarily uses the class library that comes with WindowBuilderPro, a third-party GUI development tool from Objectshare Systems, Inc., to create GUI classes. However, it was possible to reuse many of the business classes created in the daily batch portion of the system for the logic behind the windows. Also, the GUI contains a set of prewritten data access classes to reinstantiate business objects stored in the DBM and to automatically launch IMS transactions. The transactions from the PC update legacy data on the mainframe. Existing class and code reuse resulted in only 40 percent new code to support the user interface.

Data Access

As the projects progressed, issues related to client/server and beyond object orientation became apparent. Many of the object-oriented prototypes needed access to data either on a server or on the mainframes. Therefore, a set of classes (db/C), that provided a persistence framework and used API from Digitalk were developed to provide access to DB2/2 DBM. Developing the classes to provide access to IMS data on the mainframes was much more complicated since no API was commercially available.

Hardware and Software

	Hardware	Software
Interface	PS/2	OS/2
	Mainframe	MVS
Core Code	PS/2 - OS/2	Smalltalk/V
Database	PS/2 - OS/2	OS/2 ES DBM
Development	PS/2 - OS/2	WindowBuilder
Environment		Smalltalk/V

Size of the System

LAN Server   IBM PS/2 model 77

5 Mg database maintaining:

    1,300 steel part numbers

    3,000 forging part numbers

    3,000 purchase orders

    5,000 open delivery schedules

    30 forge shops

    significant inventory of on-hand steel

PC Workstations IBM/clone, 486 with at least 16 Mg RAM

    10 users

PROJECT LIFECYCLE

Analysis and Design

The Procurement Systems group of Corporate Information Systems (CIS) supporting Central Purchasing was only experienced in developing and supporting IBM mainframe COBOL systems. There was a recognition by this group and its management to support their users'/customers' desire to move to client/server. At the same time, CIS senior management was interested in evaluating the merits of object-oriented technology. They made the funds available to provide the necessary education, training, and support for some developers to begin an evaluation process through selective prototypes. This funding made it attractive to the Procurement Systems developers to learn a new technology, and affordable to Central Purchasing to have a new system developed.

To help with the initial process, David Taylor, a well respected consultant, was engaged. David helped in establishing the criteria for picking the prototypes, the tool selection, and object-oriented methodology training. The tools selected for the forging steel planning and problem resolution system were: Cooper and Peters Window Builder Pro for PM, Digitalk's Smalltalk/V for OS/2, and Team/V. Language training and mentoring were provided by Digitalk Professional Services.

The major constraint on the project was funding. The user/customer agreed to fund the project based upon specific milestones being achieved in a timely manner. The project started by early December 1992, design was completed by mid-February 1993, the initial prototype was running by the end of March 1993, the fully functional prototype was completed by the end of June 1993, and the system was to be in production by year end 1993. Funds were not available to purchase an object-oriented database system, therefore OS/2 ES DBM (since converted to DB2/2) was selected.

Another significant constraint was the lack of client/server experience and lack of a documented architecture for client/server. Thus the developers had to address many challenging issues not related to object technology.

Development

The development methodology employed was responsibility-driven design. The three-tiered object model was chosen, which resulted in a GUI model, a business or application model, and a data access model being developed.

The GUI model was developed using an iterative technique, incorporation design build, and test, with active involvement from the user. This was found very effective for generating enthusiasm from the user of the system, and to continue the funding.

The business or application model already existed. This was a re-engineering effort, replacing an IBM mainframe legacy application with a client/server application with interface to other legacy systems. Although much of the business logic was poorly documented and only existed in the COBOL code, it was a relatively simple process to develop the required object model.

The data access model had to be developed. This represented a significant challenge in two specific areas. The first was storing persistent objects created in the batch system for access by the analysts through the GUI. This required creating a persistence framework to enable the data to be stored in relational tables, with the flexibility to provide database management system independence. The second was to provide the ability to interface with IBM mainframe legacy data transparently, so that the analysts would never have to enter changes into more than one system.

A deliberate effort was made to spend time up front developing solid object models prior to writing code. This provided the basis for the developers to learn Smalltalk with relative ease, although the lack of good Smalltalk programming documentation with business examples did cause some frustration. This frustration was partially alleviated through the mentoring provided by Digitalk Professional Service.

BENEFITS

Some benefits of using object orientation in the Forging Steel system development include:

1. Responsiveness/Productivity. The Forging Steel system took 2.5 analysts one year to develop. This included three months of training. The education and training included: object orientation methodology, Smalltalk, client/server, and PC development. The COBOL/IMS mainframe system being replaced took four staff two years to develop fifteen years previously. The new system contained all the functionality of the mainframe system plus some additional features that the customer identified. The staff that developed the new system were the analysts that supported the old system.

2. Flexibility. A number of new functions were added to the system during the iterative development process that were not in the original mainframe system. These functions include:

   ■ Notes feature—the ability to apply post-it type notes within the system, eliminating the need for the steel analyst to keep separate paper records. The feature took one day to incorporate into the system. Incorporating a similar feature in COBOL/IMS application was estimated to take fifteen to twenty days.

   ■ Rolodex feature—the ability for the steel analyst to bring up all supplier contact information for the appropriate steel code. This feature took two days to incorporate into the system, versus an estimated fifteen to twenty days to do the same thing in COBOL/IMS.

   ■ P.O. Grief—the ability for the steel analyst to identify grief before final processing. This feature took ten days to incorporate. A similar COBOL enhancement would have taken fifty days.

   Even if these features had been incorporated into the COBOL system, they probably wouldn't have been as effective or practical with character-based screens in a transaction-driven environment.

3. Abstraction. Abstract classes were created so that more specific subclasses would inherit behavior from them. Purchase order is one example of an abstract class that supplies common behavior to demand PurchaseOrder and SupplyPurchaseOrder.

4. Polymorphism. A good example of this in the application can be found in the persistence frameworks. The objects know how to reinstantiate themselves from SQL rows. The message mapFromDatabase is used to take the data and create an object in memory.
5. Encapsulation. The reuse of classes used in the batch portion of the application for the GUI portion insures only one class is responsible to access data from the relational database.

The manager of the FSPPRS development project was Caterpillar Senior Systems Analyst Mike Baker. He lists a number of benefits to Caterpillar resulting from this project:

- Reduced mainframe charges.
- Developer productivity, including adding increased functionality from the users' perspective at minimal cost, made for a very happy customer.
- Improved productivity of the steel analyst. This was achieved by eliminating the analysts' need to work on their PCs in 3270 emulation, and the basic clumsiness of navigating between character-based COBOL/IMS screens versus point-and-click.
- Reduced the number of systems supported by the customer by one, by consolidating functions from the old forging steel system and the MCS Requirements system.
- Portability. The system can be loaded on a laptop and taken by the steel analyst to assist with on-site audits of forge shop inventories.

CONCLUSIONS

According to Baker, this project has confirmed to management the potential benefits of object-oriented technology. However, two issues remain to be resolved. The first is a single integrated process (methodology) that can be followed when developing an object-oriented application. The second is the scalability and supportability of shared class libraries across a large IS organization. Caterpillar is continuing to explore object-oriented development in client/server applications currently in the development system lifecycle.

Other observations from Mike Baker:

"The client/server learning experience has proved invaluable in providing input to the development of a corporate client/server architecture. As the Forging Steel system was developed, many of these issues were addressed.

"For COBOL programmers getting started in object technology, Smalltalk is a relatively easy transition once the new paradigm is accepted. Those with C experience say Smalltalk helps them understand objects. Programmers need three months to become familiar with objects and Smalltalk before they can fully address object-oriented A&D issues. Mentoring is another service to utilize, especially during the first six months of the programmer's learning curve. "

Object Technology and Cost-Effectiveness

OVERVIEW OF SECTION VI

It's easier to say things about the technical aspects than about the cost-effectiveness of object technology. We have emphasized several times that object technology represents a major shift in computing. Using object technology, companies can begin to create entirely new infrastructures for themselves. But they can also use the technology to create new client/server applications or new databases.

With any new technology, there is a learning curve. Most shops we have talked with claim that it takes at least six months for a good development team to really come up to speed with object technology. When you consider that many small object-oriented applications are done in less than six months, you realize that initial cost data is going to be untrustworthy in such cases. On larger applications, the greatest advantage offered by object technology comes from the reuse of code. Before code can be reused, however, it must be created in the first place. This means that a company must do one application, and in the process, generate components that can be reused in subsequent applications. Unfortunately, most companies report that they need to do two or three significant applications before they understand how to package code for reuse.

Finally, many stories in this book involve mixing object technology with new client/server hardware architectures, using object technology as part of a re-engineering effort, or using object-oriented methodologies to design software that is then developed with more conventional tools. In these cases it is hard to be sure just how much object technology contributes to any overall cost-effectiveness claim.

None of these comments are meant to suggest that object technology will not prove a very cost-effective way to develop software. They are intended to suggest that it is early for neat cost-benefit stories.

Some of the cases included throughout this book have, in fact, validated the claims object technologists have made for the technology. Code has been reused and significantly reduced the time it has taken developers to create new applications. Most developers do report that it's much faster to create applications using object technology approaches. On the other hand, the critical reader might be excused for believing that in several cases, benefits would have been attained with any of several modern approaches to software development. Besides code reuse, the most important claim that object technologists have made is that object-oriented systems will be easier to update and maintain. Realistically, to judge if a system is cost-effective to maintain, you need to review the data after the system has been in the field for about three years. Few large object-oriented systems have been in use for three years.

Thus, for a number of reasons that apply to any new technology and for some specific reasons that especially relate to object technology, it's early for convincing stories that prove how cost-effective object technology is. The case studies that follow and some of the stories that have appeared in other sections of this book provide some early data, but those who demand really convincing data will have to wait a few more years.

APPLICATIONS

With these caveats in mind, we have included five applications in this section. Each of these applications were winners or finalists in either the 1994 or 1995 Object World contest in the Cost-Benefit category.

Allied Signal Aerospace's SMST
(Supply Management Specialist Tool)
Winner, Category 4, 1995

This application illustrates a system developed as part of a major re-engineering effort. A fifty-two-step business process was analyzed and redesigned so it could be accomplished in three steps. In the course of this redesign effort a task that had taken seven people nine weeks to accomplish was changed into a task that took one person nine minutes.

The SMST software system presents the Supply Management Specialist with a list of parts to be procured in a given interval. It provides email to communicate internally and faxes for external suppliers. In effect, the system is a frontend for mainframe-based legacy systems and the graphical screens the Specialist uses replace some 107 IMS screens. As the user clicks on appropriate buttons, the system automatically generates keystrokes required by the various legacy systems.

The SMST system was developed in Enfin Smalltalk. It reused objects from earlier manufacturing and routing applications. The developers credit the object technology approach with significantly speeding the development and the testing of the new system. Clearly code reuse and the ability of object technology to integrate with existing legacy systems are key elements in this success story.

Bell Sygma's COORS
(Information Services Customer On-Line Order Request System)
Finalist, Category 4, 1995

This application was created to enable reality services clients to obtain fast access and quick responses and follow-through. The system is distributed on some thirty workstations across Canada.

COORS was designed using a hybrid of the Rumbaugh and Jacobson object-oriented methodologies. It was written in Enfin Smalltalk, supported OS/2 and Windows clients, and relied on Oracle and DB2 databases. The developers claim the application saved them some $332,000 and has a Return on Investment of 29 percent per year. More important, however, the system was needed quickly and object technology allowed them to develop it in an acceptable timeframe. Most important, the customers are enjoying significantly improved service.

Blue Cross/Blue Shield of Oregon's EMC (Electronic Media Claims) Finalist, Category 4, 1995

This system preprocesses and prepares electronic claims for further processing by legacy adjudication systems. This system replaces existing systems that were unable to handle the load they were being given. A new system was needed and it was needed quickly.

In effect, EMC was a re-engineering effort. Blue Cross/Blue Shield used a re-engineering tool from CACI, called RENovate—which runs on top of Rumbaugh's OMT—to analyze the problem. The actual software was designed using the Rumbaugh object-oriented methodology as instantiated on IDE's Software Through Pictures object-oriented CASE tool. An object model was developed to structure all subsequent system development. The GUI was developed with Sterling's Key:Client tool (Formerly Object View) and with C++ products from CenterLine and Microsoft.

The old system processed some 7000 claims a day while the new system processes between 10,000 and 14,000 claims per day. This results in a savings of between $6,000 and $14,000 dollars a day. The object-oriented development group claims the main object technology benefits resulted from the ease and speed of development possible with the object technology products and the quality of the resulting interface that makes the system easy to use.

Chrysler Financial Corporation's (CFC) Branch Automation System (BAS)
Finalist, Category 3, 1994

This application was developed with Next's NextStep object-oriented environment. The BAS is a suite of some twenty-four different business applications used in the sale of financial services to auto dealers and their customers. The system serves some fifty-four branches and some 1200 users. All of the applications were developed in the NextStep environment and in Objective C, C, and C++.

All twenty-four applications were developed within an eight-month timeframe. During the first four months, the development team created and delivered five of the applications. During the next four months, the team created and delivered nineteen additional applications. This application is a dramatic example of how code reuse can reduce development time. It also illustrates the fact that some initial experimentation is necessary to get the initial objects right before extensive reuse can pay off. It probably also illustrates the advantages of using a comprehensive object-oriented development environment, like NextStep, to assure that every aspect of each application is fully object-oriented.

Pacific Bell's State Transition Application Controllers (STAC I and STAC II)
Winner, Category 3, 1995

This entry is comprised of two large state machine applications that serve as interfaces between several legacy Pacific Bell applications and network carriers that need consolidated statements for network traffic routed to them. The two systems handle 2 million and 1.5 million transactions per day. The applications run on Amdahl 7670 mainframes in MVS and are written in COBOL, although the interface for STAC II was written in Smalltalk/V.

The main contribution that object technology made in the design of these applications is twofold. First, the COBOL applications were based on an event/class/operation design. In effect, the COBOL was structured as if it were an object-oriented language. The analysis was done initially via Rumbaugh's object-oriented methodology. Then, the object model was implemented in KnowledgeWare's ADW and COBOL code was generated.

This application demonstrates the power of an object-oriented approach to large system analysis and design efforts, without regard to the language or tools actually used to implement the application. The object-oriented analysis and design phase made it easier and faster to develop this system. While it was a finalist in the cost category, it could just as well have been a finalist in the legacy application category.

Taken together with other applications described in this book, these applications suggest some of the ways that object technology is making software development more cost-effective. They also hint that object technology will make the software development process even more efficient as companies gain more experience with the technology.

16

SMST: Supply Management Specialist Tool

AlliedSignal Aerospace Company

THE OPPORTUNITY

Supply management activities were being performed by seven people. Planners, buyers, and purchasing administrators created material requisition and purchase order documents with help from two computer data entry clerks. At least two other people were always involved in the process.

The business process was as follows:

1. Planner determined need using a dozen printed reports.
2. Planner wrote requirements and sent to data entry.
3. Planning data entry created a requisition for planners.
4. Planner worked on the document and interfaced with computer data entry QA, compliance, entry until the document was finalized.
5. Planner sent requisition to purchasing MDS to create purchase request document for buyer's review.
6. Buyer made notations and started the (RFQ) process.
7. RFQ was processed by the buyer, conducting many internal interfaces to justify the prices and the supplier; sent to Purchasing data entry.
8. After much reciprocation, the supplier was determined.

9. Buyer planner sent purchase request package back to Purchasing data entry to create the purchase order.
10. PO information was passed to the administrator to interface internal customers and suppliers.

These steps were done in MANUAL coordination with QA, MPS, Warehouse, Shipping, Tooling, Raw Material, Fabrication, Manufacturing Engineering, Compliance Approvers, and Department Managers. Computer data entry was done by two separate groups and printed papers were routed in plastic packages. It was costly to print many boxes of reports and difficult to train new employees, and the applications were hard to maintain.

THE APPLICATION

SMST is the enabling tool for a newly re-engineered supply management business process. It front-ends (wraps) 107 IMS green screens with object-oriented Smalltalk APPC connectivity and GUI interfaces and implements inference modules. It is used by material planners and buyers.

SMST provides an email-like component for internal interface and a fax capability for external interface. The original business process contained fifty-two steps performed by seven people in nine weeks. A team of IS professionals and process owners re-engineered this process down to three steps that can be completed by one person in nine minutes, for established suppliers, and one week for new suppliers.

Using an implementation of Smalltalk for MS Windows and OS/2, IBM's DB2/2 RDBMS, Communication Manager/2, LU6.2 (APPC), and internally developed modules, a small team of developers built the SMST system and integrated it with AlliedSignal's MVS/IMS Purchasing and MRP system in seven months. This object-oriented multi-tier client/server application was implemented on January 9, 1995. A large Amdahl computer running MVS/IMS SNA VTAM is the host, an IBM PC 295 is the area server, and workstations are OS/2.

Upon logon, SMST presents users with a list of the parts they need to buy. It shows each part with quantity, delivery schedule, and candidate suppliers. A row of icons provides inquiry on each part's supplier(s), BOM, inventory, sales order data, engineering, QA, and historical data with a click of the mouse. The system tells SMS users WHAT parts to buy, HOW MANY to buy, what to FURNISH, and WHO to buy from. Every aspect of the process is designed so that data entry is kept to a minimum. Populating screens with the latest data, such as engineering, is done by a simple click of the pertinent icon. SMST also allows SMSs to send and receive messages and faxes online across the internal and external user community.

Figure 16.1 shows the initial screen of SMST. The highlighted Parts icon indicates that the user is writing a purchase order. She could have selected to work on any other object shown on the screen.

Order	Qty	Part Number	Part Name	Comm
01/19/96	48	2304955-1	SWIRL AY 120	2962
12/21/95	39	2304988-1	MOUNT LTA	3726
01/12/96	38	2306300-1	PAN	3708
01/26/96	4	2707409-1	HSNG ASSY	3735
02/02/96	183	2707920-2	STUD LTA	3726
02/09/96	30	2708020-2	CARRIER LTA	3726
01/26/96	40	2709623-1	COVER LTA	3736
01/25/96	37	2710193-1	END BELL AY LTA	3735
05/23/95	22	2743571-1	SPACER LTA	3726
01/19/96	8	2743667-5	BRACKET LTA	3735
01/12/96	4	2782794-1	HSG. OUTER	3726
01/30/96	2	2783185-1	STRUT ASSY	3704
01/12/96	41	2783920-1	IMPLR. MACH LTA	3737
08/29/95	6	30712-10	SHIELD	2988
02/08/96	3	31486	RETAINER LTA	2856
12/14/95	76	46701-5	END BELL LTA	3735
01/26/96	26	47314-1	CLAMP	3256
12/07/95	87	49156	BUSHING LTA	3726
01/26/96	21	515987-3	HOUSING LTA	3736
01/26/96	5	516009-1	END BELL LTA	3735
01/19/96	33	516889	PLATE	3708
01/26/96	15	516979-8	HSG AY	3736
12/14/95	48	519972-5	COVER LTA	3725
01/19/96	44	529223-1	HSG AY LTA	3735
02/02/96	7	531918-1	NUT GUIDE LTA	3726
01/12/96	633	584262-2	SPACER PLT LTA	3726
01/26/96	28	586169-2	TORUS AY LTA	3703
01/26/96	5	605257-4	HSG AY LTA	2983
01/19/96	49	605175-2	SPACER	3726

FIGURE 16.1 SMST initial screen.

Figure 16.2 shows the SMS working on Part 2304955-1
Swirl AY 120. The tools on the left vertical band help the SMS
determine what to buy (W2B), what to furnish (W2F), and who
to buy from. Information is incrementally gathered and shown
with the "i" button.

Upon configuration of a purchase order, the SMS clicks on
the AWARD icon. This triggers the SMST application to replicate,
in an interactive manner, all human keystrokes required by the
MVS/IMS host transactions to create the order. On-line GUI feedback to the user reports the actual transaction that is being
processed while delivering full Checkpoint and Restart capability.

There were many classes derived from pre-existing class
libraries. This was AlliedSignal's second object-oriented applica-

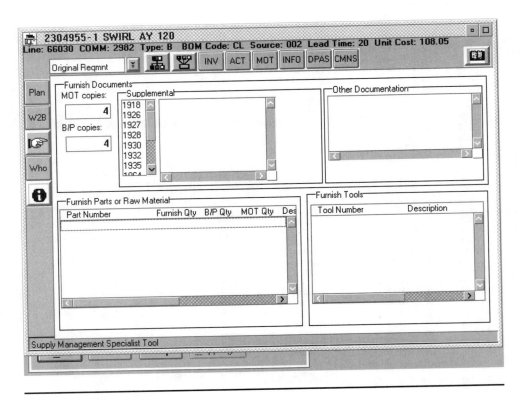

FIGURE 16.2   SMST—"Swirl AY 120."

tion. They had already created an object-oriented tool for Manufacturing Engineering and Routing purposes, and many of the objects of that system were reused. Some of the objects were also provided by the consultant on our team, as well as many of the Enfin-provided APPC/APPN objects for IBM host connectivity.

Size of the System

SMST contains nearly 1800 user interface objects that operate its screens.

Hardware and Software

	Hardware	Software
Interface	IBM PC	OS/2
Core Code	IBM PC	Smalltalk
Database	IBM PC Mod 295	DB2
Development Environment	IBM PC	Enfin

PROJECT LIFECYCLE

Analysis and Design

Potential benefits of the SMST system were:

- Reduce training costs
- Take advantage of productivity of object-oriented and GUI technology
- Replace cumbersome legacy system user interface with agile three-tier client/server solution for decision support
- Integrate SNA VTAM based purchasing and MRP system
- Allow Supply Management Department to keep writing purchase orders when the host computer (SNA/VTAM MVS/IMS) is down

An object-oriented approach was chosen because manufactured parts (objects) are well suited for object-oriented design and development. Object orientation provides ease of maintenance through the mapping of the physical part to reusable objects.

Developers were glad to use the intuitive power of PC Windows, mouse, icons, and pointers to bring a real-world concept to the business of manufacturing parts, replacing abstract lists.

A conventional approach wasn't pursued because in manufacturing, the number of entities and attributes used are not great but their usages vary, making data hiding, inheritance, and other features of object orientation attractive. Too many scattered parameters must be simultaneously compared to make the correct decision on determining what parts to buy, what to furnish with the purchase orders, and who to buy from.

Among the significant constraints in the domain was making a Smalltalk application communicate with IMS remote procedures. This was initially difficult but it was resolved quickly with help from Easel Corporation.

Total leadership concepts were used in forming the team, identifying the barriers, and agreeing on the process re-engineering and its entitlement. This involved one person from Information Services leading the JAD effort and eleven people from user community. The users were the Material Planner, material buyers, purchasing administrators, computer data entry, Quality Assurance, Compliance Administrators for government and company, Small Business Administrators, fabrication and assembly representatives, Raw Material Representative, and process managers.

The paradigm was very easy to communicate to the users with a manufacturing background. An internally developed methodology consisting of planning, requirement, external design and prototyping, internal design, testing, conversion, implementation, and tuning was used.

Development

The solution is mixed object orientation and non-object orientation. The portion of the solution that interfaces with the MVS/

IMS is coded using COBOL and other procedural languages. All desktop client modules are object oriented. Speed of development and quick test results are the most important benefits.

Ahmad Asadi of AlliedSignal's IS department led the development effort. He observed that having to implement the discipline to maintain classes and objects is not easy.

One IS developer wrote the interface to the MVS/IMS and the modules to populate the server database. IS developers and a consultant wrote the Enfin Smalltalk portion.

The development effort took seven months and consumed 1200 person hours.

The team compared many implementations of Smalltalk and C++. They decided on Enfin for OS/2 to be most suitable to their very IBM saturated environment.

According to Asadi, Communication Manager/2 proved to be the key component to their success

The approach to development was incremental. As they were developed and tested, objects were released to a selected user on an incremental basis. One trainer was trained and she trained the rest of the department on a part-time basis.

Deployment

The user community did not have experience with PCs, LANs, or object-oriented GUI solutions. Every PC, communication component, LAN, and server, down to wire, bridges, routers, and controllers had to be acquired and installed for the entire user community.

Having used ugly green screens for many years, the users treated us like heroes. This represented a significant quality of life improvement among users.

Maintenance

There is very little maintenance required. There's been no major problem with the application since implementation. Most of the problems deal with communication and equipment failure. Integrated Systems Solutions Corporation, a subsidiary of IBM, does the maintenance and production support. They handle everything except application failures. The component that interfaces the MVS/IMS is monitored on a once-daily checking basis. Software fails less frequently.

BENEFITS

Ahmad Asadi lists many benefits from the SMST project:

> "Every one in the company wants one. Cycle time was reduced from nine weeks to nine minutes for established suppliers and one week for new suppliers. One person does the job of seven people. A novice is doing the job of an expert using the interactive guides of the object-oriented system. Combining many tasks to one desktop freed up real estate and office equipment. Cycle time was reduced. Quality of life improvement, employee satisfaction, and productivity were attained. There are very few entities and attributes when dealing with the entire set of data."

CONCLUSIONS

Asadi offers the following observations regarding his project:

> "Data hiding can save the company money. Data warehouses are good matches for an object-oriented environment. Developers work harder on object-oriented solutions than on the old fashion ones. Object orientation requires discipline and version control.
>
> "Once started in object orientation you should stay with it; you cannot regress. We are building the data warehouse with object-oriented objects developed for its entities. Make sure you shift your paradigm before you enter into object orientation. Learn object-oriented design before starting development."

17

Customer On-line Order Request System (COORS)

Bell Sygma, Inc.

THE OPPORTUNITY

Real estate management within Bell Canada is handled by their Realty Services department. This department is divided into two groups, Property Management and Client Services. Property Management administers the nonbillable services to the client, which includes changing light bulbs, snow removal, fires, spills, and general maintenance. These services required a district office contact, such as a building manager or security guard. The Client Services group handles billable items, such as client relocations or work orders. Each group had its own systems for handling its aspects of property administration, however, neither group was satisfied with the effectiveness of these systems. Using district offices as a go-between for customer requests negatively impacted the responsiveness and timeliness to the requests. Individuals dispatched to repair or investigate a call were sometimes given the wrong client address. Customer complaints were frequent.

Both Property Management and Client Services wished to increase levels of customer service by providing a uniform way to help all their clients. Instead of using district offices as a go-between, they needed to contact directly the person responsible to handle customer requests. The new system must also provide reporting capabilities as well as integrate with their current applications on their IBM mainframe.

THE APPLICATION

The Customer On-line Order Request System is a client phone center system providing the clients of Bell Canada's Realty Services with a convenient point of contact 24 hours a day, 7 days a week. It is a mission-critical, multipurpose system that is integral to Bell Canada's Realty Services' business. It collects information on clients, contacts, and locations. Using a 1-800 number, Bell's clients can now access a full range of products and services. COORS empowers the agents by giving them a tracking system for services requested. It also serves as a financial data storage and billing system, as well as an easy-to-use communication and dispatch system.

COORS enables Realty Services to provide easy access, fast response, and consistent follow through to clients in any location. The system handles requests from two areas within Realty Services—Property Management and Client Services—and funnels the information to the proper person. COORS is also fully integrated with Realty Services' current systems, including their mainframe, manpower, invoicing, and email.

Based on the nature of the call, a client using the 1-800 number is guided through a series of prompts and routed automatically via an ACD (Automated Call Distribution) unit to the appropriate Client Centre agent. These agents are located in major cities throughout Ontario; however, the corporate customer data is stored in an Oracle database at the home office in Toronto. COORS downloads this customer information weekly from Bell's Corporate Communication Directory located in DB/2 files on their VM-based mainframe. The agent gathers and verifies all the necessary information on the client and records the request.

Depending upon the client request, COORS's work flow engine initiates the proper transactions to support the required services. Using Bell's existing email system, an electronic confirmation is automatically sent to both the client and the Realty Services prime contact. Financial information also is downloaded weekly to the Oracle database from several different DBase 3 systems. Monthly statements are electronically sent to the clients, followed by a bill for any labor and material charges associated with the request.

COORS is comprised of one Netware 4.01 File Server used to distribute application releases, two Oracle 7.0.12 database servers (part of a Fault Tolerant System) to house the extensive COORS data, one VM Communication Server to connect to the IBM host, one Windows Dial-in server used for remote database connectivity, and approximately 25 to 30 OS/2 and Windows client workstations running COORS.

The application was developed under OS/2 using Enfin Smalltalk, an application development environment from Easel Corporation. Currently there are seven programs that make up the entire system. Each one utilizes a notebook paradigm. By "opening" a particular notebook, users can easily and seamlessly navigate between programs. Clicking on the tabs representing the notebook pages enables the users to maneuver within an application. Figure 17.1 shows the COORS main application screen.

Figure 17.2 shows the Case Review screen, for viewing all existing cases meeting search criteria. Based on the agent's requirement, he or she can access billing or client information, open and work on an existing work order, print confirmations, view and send messages to the clients and to Realty Services contacts, and perform searches based on a variety of criteria.

The seven programs making up the entire COORS are:

- COORS (Main): The main version used for recording new cases in the system, as well as for modifying customer, contact, and location information.
- COORS Lite: An OS/2 contingency application that gives the agent access to location and contact information in case of connectivity or hardware problems.
- COORS Admin: Provides a user front-end window to database maintenance. Only users with the necessary privileges would be able to add or modify this information.

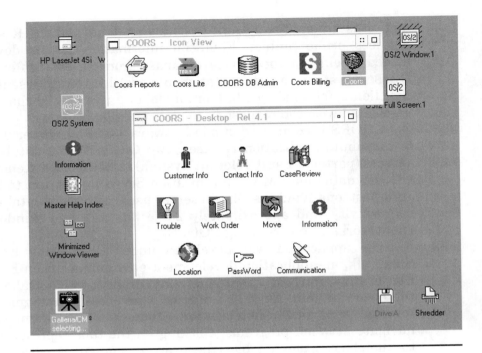

FIGURE 17.1 COORS main application screen.

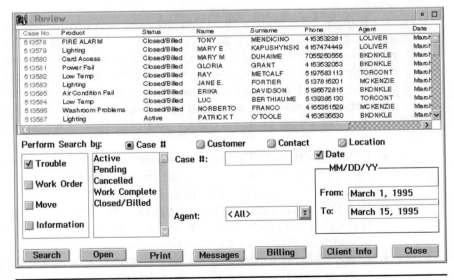

FIGURE 17.2 COORS Case Review screen.

- COORS Billing: Gives the billing administrator an access to billing-related modules. It also downloads financial data from other systems (time and material costs).
- COORS Reports: Generates and distributes reports to the users based on a predefined schedule.
- COORS DataLoad: Performs multiple functions such as downloading data from a mainframe and updating customer information. It also creates contingency files.
- COORS Messaging: Supports distribution of reports, confirmation, and statements to a VM-based email system.

Following is a list of the classes used in COORS:

BSSql
  BSBilling
  BSAdjustment
  BSBillingError
  BSBillingFiles
  BSBillingValidations
  BSStatement
  BSBillingContract
  BSCommitment
  BSCommunication
  BSLocalPrint
  BSMessage
  BSMessageReview
  BSPrintFile
  BSSendAnyFile
 BSCompany
 BSContract
 BSCustomer
 BSDataFile
  BSBillingStatus
   BSStatementStatus

BSDataBillingSource

BSDataContract

BSDataCSM

BSDataHistory

BSDataLocation

  BSDataLocationMaintenance

  BSDataRole

BSLocation

BSProductCode

BSRequest

  BSContract

  BSInformation

  BSMove

  BSTrouble

  BSWorkOrder

Some classes subclassed some of the classes provided by Enfin in the development environment—for example, the array, date, string, and button classes were modified.

The application currently is deployed on thirty workstations across Bell Canada, and is approximately 3 megabytes in size.

PROJECT LIFECYCLE

Analysis and Design

Bell Canada has a prior history with object orientation—intermediate to advanced.

Potential benefits of the project included providing added levels of customer service/increasing competitive advantage, increasing productivity by eliminating need for the district offices, decreasing cost of doing business, and leveraging current systems/technological investments.

An object-oriented approach was chosen for speed of development as well as flexibility of design. The application also needed to access data across multiple platforms (mainframe and PC based), and the object-oriented tool they were using supported this easily.

The application was quite complex, and was needed within a very short timeframe (three months for the initial release!). Utilizing an object-oriented development environment enabled the development team to complete the project within that time-frame. They also would not have been able to accommodate the changing business rules as easily, but using an object-oriented approach, only small methods need be rewritten. The GUI nature of the object-oriented tool enabled the team to rapidly change the front-end screens to accommodate the ever-changing user requirements. Enfin also supported the multiplatform environment crucial to COORS.

Other constraints on the design of COORS were the legacy information on the mainframe, the necessary learning curve of the developers who were new to object-oriented technology and Enfin as well as architectural issues such as remote connectivity problems and integration issues.

The opportunity was identified by the user, Bell Canada, during a Bell Canada/Bell Sygma Information Services meeting. Bell Canada wished to increase levels of customer service and still be able to downsize their organization. Their old systems were patchwork at best and cumbersome. Numerous customer complaints occurred because their requests were not met within a timely manner. The agents could not handle their workload effectively; individuals were often dispatched to the wrong site.

The A&D team consisted of project managers, a Realty Services user, tier B (equivalent of section chief) from Bell Canada, and one project leader and two developers from Bell Sygma Information Services.

Non-object-oriented approaches considered included Focus (4GL) from Information Builder, SQLWindow (4GL) by Gupta, and Uniface (4GL) by Uniface.

The methodology employed was Joint Application Development (JAD) sessions. Rapid prototyping and iterative development cycle produced initial prototype in very little time.

Development

The development methodology employed was a hybrid of Rumbaugh (OMT) and Jacobson. Added to the group that did the A&D was one senior developer from Mark Winter & Associates to begin development and provide knowledge transfer in object-oriented technology.

Elapsed time for development was:
3 months for the core system (COORS Main, first release, using three developers)
9 months for the entire system (all seven modules—two developers for the final six months)

Person hours:
Approximately 500 hours for core system
Approximately 9500 hours for the entire system

According to Bell Sygma project leader Roland Mathis, the development tool had to be object oriented and provide multi-platform/multiuser support. After seeing a demonstration of Enfin, developers felt that it met these criteria. Other tools were deemed too new (i.e., only beta versions available) and not portable across platforms. There were also connectivity and performance problems with Oracle and Netware.

Iterative and rapid development cycle enabled the developers to deliver a fully functional application within the allotted time. Flexibility inherent in the object-oriented development environment also facilitated changes as the system evolved.

Deployment

Bell Canada users, the Realty Services Systems Team, aided by mentoring from Bell Sygma Information Services, installed the hardware. Software installation, including COORS, Oracle, and Netware Requester, was done by Bell Sygma Information Services. New releases of COORS are distributed to the users automatically.

New equipment required included fault-tolerant servers (Pentium based-PC 95, PC 500, Raid Tower), and eighteen client workstations, split between IBM PS/2s and Dell.

The iterative development cycle that Enfin and object-oriented technology facilitates created extensive user involvement throughout the course of the project's development. Because the users were so involved in the actual development cycle of the application, end-user training for Bell Canada's system team (they maintain the COORS application) was minimal. One of the system team members then went on to provide the formal training required by the other users of COORS—client center agents, property managers, and planners.

Roland Mathis states: "User acceptance has been extremely positive; however, because of the rapid prototyping capabilities, user requirements would also change rapidly. We eventually had to set a cutoff date for acceptance testing."

He cites the fact that Enfin generates a single image (one file), and therefore distribution procedures are easier to roll out.

Maintenance

Maintenance is limited to client requests to Bell Sygma Information Services for new development. Maintenance and upgrades are completed in a fraction of the time compared to traditional 4GLs.

BENEFITS

The major benefit derived from the application has been one of improved customer service. In addition, the system enables Bell's Realty Services to leverage current investments (i.e., invoicing, email, manpower systems).

With the user-friendly graphical interface, users are more productive more quickly—extensive training to use COORS was not necessary.

Tangible benefits include cost effectiveness: $332,000 annual savings through downsizing, which amounts to a Return on Investment of 29 percent per year.

Mathis praises the speed of object-oriented development: "The speed with which the application was developed and is continuing to evolve to meet our dynamic business requirements impacts both customer service and the cost-effectiveness benefits."

CONCLUSIONS

Mathis has these words for those contemplating a similar development effort:

> "The benefits derived from using object-oriented technology (as opposed to structured programming) are real!
>
> "Bell Sygma, Inc. has created an object-oriented alliance to implement a corporate-wide strategy for object orientation. Our group has made a significant contribution.
>
> "Do not rush through the analysis and design phase. Smaller and more frequent releases are much better than a "perfect" product done in one major release. Also, if your organization has decided to make the commitment to adopt object technology, consider an outside expert source for mentoring or 'knowledge transfer.' After eight weeks of mentoring we were able to continue development on our own—in a very complex environment, and still deliver a quality product on time and within budget."

18

Electronic Media Claims (EMC)

Blue Cross/Blue Shield of Oregon

THE OPPORTUNITY

The purpose of the Electronic Media Claims (EMC) application is to edit, preprocess, and prepare electronically submitted claims for further processing by claims adjudication systems. The project was basically a systems re-engineering project with the objective of recovering and moving the functionality of EMC to object-oriented and client/server operation environments. The legacy application had a backlog of requirements and was unable to handle the growing number of electronically submitted claims. Blue Cross/Blue Shield of Oregon (BCBSO) saves money on each claim that gets into the system electronically.

The application was old, difficult to maintain, and required numerous enhancements to improve user interaction, business edits, and new claims rules. The cost to effect the changes was equal to or greater than the cost of a full re-engineering of the business logic.

The greatest potential benefit of the re-engineering project was to increase the number of claims that enter the system electronically. Providing better user access to the data and reducing the user effort to manage the electronic claims that are submitted were also important benefits.

THE APPLICATION

EMC is a client/server application with the client operating on MS Windows and the server operating on Sun server with Oracle 7. The core of the application was designed and developed using the Rumbaugh OMT methods realized in C++. All design, code generation, persistence code, data models, and test plans were done in Interactive Development Environment's Software through Pictures/OMT and /IM. The client–user interface is developed in a client/server data access tool ObjectView (now Key:client) from Sterling Software and ClearAccess GUI report developer. Graphical user interface testing was done in Mercury Interactive's WinRunner. C++ compilation and debugging for the server code was done using CenterLine's ObjectCenter and the client code was done using Microsoft's Visual C++.

The primary object model defined classes of objects that represent the core business functions at BCBSO. The business object model consisted of sixty-five classes, which are too voluminous to depict here. Described below are three class hierarchies that are a subset of the BCBSO business object model:

- Claims classes define the type of claim being submitted (medical, dental, etc.). This class hierarchy also includes relationships to patient, diagnosis, and service classes. An abbreviated OMT model is shown below in Figure 18.1
- Member classes represent the insured members and the associated coverages for the BCBSO plans, as seen in Figure 18.2
- Provider classes represent the professional health-care providers that submit the claims for services rendered. An abbreviated OMT model is as seen in Figure 18.3

None of the classes were derived from pre-existing class libraries. A domain search was done to find health insurance classes that support claims processing. None were found.

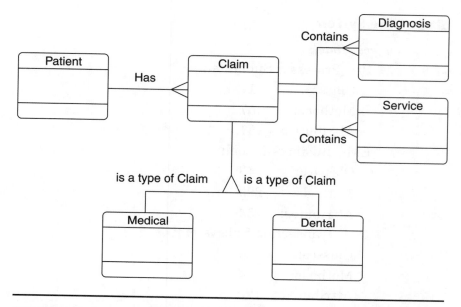

FIGURE 18.1   Overview of EMC claims classes.

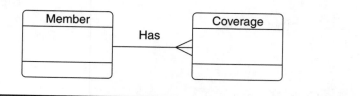

FIGURE 18.2   EMC member class overview.

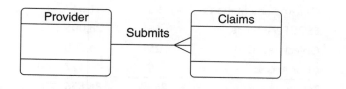

FIGURE 18.3   EMC provider class overview.

Size of the System

Object Models

Pre_Processor Subsystem

Classes:	17
Methods:	57
Attributes:	151

EMC Business Model:

Classes:	48
Methods:	299
Attributes:	254

CAS Transaction Subsystem:

Classes:	4
Methods:	4
Attributes:	120

Average Associations per class	1.3
Average Depth of Inheritance Tree	0.3
Transactions:	23 (of which 15 are report related)
Test Plans	23

Code Metrics

Component Type	Count	Lines of Code
C++ header	73	12,787
C++ Implementation	90	41,647
ESQL Persistence	66	28,005
ObjectView C	25	4,290
Clear Access	5	127
Totals	259	86,856

Object-Oriented Features of EMC

Following are many of the object-oriented features included in the EMC development effort.

1. The application used objects to encapsulate all the business rules and processing of Claims, Member, Coverages, Provider, Patient, and Diagnosis as well as several supporting classes of objects.
2. Class instances are realized and instantiated using C++ with embedded SQL hooks to Oracle to provide persistent storage. Refer to the metrics above for the number of classes in the design.
3. Private methods were used in C++ to hide the business object with public methods used as interfaces to the objects. IDE's StP/OMT was extended to automatically generate access to class attributes via public "Set and Access" methods. All attributes were defined private or protected. Refer to the metrics above for the number of methods in the design.
4. Inheritance was used to specialize classes of objects. For example, claims specializes to dental and medical classes.
5. Polymorphic classes were only required in some of the technical classes such as report classes, mainframe transaction files (implemented as stream classes), and so on.
6. Objects were persisted to Oracle databases. Embedded SQL was generated using extensions to the StP/OMT tool. The external Pro*C code was maintained in the StP repository and included as part of the object model design.
7. All code was C++ business-related code.
8. Developers used ObjectView and ClearAccess from Knowledgeware (now Sterling Key: client products) to prototype and develop graphical user interface.
9. Some DDE and ViewScript code was developed to support Windows interfaces in the ObjectView tool. IDE's StP provided a graphical repository browser as part of design/development tool. The application used CenterLine's ObjectCenter to perform animated method and code tracing during debugging stages.

10. Links to Oracle tables for persistent storage were linked into the ObjectView tool to assist in prototyping and client programming.

11. The application used Booch Components class library for collections and date/time functions. It used CenterLine's ObjectCenter for C++ checkers and IDE's StP for OMT model consistency checking and C++ editors. It used IDE's StP core repository for all analysis, design, code, and test artifacts; BCBSO's information warehouse for operational static data; and IDE's StP version control capability to control all analysis, design, code, and test artifacts.

12. C++ code was generated from StP/OMT tool. DDL was generated from StP/IM.

PROJECT LIFECYCLE

CACI of Arlington, VA, contracted to re-engineer the application using its RENovate re-engineering process. RENovate is a repeatable and defined software re-engineering process that provided the framework for planning, analysis, and legacy decomposition of logic; reconstitution/design of the new application architecture; and implementation of the code.

Analysis and Design

The opportunity demanded an object-oriented approach because the application touched most of the claims-based areas of the business. Therefore, claims-based generic classes would result in future reuse in new or re-engineered applications. It was also the first operational system at BCBSO to target the client/server environment.

Conventional approaches wouldn't have solved the problem, because the application would require complete overhaul on the COBOL mainframe environment to effect the required improvements. Since client/server is a strategic goal of BCBSO, it made more sense to target that environment, which demanded a different technical approach to application development.

A significant constraint in the domain was that the application had to be fed with Member and Provider data from the mainframe. This required periodic data extracts from the VSAM files that are loaded into Oracle to support Object instantiation from persistent storage.

BCBSO had little experience with object orientation; CACI has significant experience with object orientation.

The problem was identified by the end users' objectives documents that defined the required enhancements and business drivers for re-engineering the application.

End users and CACI and BCBSO CM, QA, analysts, database specialists, and BCBSO management were all involved in the design effort.

Development

Elapsed time:	Eleven months
Person hours:	6502 CACI
	4000 BCBSO (estimated)

Based on the performance requirements, C++ was chosen as the target language.

The only drawback of Object Orientation in development was that the BCBSO staff had to learn the object-oriented approach as the project was proceeding.

Deployment

BCBSO standard distribution procedures for client software to PCs were used. Test platforms were used to support parallel testing on the servers.

Deployment of EMC required the installation of new PC Windows platforms. The learning curve for the end users created a strain, due to having to support existing legacy system while testing and installing new system.

Maintenance

The system is maintained primarily with one BCBSO analyst, with the first four months of the maintenance period involving a CACI mentor.

In order to maintain this application it is a prerequisite for staff to go through the training program that includes object-oriented concepts, tool, C++, and technology training.

The object-oriented approach provides improved maintainability and quality of the application by using the design in StP to maintain the application.

BENEFITS

John May, Vice President of BCBSO's IS division has a long list of the benefits of using object orientation to attack the EMC re-engineering project.

The application now includes the backlogged enhancements required by the end user. It also has doubled the number of electronically submitted claims that are received into the system daily. Class designs resulting from this application are already being reused in other BCBSO applications.

By re-engineering the application, it can now handle up to 200 percent of the claims that the legacy system processed.

Ease of Use

- User involvement. The end user was involved in each of the activities, including user interface prototyping, object modeling, and testing. This approach, along with the formal training program, provided a supportive environment for learning the application.
- Adherence to interface standards (where applicable). The GUI was designed with a standard look and feel that was developed at the start of the project for BCBSO MS Windows applications. The BCBSO look and feel was a standard on top of the CUA standard.
- Polished appearance and design. The design of the application appearance went through a user interface prototyping activity and was developed with a standard and feel to ensure consistent screens across the application.
- Quality of on-line help and documentation. On-line help was provided with a standard pushbutton on the screens as part

of the standard user interface. The help is context sensitive for the activity being done on the screen.

Ease of Development and Maintenance

- Uses of modular design. The RENovate repeatable process provides for modular design using industry accepted notations and methods such as Rumbaugh (OMT). The StP/OMT models and GUI prototypes were used throughout the application development phases to communicate the design.

Tangible Benefits

The tangible benefits are primarily in the area of being able to process more claims electronically through the system. The old system could handle about 7000 claims per day with a savings of $2.00 average per claim. The new system is already handling about 10,000 to 15,000 claims per day, which equates to an additional $6,000 to $14,000 per day in savings. This was the primary business driver for re-engineering the application, along with improved user access to the data.

- Development savings. The application was re-engineered at a cost of about 50 percent of what a new development would have cost. The primary leverage in development savings is the large number of business classes that provide a building block for other BCBSO claims-based applications.
- Maintenance savings. The application maintenance savings will be recognized primarily through the reuse of the base classes in other projects. The backlog of requirements was the primary driver for the project, more so than maintenance savings.
- Learning/training savings. The new system will allow for easier training of EMC specialists in the future. The old system was not conducive to training new specialists. This is realized primarily through the use of the GUI interface, automated file transfer, and ad hoc reporting capability from the desktop.
- Downsizing savings. This was not a downsizing effort; however, it leverages the client/server platform to move process-

ing from the mainframe. The application is also open, portable, and scalable. Processing power can be increased by simply adding additional servers, with no impact to the application code.

Information Access

- Gives end users better access to important information. The GUI client interface provides for improved access to the data. The RDBMS persistent stores also open up the capability for end user ad hoc queries. This is being exploited by the EMC users.
- Presents information in easy-to-understand formats. The GUI interface was developed with user involvement and provides data formats that are much improved over the old system. In fact, the old system was a batch system with most of the user interface coming from report listings.
- Integrates data from multiple sources. The data for the application is based on two sources. One is the claims data submitted electronically from the health-care providers. The other is from the static legacy databases from the mainframe such as Member, Coverages, Providers, and so on. The legacy data is extracted and loaded into Oracle periodically to support the construction of objects at runtime for the static data. This provides integrity between object associations in the new application.

Innovation

- Breaks new ground. This project was the first object-oriented client/server project undertaken at BCBSO. It tested all the cultural discomfort from management to the users. The project's success can almost be measured totally on this subject from a technical standpoint.
- Pioneers new computer concepts or techniques. No new computer concepts or techniques are being used here. However, the concepts and techniques were totally new to BCBSO.
- Provides ease of use enhancements and improvements. The application has demonstrated very good maintainability. The maintenance of the application has been handled with one analyst from BCBSO.

■ Exploits the full capabilities of the environment. The application fully supports an open and interoperable environment. The application shares data with legacy mainframe files, BCBSO information warehouses, and windows ad hoc reporting tools. The application runs on a TCP/IP network that allows the user to connect to different versions of the data bases for testing, development and new releases.

CONCLUSIONS

John May observes that testing time was not sufficient in the original plan. Feedback into the RENovate process will allow for additional testing time when a completely new domain is being considered for re-engineering.

There are lingering performance concerns. These are being addressed by selectively converting I/O to stored procedures. This is a step away from the original objective to build a "completely open" system.

In conclusion, May says that the project has proven to BCBSO that critical applications can be implemented using object orientation as well as client/server techniques.

19

Branch Automation System

Chrysler Financial Corporation

THE OPPORTUNITY

Chrysler Financial Corporation (CFC), a subsidiary of Chrysler Corporation, provides financial products and services to more than 5000 automotive dealers and their customers throughout North America.

In the highly competitive financial marketplace, time to market of mission-critical applications translates to real profit (or loss) opportunities. CFC sought to deliver applications faster, adapt to changing regulations, reduce maintenance cycle times, and provide users with an easy-to-learn interface.

To strengthen its competitive position in the financial marketplace, CFC sought to adapt more quickly to changing financial and legal regulations; respond to competitive challenges from other financial institutions; empower developers to quickly build high-quality database, client/server, and GUI-based applications; empower users to make faster and smarter decisions; contain operational costs; and replace legacy systems.

Specifically, CFC identified twenty-four existing business applications needed to manage their branch financial operations in North America. Using object orientation, CFC developers reimplemented and deployed these applications in much less time than expected. Leveraging NEXTSTEP to build reusable objects, as well as using its built-in objects, meant CFC programmers spent less time writing code and more time solving CFC's business problems.

THE APPLICATION

The company's solution was to employ object-oriented technology to increase the speed, scope, and quality of application development. The solution underscores the benefits of reusable code and clearly identifies the productivity gains achieved and quality of software delivered.

CFC purchased NEXTSTEP to develop and deploy client/ server applications using objects. Using the environment's object frameworks and development tools (which include the ApplicationKit, DatabaseKit, ProjectBuilder, InterfaceBuilder, C/Objective C/C++ compilers, debuggers, and class browsers), CFC reimplemented more than twenty-four legacy applications to run its daily branch office operations. Example applications include FleetMaintenance, LoanTerms, and NewBusiness. These applications, coexisting with bundled and third-party office productivity applications such as NeXTMail and WordPerfect, have been deployed to more than 100 branch offices and 2500 desktops throughout North America.

CFC required a true client/server architecture on which to deploy custom applications to remote sites. NEXTSTEP, based on UNIX/Mach, provided networking and infrastructure to configure the network topology; administer network-wide data; deploy and update applications; share resources such as files, printers, and faxes; and help remote branch office users by connecting directly to their systems and applications.

Since NEXTSTEP runs on Intel-based hardware, many hardware configurations were considered. CFC ultimately decided to deploy LGI hardware to the branch offices.

End User Hardware Configuration (supplied by LGI Systems)
    Intel 486/66 processor
    20MB RAM, 170MB IDE disk

ISA bus

Localbus Wingine 16-bit color video

10BaseT ethernet

Software Configuration

Business Applications Developed by CFC

- FleetCashApp, FleetMaintenanceApp, FleetNewApp
- HolidayApp, NewBusinessApp, CashApp
- RetailNewBusinessApp, RetailTermsApp
- WholesaleCashApp, WholesaleMaintenanceApp
- RetailLoanInquiryApp, RetailContractBuilderApp
- BranchAdminApp, BranchChangeApp

From NeXT

NEXTSTEP User

- NeXTMail, for inter- and intra-office multimedia e-mail
- DigitalLibrarian, for searching large collections of CFC procedures
- DigitalWebster, as a desktop user reference
- TCP/IP, NFS, NetInfo, for network connectivity, management, administration
- printing, faxing
- DisplayPostscript

NEXTSTEP Developer

- ApplicationKit, DatabaseKit
- InterfaceBuilder, ProjectBuilder
- C/Objective C/C++ compiler, debugger
- Edit, HeaderViewer, DBModeler

From Third-Parties

- WordPerfect, from WordPerfect
- 3270Vision, for mainframe connectivity, from Conextions
- Mesa Spreadsheet, from Athena Design
- ScreenCast, for remote screen sharing, from Otherwise, Inc.
- AccessKit, for business object modeling, from VNP Software
- DevMan, for source code control, from VNP Software

Developers leveraged CFC's client/server architecture to facilitate the sharing of source code, object libraries, development tools, and on-line documentation. NEXTSTEP's support for remote compilation on fast servers reduced developer downtime (i.e., the time spent waiting for applications and objects to compile).

CFC subclassed (i.e., derived) classes from NEXTSTEP's preexisting object frameworks, such as the AppKit and DBKit, to match CFC's application requirements. For example, with minimum effort CFC subclassed the TextField class to add data validation capabilities, then reused the new class, CFCTextField, in other applications.

CFC also created its own library of pre-existing classes that were explicitly designed to be reused through subclassing. These general classes encapsulated similar behavior for many applications, yet were meant to be customized—as required—for each application.

Figure 19.1 shows many of the object-oriented applications used daily by CFC employees. These applications have been deployed to over 2500 desktops in CFC's North American branch offices.

Figure 19.2 shows an example of a custom Inspector written by CFC's developers for the CFCNumParser class. This custom class reuses (i.e., inherits) much of the functionality of NEXTSTEP's TextField class, but adds specific functionality required for input validation. CFC made this object available to all CFC developers by dynamically loading its implementation into InterfaceBuilder.

Size of the System

Number of applications: 24

Average number of classes (objects) per application: 19

Number of classes (objects) reused by the applications: 13

Number of general classes designed to be subclasses: 4

Lines of code (avg/class): over 70,000 (including comments)

Size of database: 70MB at each branch office

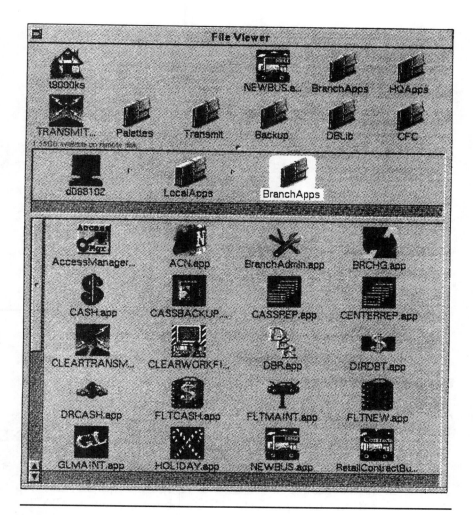

FIGURE 19.1 CFC custom applications.

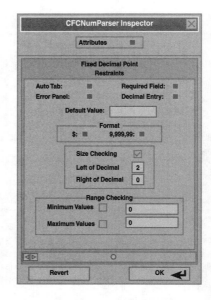

FIGURE 19.2 CFC custom reusable objects.

PROJECT LIFECYCLE

Analysis and Design

CFC chose to develop its branch office applications using NEXT-STEP because:

1. It provided tools for CFC developers to quickly develop applications using objects. CFC's objects, such as CFCTextField and CFCMessageHandler, were reused throughout all applications, saving programming costs, delivering applications faster, and ensuring consistency.
2. Its intuitive GUI was easy to learn by CFC's users, which significantly reduced training costs. NEXTSTEP's GUI objects provided a consistent look and feel for all applications developed by CFC.
3. It provided networking tools to manage the remote branch offices, eliminating the need for on-site systems administrators.

Development

The MIS development team used to develop the twenty-four applications was headed by Mike Adelson, MIS Manager at CFC, and consisted of one object architect, three application developers, one end-user operations representative, one database analyst, and one systems administrator.

Using object-oriented techniques and tools, CFC developers were able to identify shared behavior across many applications. Common business or user-interface logic was encapsulated in objects, thus enforcing consistency and isolating changes to those specific modules. Once constructed, objects were reused by developers in many applications. Also, modifications to these objects, when necessary, were reflected across all applications.

Subclassing NEXTSTEP's GUI objects allowed CFC to leverage existing user interface elements without having to rewrite them from scratch. For example, CFC created a CFCTextField object that contains all the functionality of NeXT's TextField, but added input validation, error handling, and new functionality requested by CFC's users.

Reusability was key in meeting the very aggressive rollout schedule. CFC used many of the pre-existing classes supplied in NEXTSTEP. Its classes were subclassed (inheritance) to implement behavior specific for CFC's developers and users.

By taking advantage of dynamic binding and real message-passing, CFC was able to load classes and create objects on the fly during program runtime (rather than compile time). As well, CFC was able to dynamically extend the development environment so that custom classes developed by CFC could be shared and reused by all developers.

During the transition to object-oriented development, the CFC development team was reorganized to promote code reuse and better understand end-user requirements.

To encourage reuse, an object architect was identified to create custom objects (NEXTSTEP palettes) that were made available to all application developers.

Just as importantly, CFC employees provided input and feedback to developers on application design and look and feel. Using InterfaceBuilder, developers quickly prototyped an application, gathered feedback from end users, customized objects and refined the design until it met or surpassed user expectations.

Deployment

CFC's solution (twenty-four custom branch applications) was deployed to the first branch office in Troy, MI on June 15, 1993. Currently, 100 branch offices (more than 2500 users) are using them. Deployment was completed in September 1994. The solution has been in full production for at least thirty months.

Maintenance

Maintenance cycles have decreased because bug fixes and modifications to CFC objects have much less effect on the overall program. This is due to encapsulation. Also, CFC's programming team has been able to partition application logic and programming assignments in ways that are much easier to understand and implement because objects encourage them to model real-world behavior better than previous (older) programming approaches.

BENEFITS

CFC chose to focus on the architecture of its development environment rather than short-term hardware and software costs, because over the lifetime of custom business applications, the capital costs are significantly less than development and maintenance costs.

In the short term, CFC realized cost savings by deploying the branch office applications faster and more reliably than expected. In addition, the move to an object-oriented approach, as evidenced by this past year's efforts, is expected to significantly lower long-term costs by improving developer productivity, delivering applications critical for business decision making, lowering the learning curve and training requirements for end users, and reducing the maintenance cycle times for production applications.

NEXTSTEP's network tools also dramatically reduced the costs associated with managing a complex network of distributed machines.

1. Reusability: Up to 50 percent of CFC's custom objects were reused in each of the twenty-four applications, including business logic objects, database access objects, and user interface objects.
2. Time Savings: Leveraging reusable objects and pre-existing objects, CFC deployed twenty-four client/server, GUI-based, database applications in just eight months.
3. Increased Productivity: In the first four months, CFC built reusable objects and delivered five applications. Using these objects, in the next four months, CFC delivered nineteen more applications.
4. Cost Reduction: CFC's applications were developed by a small team of developers, analysts, and end users. Maintenance costs decreased because changes were applied to encapsulated objects minimizing the impact on the rest of the application(s).
5. Decreased Training Costs: All applications consistently use the same NEXTSTEP and custom GUI objects, therefore, users at remote branches learned to use all twenty-four applications (plus third-party office productivity applications) in much less time than expected.
6. End-User Satisfaction: Because of rapid prototyping and step-by-step refinement of applications and user interfaces, end users at CFC were able to participate in the specification and testing of applications, leading to end-user "ownership" of the final product.

CONCLUSIONS

CFC's ability to adapt to changing business requirements is its primary competitive advantage. Object-orientation has decreased the time needed to develop, deploy, and maintain applications that reflect current market conditions. These custom applications provide better, faster, and more consistent access to information for end users.

The original system was a terminal-based environment, written in procedural COBOL, using 3B2 machines at the branch offices. Compared to the old system, the object-oriented, client/server environment approach reduced the time needed to develop custom applications, offered a consistent set of objects for all application developers, promoted the construction of reusable objects, and provided a friendly user interface to reduce training costs and maintain consistency.

CFC's developers are transitioning to object orientation using NEXTSTEP. The move to objects has changed CFC's approach to building business solutions. CFC's experience has resulted in the creation of an organization, the Data Object and Technology Team (DOTT), for creating and managing enterprise-wide objects. DOTT is expected to influence other organizations and projects throughout Chrysler Financial Corporation.

20

STAC: State Transition Application Controller

Pacific Bell

THE OPPORTUNITY

Pacific Bell provides billing services to other companies, primarily long distance telephone carriers and other telecommunications companies providing network-related services. The service charges of these companies are incorporated into a consolidated telephone bill sent each month to Pacific Bell customers. This requires that the detailed service charges of each company be transmitted to Pacific Bell, edited, and printed together in a separate set of pages in the format specified by the company. The amounts owed to each company are then included in the total amount billed. Each company may also include service announcements, advertisements, and other sales materials, in a format specified by the company, in the consolidated bill. Generating these consolidated telephone bills is quite a complex process requiring the processing of large amounts of data from a variety of sources and its presentation using a very flexible, user-specified formatting scheme.

As part of the effort to provide these services to its third-party customers, Pacific Bell has established the FIRST (Flexible Invoice Ready Systems Technology) organization. The applications that FIRST designs, develops, implements, and maintains provide the data and process interfaces between Pacific Bell and its third-party billing service customers. These applications are significant components of Pacific Bell's third-party billing service.

Initially, the interface applications were custom designed to meet the requirements of each company. However, it became apparent in the late 1980s that the variety of network-related services and the market demand for them was dramatically increasing and that this trend would continue. A number of new organizations providing these services expressed interest in Pacific Bell's third-party billing service. FIRST recognized the need for a more efficient and cost-effective means of providing such an interface without developing a whole portfolio of custom-designed systems meeting individual customer requirements. This led in 1990 to the design and implementation of CAMS, an application architecture and state machine engine for creating highly modularized yet customized interfaces. CAMS runs on the MVS/DB2/COBOL platform. Since its initial implementation, CAMS has been renamed the State Transition Application Controller Version 1 (STAC I).

The concept underlying the design of STAC I was the state machine. STAC I is an engine that reads and executes a set of process control statements specified by a business application developer. STAC I provides for the creation of highly customized, reusable processing modules executed by a single driver, thereby allowing FIRST to provide necessary feature customization without having to develop a new application architecture for each of Pacific Bell's third-party billing customers. The table-driven character of the application control statements also allows for the rapid and efficient addition or modification of customized features, greatly reducing the costs of maintaining the third-party interfaces. A significant portion of the interface to Pacific Bell's third-party billing service for two customers runs under the STAC I application architecture.

STAC I constitutes a particular approach to the physical implementation of the event/class/operation relationship structures of OMT (Rumbaugh), Fusion, and so on, for a particular application domain.

Factors requiring the development of STAC II included:

- An increased demand for a cost-effective and easily adaptable "generic" third-party billing interface. The need for a generic, yet customizable interface and process has significant application architecture implications in addition to business process implications. It has become clear that the requirements of the business and information system views of such a generic billing service are different.

  From the business perspective, in order to market and bill for a specific generic product, the functionality and data of the generic billing product must be clearly distinguished from the functionality and data of any and all customized product features required by particular third-party customers.

  From the information system perspective, however, it is essential to implement the generic and customer specific features within the same application architecture and in exactly the same way. The need for such an architecture caused FIRST to re-examine the architecture of STAC I to determine whether it could be enhanced to meet generic third-party billing requirements.

- An increased awareness of STAC I functional limitations. Although the STAC I state machine appeared to be flexible, it became apparent that it could not accommodate various types of processing requirements. STAC I was built for a particular process (the reading, editing, and writing of file records) within a particular application domain. (In fact, the STAC I state machine engine had to be modified for a second application to run under it. There are, in effect, two STAC I state machine engines.)

  To meet the business challenge of providing a generic system interface to customers, it became clear that the functionality of STAC I would have to be extended to other kinds of processes and to other application domains.

- An increased need for a more friendly user interface. In order to become widely used, STAC I needed a better user interface and better documentation.

■ An increased need to provide for both legacy systems and object-oriented development. The STAC I engine also needed to be more flexible to provide for applications developed through the use of object-oriented techniques and methods. The transition to object technology within the large system environment can only be accomplished in stages. Some legacy code will have to coexist with object-oriented applications for years to come. There was a need, therefore, for a state machine engine that could handle both object orientation and traditional applications.

THE APPLICATION

STAC versions I and II are state machine engines that execute highly customized applications within the Pacific Bell billing organization. These applications provide the data and processing interfaces to the users of Pacific Bell's third-party billing service. This service provides for the generation of complex, consolidated telephone bills that invoice for the network-related services provided by a number of telecommunications companies. STAC I and STAC II provide for the rapid development and cost-effective implementation of the highly customized software needed to incorporate a new service provider into the consolidated telephone bill. Both STAC versions run on the MVS/DB2/COBOL platform. STAC II also runs on the OS/2-Windows/MicroFocus COBOL platform. STAC was implemented in 1990 and has provided significant benefit to Pacific Bell. STAC II was designed and constructed using Knowledge-Ware's Application Development Workstation CASE product (a non-object technology product). Among other things, STAC II provides increased application domain and application process extensibility to the functionality of the STAC I state machine engine.

Both STAC versions are based on business application developers' specification of the event/class/operation structured relationships described in the object technology analysis and design literature. The development and evolution of STAC has involved a combination of traditional and object technology methodologies, platforms, and languages. STAC provides a path for the migration of legacy applications to object technology architectures using traditional tools and languages.

The number of lines of code is large. The two applications running under STAC I contain 78,242 and 92,050 lines of executable code and process about 2 million and 1.5 million records per day. The first application to run under STAC II is expected to process about 500,000 records per day.

The applications running under STAC are just a small portion of a much larger Pacific Bell billing system context and involve a large number of input and output data flows/processes. STAC runs on platforms and under operating systems traditionally associated with large systems.

Major design principles applied to the development of STAC II included the use of one of the more robust methodologies of object-oriented A&D to provide enhanced application function and data analysis capabilities to STAC.

Another principle was to leverage the existing and extensive FIRST I-CASE application development infrastructure by using KnowledgeWare's analysis, design, and construction workstations to develop STAC, and to leverage the design architecture and implementation programs of STAC I as appropriate through the development of a mapping of the STAC I structures to the STAC II Object Model.

Hardware and Software Used

STAC I

	Hardware	Software
Interface	Amdahl 7670	MVS COBOL II
Core Code	Amdahl 7670	MVS COBOL II
Database	Amdahl 7670	MVS DB2
Development Environment	Amdahl 7670	MVS COBOL II

STAC II

	Hardware	Software
Interface	486/Amdahl 7670	OS/2/ MicroFocus COBOL MVS COBOL II
Core Code	486/Amdahl 7670	OS/2/ MicroFocus COBOL MVS COBOL II
Database	486/Amdahl 7670	.DBF file format MVS/DB2
Development Environment	486	OS/2: KnowledgeWare ADW; Windows: Smalltalk

Overview of STAC II Object Model

Figure 20.1 shows the STAC II Object Model.

The STAC Object (Entity-Relationship) Model contains classes (entities). Based on Derek Coleman's Life Cycle Model, which defines the allowable sequences of interactions a system may engage in its lifetime, developers consider the creation of the EVENT CLASS SEQUENCE class one of the most important concepts to emerge from the STAC II project.

The elements making up STAC I and STAC II have different names and, at first glance, it appears that the architectures of the two systems are different. In fact, however, the fundamental elements of the two systems are the same. The STAC II Object Model amounts to a normalized view of the data elements found in STAC I.

Potential benefits from STAC II development:

- A simplified approach to the implementation of business requirements. Application programs in the two applications running under STAC I can be accurately coded with little more than the COBOL linkage rules and a statement of program function. Because STAC provides application control functionality, the application programs were easily created by programmers just out of training. The information

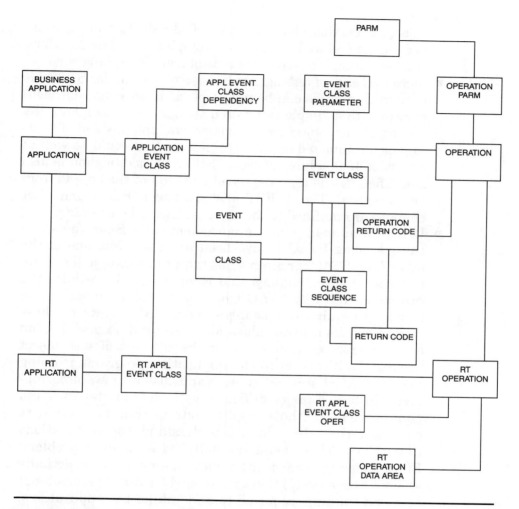

FIGURE 20.1 STAC II Object Model.

required for specifying application control functionality within the state machine tables also proved straightforward for the designer assigned to their creation. In contrast, the other (non-STAC) programs in these two appellations required the use of the most experienced programmers available.

- Increased software quality and reliability. Because the interfaces among application objects are specified in the STAC I object tables, there has been a marked reduction in the number of errors related to functional complexity and mishandling of cases through the complex code of traditional programs.

- Increased ease of testing. Application testing under STAC I is easy in that stubs can be put in place for missing (uncoded) objects with a simple return code generator. This allows the testing of each object as it becomes available instead of waiting for a completed application process that could be well in excess of 40,000 lines of code. Testing of modification is also simplified by the high degree of isolation of the objects from one another. The FIRST test manager has found that changes are confined to the object submitted for testing.

- Lower maintenance and enhancement costs. Since the applications using STAC I have been in production, one of the other (non-STAC) programs has required a complete rewrite because of its unmanageable complexity. Meanwhile, the programs called by STAC I have only needed modification based on requirement changes. The STAC I state machine engine and its control tables have required no modification or maintenance other than for the creation of new object tables. Modifications to the application programs running under STAC I are easily accomplished by new programmers. In fact, a major difficulty with the maintenance and enhancement of these applications is that programmers complain that they do not understand the applications themselves. This would normally be seen as a problem. From a management point of view, however, this is actually a benefit because (1) there is no need for every programmer to spend the time required to understand the applications, and (2) the changes that are made to the application are made with a high degree of accuracy.

- Increased reusability of business application code. The encapsulation of operations within application classes makes it easier to develop reusable software. Figure 20.2 is a table of statistics describing the size of the application running under STAC I and the extent to which the use of STAC I has facilitated application code reusability. (The actual size of the core code of STAC I is not large. However, because STAC I has

	Application 1	*Application 2*
Application Transaction Records Processed per Day	~2,000,000	~1,500,000
Total Lines of Application Code	78,242	92,050
Total Lines of Application Code Running Under STAC	36,689	48,123
Total Lines of Application Code Not Running Under STAC	41,553	43,927
Average Lines of Application Code per Program Running Under STAC	456.6	528.8
Average Lines of Application Code per Program Not Running Under STAC	719.4	861.3
Average Lines of Application Code STAC to no-STAC Ratio	.63	.61
Number of Project Hours to Build	19,976	7,949
Average Number of Code Lines per Project Hour	3.92	11.58
Number of Application Objects Running Under STAC	91	
Number of Rows (Events) per Object	minimum is 4 maximum is approxmately 60 mean is approximately 40	
Number of Application Programs Not Running Under STAC	51	

FIGURE 20.2 Application statistics for STAC I applications.

been customized for each of the applications that use it, its actual size is difficult to estimate.)

■ No impact of requirements specification on application architecture design. A major difficulty faced by developers is the fact that requirements specification is seen as having significant consequences for the design of an application's architecture. The use of STAC and its application control functionality removes the need for application requirement to be completely identified before the design phase begins.

■ Provision of an approach to the transition to object technology. The fact that applications of both traditional and object technology may run under STAC means that developers of both types of applications must think in terms of the same categories. Over time, this provides a means of smoothing the transition to object technology.

Two fundamental business requirements demanded an object technology approach: the need to implement the business requirements quickly and cost effectively, and the fact that the design of an architecture had to take place before all business requirements were known. Conventional approaches wouldn't have solved the problem. The object technology approach encapsulates processes with the appropriate class. The conventional (process-driven) approach does not have a single organizing element to which functions must be attached in either the analysis or design phases. In the conventional approach, there can be multiple major design architectures to solve the same problem. A process-driven conventional approach would require that application specifications be complete before the design could be completed.

A conventional approach has no straightforward design and implementation path from the analysis phase. Instead, one can only design the application architecture after specifications have been completed. This clearly won't lead to the rapid implementation of the requirements.

At the start of the STAC II project, developers did not fully appreciate the fact that the STAC domain is different from a business application domain. They knew that to meet the business requirements they had to provide a software architecture.

The objective of STAC is to provide a software architecture that tackles the issue of control in software products. The difficulty of taking on this task is that it immediately brings everyone's competing vision of software development to the forefront. The most significant constraints in the STAC domain are aspects of this point.

Conflicting application development paradigms was a major constraint. The development of STAC II required that FIRST confront the conflicting visions of the software development process.

Another constraint was misunderstood application development paradigms. Despite their differences, there also exist clear similarities between the object technology approach and the approaches traditionally used in large systems development environments. Despite this fact, it is often not clear what these similarities are. Adherents of the two approaches often do not appreciate the value of the alternative approach. Many adherents of the object-oriented paradigm cannot imagine that object technology based application can be built on large system or legacy platforms with conventional tools. Similarly, many of those familiar with large platforms are reluctant to make the effort to understand or embrace object technology concepts because they consider it irrelevant to large, legacy platforms.

With regard to the COBOL-generated portion of STAC II, no classes were derived from a pre-existing class library.

Object-Oriented Features Used

- Classes/instances. All the classes shown in the object model have actual instances.
- Inheritance/specialization. Several classes, such as Event and Operation, have inheritance/specialization. These were discovered during the design/prototype phase when expressing the unique behaviors of the specialization. The Event class, for instance, specializes into Event types: Random, Temporal, Scheduled, and so on.
- Methods/messages. STAC's use of methods/messages were originally expressed as data flow lines between the objects, using data flow diagrams similar to OMT.
- Virtual methods/polymorphism. Runtime objects, such as RT APPLICATION and RT APPLICATION EVENT CLASS

share common functionality such as receiving and validating message requests. Although message/methods names are the same, the underlying behavior is different.

Advance Object-Oriented Functionality

- Persistent objects. All the classes shown in the object model provide methods for the storage of persistent objects. The semantics of STAC persistent objects are of two kinds. The "static" class persistent objects are the elements of a business application that runs under STAC. The runtime classes are the elements that contain the runtime trace of an application running under STAC.
- Graphical developer interface. The STAC II developer interface and state machine engine trace environment was developed using Digitalk's Smalltalk/V for Windows.
- Graphical browsers. The Class browsers within Smalltalk/V were used as the primary development environment to develop the STAC II developer interface. These browsers provide the capabilities to create new classes and methods as well as augment and enhance current classes within the environment.
- Internal/external class libraries. The developer interface was created using Smalltalk/V internal classes as well as several other classes from third-party vendors. In addition, approximately forty-two classes were developed to support the developer interface.
- Graphical tool for user interface development. Smalltalk/V with WindowBuilder Pro was used to develop the STAC developer interface. KnowledgeWare's ADW design workstation was used to develop the TSO/ISPF user interfaces.
- Tools for target operating systems interface layout available. Smalltalk/V provides a reasonable level of portability between Windows and OS/2. The STAC developer user interface can easily be ported to OS/2 to use OS/2's true multitasking abilities.

Storage Management

Repository available. KnowledgeWare's ADW encyclopedia is used to store all object-oriented A&D information.

Code Generation

Language code generated. STAC II was developed using KnowledgeWare's ADW product that generates COBOL for the MVS and OS/2 components.

WindowBuilder Pro was used to generate the Smalltalk/V code for the STAC developer user interface.

PROJECT LIFECYCLE

Analysis and Design

Pacific Bell is a large organization that is supported by several application support groups. Each group is responsible for the standards, methods, and procedures that are employed. This effort was initiated and developed by the FIRST organization whose primary system development lifecycle was structured design and, most recently, information engineering. The migration to object orientation was a natural extension of their current path.

Two fundamental business requirements were important in leading FIRST to identify the business problem. These requirements were first the need to implement the business requirements of a third-party billing service customer quickly and in a cost-effective manner, and second, the design of the architecture had to take place before all business requirements were known.

The "sale" of object orientation was delivered only with the context of meeting the application requirements. That is, they did not use the solution in search of a problem approach. Through clear domain specific explanations, management understood the benefits and supported the object-oriented approach.

Rumbaugh's OMT methodology was used as the basis of a "synthesis" approach. Developers used many of their current diagramming tools to express OMT models by modifying and extending semantics.

Object and dynamic models were created for STAC II using the KnowledgeWare ADW toolset. This was done according to a particular specification of the relationship between the ADW toolset and the OMT methodology.

Obvious benefits of object orientation during analysis and design were the savings of time and money by reusing current tools. Developers were able to quickly express requirements without initially sustaining the learning curve associated with new tools. A drawback was that they could not be more academic in approach, which might have expedited the education process.

Development

Methodology employed for development was a synthesis of Rumbaugh's OMT, Wirfs-Brock, and other methods. The STAC II developer user interface application was prototyped and delivered in two months. Development is continuing on the STAC II state machine engine.

The mainframe portion of the application was chosen due to its integration with the I-CASE tool. Smalltalk/V was chosen as the desktop application development software due to its pure object environment. Smalltalk allowed the expression of the object-oriented A&D models very closely. Also, Smalltalk lends itself to a quick, iterative development process.

The object-oriented analysis models naturally evolved to a design/implementation expression of the application requirements. The development of the application went very quickly, and by using object-oriented tools, developers were able to quickly demonstrate proof of concept, as well as evolve an application that met the requirements.

Deployment

Through the development of classes, the procedures for creating state machines (instructions for STAC) makes the user procedures clear. Each class represents an informational need and business requirement. This assists the user in understanding and determining the most effective way to assemble application suites. User procedures are provided through on-line help within the STAC II developer user interface application.

Since STAC II supports the application development domain, only members of the application development organization have been involved. Deployment involves a representative from the

FIRST quality organization who is performing rigorous testing of the environment before and after implementation.

No new equipment was required for STAC I. STAC II requires only a PC compatible machine running OS/2.

STAC II's development environment provides access to all of the STAC components (Events, Classes, Operation). The user interface was designed to provide a logical path for the user to follow to ensure that the STAC components are entered accurately. Users are able to test the result of their work at the desktop before committing changes to the mainframe. This ability not only protects the production environment from error but also provides the user with the ability to do "what-if" scenarios.

Throughout the development of the STAC II development environment, the iterative development process was encouraged due to the object-oriented approach. The openness of the architecture allowed many interface changes without disturbing the essence of the system. This saved significant time and money as a non-object-oriented environment would have discouraged the kind of changes that were incorporated.

Maintenance

Little or no maintenance is required on the STAC I driver. The maintenance required for an application is also minimal. It involves two elements: the updating of the application program that uses the STAC engine for control functionality, and the changes required to STAC tables for changes to that control functionality.

There are a few special maintenance considerations. When one maintains the application, one must actually change at least one but perhaps up to three distinct portions of the application: application code, EVENT CLASS SEQUENCE table, and the STAC engine code itself.

The major benefit of object orientation in this phase is that when maintenance changes have to be made, the changes are discrete because of the relationship of methods to particular classes.

With an object-oriented approach developers are able to plan and extend functionality in a more predictable manner. By adding new classes or extending current object behavior maintenance is greatly simplified. Since additions and changes are localized to discrete classes, testing is more complete and confident, and changes can be delivered more quickly.

CONCLUSIONS

David Pett, technical director of Pacific Bell's FIRST program has these observations regarding the development of STAC:

> "The objective of the STAC application is to provide future projects with a mechanism for application control that will work in a consistent manner across applications. The most important lesson learned from this project was how to express requirements using object-oriented A&D."

His advice to others contemplating a similar development effort:

- Pay attention to the problem to be solved, not to producing a textbook object-oriented product. Once the object orientation development team is convinced they have an appropriate vision, they should proceed with determination.
- Sell the project as a profitable solution to a business problem (better, cheaper, faster), and not as an interesting experiment in object orientation. Mention object orientation as an aside if the company has demonstrated an interest in object orientation.
- Minimize discussion about terminology and whether some application element is an event, class, or operation.

Conclusion

Commercial object technology is developing and changing very rapidly. A book like this is like a snapshot of some fast-moving animal. In the lights of our camera the animal has paused, momentarily, to look at the camera. But we know that an instant later, just after the photo was taken, the animal ran off in a new direction.

The applications that were finalists and winners in the 1994 and 1995 Object World contests were developed between 1992 and 1995. To participate in the contest, the company submitting the application had to assure the committee that the application was already in use. Thus, even as these applications were being judged, changes were taking place in the object technology market that would date these applications. New products were being introduced. New standards were being agreed upon. Organizations were working together to create industry frameworks. New methodologies and books were being published. And everyone was learning more about the process of developing effective object-oriented applications.

At this point, if you have examined the application stories that have been described in this book, you probably already have your own ideas about the trends that are illustrated by these applications. The application stories include conclusions drawn from the experienced practitioners who created the winning object-oriented applications. In this last chapter we simply want to go over the main themes again, quickly, to summarize that state of commercial object technology in early 1996 and to suggest some of the emerging trends the authors anticipate in 1996 and 1997. To organize our conclusions, we'll follow the same outline that we used when we described each of the applications in this book.

THE OPPORTUNITY

As you review the applications described in this book, you realize that object technology opportunities are everywhere. Some companies have explored the use of object technology by tackling small problems to give themselves time to learn more about the technology. Others, with more experience, have used object technology to attack very complex problems that could not be solved by conventional means. As you might expect, most of the winning applications come from industries that are sophisticated users of computer technology and tend to adopt new technology earlier than other industries. These early adopters commonly include telecommunications, finance, manufacturing, computer companies, and the military; each is well represented among the Object World winners.

What will probably surprise some readers is the variety of the applications. Many managers and developers tend to think of object technology too narrowly. Thus, when they hear of an object-oriented application, they are likely to think of an application involving a graphical user interface or something programmed in C++. The use of object technology to integrate and access legacy applications may seem unusual to some. Others may be surprised by the important role that object technology is playing in the development of the distributed, client/server market. Similarly, some readers will be surprised to read of applications that were analyzed by means of object concepts and then developed by conventional means. The key thing to remember is that object technology is not a narrowly focused technology or a set of products: It is a major shift in how people think about software development.

It would be nice if we could give a formula that would help readers identify applications that were especially suited to an object-oriented approach. The fact is, however, that object technology is a better way to approach software development and that any software development effort can benefit from the use of object technology. Having said that, however, we must quickly add an important qualification: It takes time and effort to learn to use object technology to develop applications more efficiently. Your first object-oriented application will take longer to develop than it would take if you developed it in some conventional language. Most companies report that it takes at least six months to train a programmer to work effectively in an object-oriented language, and a year or more before that programmer becomes really creative in the new approach. In a similar way, most companies report that it takes three years and several significant applications before a company becomes efficient in creating components that can be successfully reused in other important applications. Thus, although the opportunities abound, the learning curve is steep. Without a serious commitment and some experienced help, a company may begin, have a bad first experience, and decide to avoid the investment that object technology requires. Thus, although opportunities abound, caution and a systematic, committed approach is required if your company is to really benefit from this new approach to software development.

THE APPLICATION

The applications vary widely. Some solve very specific end user problems. Some solve complex corporate problems. Some involve the use of 300 classes while one involves the use of over 800,000 classes. Some were prototyped in two months while others took much longer. The scope and focus of the applications varied widely and so did the hardware and the software that was used.

Hardware/Software Used

As you can tell from looking at the matrix (Table 1) that appeared in the Introduction, the applications in this book involved a wide variety of hardware and software techniques. Some ran on PCs, and some on workstations or mainframes. Most were distributed, client/server applications and combined multiple platforms.

The applications were developed in a variety of different ways. Some were written in object-oriented languages, some were developed with tools, and some were developed with object-oriented databases.

The largest number of applications written in languages were developed in C++, followed by Smalltalk. This corresponds to the overall use of object-oriented languages. Two years ago, one might have said that C++ was the dominant object-oriented language. Since that time, we've seen a surge of interest in Smalltalk, especially for use in enterprise applications. We expect that next year's contest will see the gap between C++ and Smalltalk narrow a little. Other object-oriented languages like Objective C and CLOS are represented by one or two applications, again reflecting their relative strength in the market. Ada is an object-based language that is used by the military. In addition, CORBA's Interface Definition Language was used in a couple of cases where the developers wanted the abstract openness that IDL provides.

Several implementations of CORBA were used and at least one proprietary ORB was used. We expect that occurred because the application was developed before the CORBA2 standard was complete and that future applications will rely on products that implement CORBA2.

Over half of the applications relied on class libraries and components for code reuse. In most cases, the developers used class libraries available with the language or tool they were using. A few applications used more complex technical frameworks and a few others used business objects. Again, this reflects the time in which the applications were developed. Technical frameworks and tested sets of business objects are just becoming available. No company talked of having a corporate library of business objects they could draw upon and no application was developed using a business object framework developed by an industry consortium. These more sophisticated collections of reusable code are just now becoming available. Still, even though the applications described here were really only experimenting with business object reuse, a few of the applications are quite interesting because they use a variety of different types of components and because the developers are speculating on how the effort might be better organized. Compared with the applications we reviewed in 1992, these applications are much more sophisticated in their use of components.

A small number of applications were developed in tools rather than languages. The most widely used tools were those that help developers create graphical user interfaces for specific operating environments. Beyond that generalization, the tools are mixed: several object-based 4GL tools, several object-oriented CASE tools, and several advanced object-oriented AI tools. Again, this reflects the time these applications were developed. Since 1994, the use of object-oriented tools of all kinds has increased and the use of object-oriented languages has declined. This change is mainly the result of better tools being introduced, but most of the applications described in this book were developed just before the language-tool transition began to pick up speed.

Over half of the object-oriented applications developed in this book were developed by means of object-oriented methodologies. The methodologies varied quite a bit, but Rumbaugh and Booch predominated, just as they have in the market in general. These applications were developed before Booch, Rumbaugh, and Jacobson joined together to create a new "Unified Method," but it's probably fair to say that most would have used the new methodology today.

Most of the applications described in this book relied on relational databases. A few relied on object-oriented databases. This also reflects the general market. The widespread use of object-oriented databases depends not only on the availability of powerful object-oriented databases but on the identification of applications that really require the superior characteristics of object-oriented databases. Otherwise, inertia will lead companies to stick with what they already understand. Most of the applications described in this book used object technology to simplify development, but only a few involved the use of massive amounts of complex data and hence only a few applications really demanded the use of object-oriented databases. Once again, this reflects what we see in the general market. The object-oriented database standards will probably make object-oriented databases more acceptable, but they are just now becoming available.

With a few exceptions, the applications described in this book could have been done with conventional technology. They were done via object technology to allow the company to explore object technology and to give the developers a change to experience some of the benefits that object technology could provide. The applications are more sophisticated than those that won the Object World contest a few years ago—clearly some companies are learning to take advantage of the technology, but they don't constitute a whole new class of applications and they are not consistently object-oriented. Some applications take advantage of one part of object technology while others use another part of object technology. The comprehensive object technology infrastructure that will allow for consistent, large-scale object-oriented applications that integrate all that object technology has to offer is still a few years off. The standards and infrastructure are only now being put into place and probably won't be fully used in winning Object World until 1997 or 1998. What these applications do represent is active experimentation and quite a bit of progress over earlier applications.

PROJECT LIFECYCLE

Few companies have well organized, formal object-oriented development procedures in place. Indeed, few companies have settled on a single object-oriented methodology; most are experimenting with several. This is really the only course open to most companies since object technology is still changing so fast. Standards that any methodology needs are only now evolving. Similarly, any mature object-oriented methodology will describe a major role for corporate component libraries, but at the moment those libraries are only beginning to come into existence and no one is in a position to say exactly how they will be used.

Complicating things further, different companies are using different pieces of object technology. Some are using an object-oriented methodology for analysis and design and then shifting to conventional approaches for the actual development effort. Others are using object technology to develop distributed networks. Others are only using object technology to simplify the development of GUIs, while still others are using object technology to stitch together complex legacy applications. Each of these rather different efforts would seem to demand a different lifecycle and it's hard to generalize at this point. We'll consider each of the different phases in a traditional lifecycle and see what conclusions we can reach.

Analysis and Design

As we have already noted, object-oriented analysis and design methodologies are popular and were used by half of the application developers, but their use varied widely. Some used relatively informal object-oriented methodologies, like Responsibility-Driven Design, while others used more rigorous methodologies, like Rumbaugh's OMT. Few complained about the usefulness of the methodology they used, but many faced problems that were not specified by the methodology and simply had to develop their own approaches. The use of components, as we have also noted, is not very well handled by any of the current methodologies, and over half of the developers were exploring the use of components.

Development

Development patterns were much more varied than the use of methodologies, reflecting, in part, the wide variation in the applications. We have already cited the wide mix of languages and tools used in the development of these applications. For most readers, however, reading about the steps that specific development groups went through and the kinds of problems they overcame will constitute one of the great values of this book.

Most of the development teams cited the importance of strong support from senior management. Several cited the fact that they had already used object technology to solve a similar problem and were called in when another problem like the first was encountered.

Most applications were developed by a small team of highly skilled developers. These stories do not describe routine development efforts; they describe exploratory efforts by teams trying to introduce object technology at their various companies. On the other hand, unlike applications that were described a few years ago, most of these applications are second generation applications and the developers are able to report improvements in their overall approach to object-oriented development.

Deployment

The Object World contest requires that companies submitting applications specify that they are fielded. Most, in fact, were fielded just before the contest closed and thus the companies have little data on the deployment of the applications. Moreover, since most of the applications are narrowly focused, they were probably easier to deploy than more generic applications typically are. In addition, most of the applications involve distributed, heterogeneous systems, and most companies are just beginning to understand how to approach these new architectures. A few applications provide good advice for object technology developers who are introducing their first object technology system.

Maintenance

Several developers cited ease of maintenance as one of the benefits derived from the object-oriented approach, but few offered concrete data. If you consider that one hardly really understands the maintenance requirements of a large application until after it's been in use for three years, then it's clear that most of the applications described in this book have not been in use long enough to have a real maintenance record.

Clearly the companies hope to achieve maintenance benefits, and several of the application developers claim they specifically chose object technology because they faced a situation in which the user was going to continue to change the overall nature of the application and the developers wanted to be in a position to respond quickly to requests for changes and updates. Some even claim that they have responded to some of these requests and that the applications have fulfilled their expectations.

The desire for ease of maintenance was probably what led most of the developers to rely so heavily on the use of components.

BENEFITS

The benefits most universally cited, by the developers of the applications in this book and by object-oriented developers in general, are ease of development and the reduction of development time. Everyone admits that the initial learning curve can be steep and that the first or second application may take more rather than less time, but once developers become familiar with object technology, they almost all claim they work faster and achieve more in less time. Since most of the applications described in this book were developed by experienced object-oriented developers, these claims predominate. Moreover, these claims are important, since many companies are exploring object technology precisely because they hope to achieve just such benefits. For many companies, object technology is the key to re-engineering their entire software development effort to make it more responsive to the increasingly urgent demands for new strategic systems, and for systems that can replace or reduce the maintenance demands created by many large legacy systems.

After the savings of time and the ease of development, the next most cited benefit is user satisfaction and the saving of user time. This is undoubtedly primarily attributed to better graphical user interfaces, but in several cases it also reflects the fact that end users are able to quickly make their own changes in the system.

The next two benefits cited were reuse and complexity overcome. Reuse resulted from the use of class libraries that accompanied object-oriented languages and tools and from the use of component frameworks. A few applications cited the reuse of business objects. Everyone is interested in exactly how much reuse object technology is going to deliver. It's hard to reach any firm conclusions from these applications because they vary so much, but the developers, at least, seem satisfied that it is occurring and that more can be expected as the component libraries grow and are better understood.

When developers claim that they have overcome complexity that had limited development by conventional means, that's especially important, since it points to applications that take unique advantage of object technology. The examples cited here mostly depend on very large numbers of formats (forms, diagrams) or complex decision making, which is usually solved with a combination of object-oriented and AI techniques.

Several application teams report very impressive savings, but most of the savings are hard to disentangle from serious re-engineering efforts that would probably have led to large savings without regard to how the new software had been developed. As with other new technologies, those that take risks will gain rewards, and those that wait for a clear-cut financial case will miss out on the strategic opportunities that are available from the early deployment of object technology.

There have been a few impressive studies made of the use of object technology when it was carefully contrasted with similar conventional approaches. Work by EDI is often cited, for example. But none of the applications in this book are based on controlled research that results in a very clear financial case. In the best cases, the developers claim that teams trying conventional approaches were frustrated and that object technology was able to solve the problem. This is impressive from a technological perspective, but the bottom line, in such cases, depends on proving the solution was really valuable and therefore worth any effort at all, and few of the applications present this kind of hard data. We're confident that object technology will be widely accepted as the most cost-effective way to develop software within a few years. Before that conclusion is widely accepted, however, companies will have to develop component libraries and company-wide methodologies. They will have to demonstrate that they can routinely create complex applications with object technology and consistently respond to user requests faster than they could in the past. Moreover, they will need to demonstrate that the object-oriented applications they build can be maintained more easily than the legacy applications that now burden companies. There is a "chicken-and-egg" aspect to this kind of proof. Until a company invests enough to really learn about the new technology and put an object technology infrastructure in place, it can't begin to get the sort of results than can provide iron-clad proof. Most of the applications cited in this book represent efforts to put an object technology infrastructure in place and it's a little early to look for the kind of proof that will convince real skeptics. A few of the applications in this book come close, but a completely convincing case for object technology will have to wait for a few years and the more widespread use of object technology by average developers.

TO THE FUTURE

The applications described in this book should inspire those who are considering introducing object technology at their own companies. Even though object technology is still rather immature, many companies have been able to use it successfully. In some cases they have solved problems more efficiently than they would have otherwise. In a few cases, they have solved problems that they would not have been about to solve with conventional technology. In all cases, the companies have learned from the experience and are now ready to take advantage of the latest advances in object technology. They are, in other words, ready to extend the competitive advantage they have already developed by learning to create and modify software more efficiently than their competitors.

It would be nice if you, the reader, could study and apply what the companies whose applications were described here have already learned. Returning to a point we have made before, however, object technology is moving very rapidly. In many cases, the developers who created these applications would probably use different tools and techniques if they were to redo these applications in 1996.

In 1994 and 1995, when these applications were developed, for example, CORBA2 and a variety of Object Services associated with the CORBA standard were unavailable. Applications written within that timeframe had to choose between one or another specific implementation of CORBA. Large applications written in 1996 will be able to mix various CORBA implementations, using one version for PC platforms and another for mainframes. Applications created before 1995 had to choose a specific object-oriented database. Applications written after 1995 will be able to rely on the ODMG object-oriented database standard and mix object-oriented databases if appropriate. Similarly, the major RDB vendors did not offer object-oriented front ends in 1995. Those front ends will begin to make their appearance in 1996. The new "Unified Method" that combines the methodologies of Rumbaugh, Booch, and Jacobson will make its initial appearance in 1996. Most important, in 1995 only a few companies had business objects that they could reuse in subsequent applications. In 1996 and 1997, as companies develop new applications and begin to expand their business object libraries, new magnitudes of productivity should become possible.

We say all this simply to remind readers that these applications must not be considered definitive. They do not offer examples of the one right way to do object-oriented development. What these applications do illustrate is the attitude and the overall approach to object-oriented development that prevailed by 1995. They illustrate some of the benefits attained with products current before 1995 and they describe the problems and the solutions used by skilled developers during that timeframe. If you or your company plans to undertake an object-oriented project in 1996 or 1997, you should certainly study how others did similar projects in the years immediately prior to 1996. Then you should consult other sources to determine how the various products have evolved since then in order to combine the best of what was known in 1995 with the products and techniques that have become available since then.

Object technology is going to continue its rapid evolution through the end of this decade and beyond. The lines between products are going to continue to blur as developers learn how to take advantage of component-based development. Management techniques and development tools are going to change in the process. Who knows, for example, what role the Internet will play in corporate computing through the remainder of this decade? Who knows if the RDB vendors will simply make a slight bow to object-oriented front ends or plunge into the object-oriented database market in a serious way offering products that will quickly move companies from their current reliance on RDBs to object-oriented databases? We'll all simply have to wait and see how things evolve. Some might think the uncertainty surrounding many aspects of object technology is a reason to put off exploring this new approach to software development. That's a dangerous notion: Any company that waits until object technology is completely mature will have already lost the competitive edge within its industry.

What's certain is that object technology will continue to grow and that companies that learn how to take advantage of the new technology will position themselves to be successful users of software in the next decade while those who hold back will become increasingly burdened by out-of-date technology and by applications that will be difficult to modify and maintain. This book provides some good examples of what companies that plan to succeed in the next decade have been doing to assure they master the technologies that will assure them success in the near future.

Computerworld/ Object World Finalists and Winners 1992–1995

The Computerworld/Object World Contest began in 1992 and has been held each year since. Applications are documented on an application form that is available from Object World/OMG in the spring of each year. The contest is open to any company that has an application that fits within one of the categories and is actually in use within the company. The category titles have changed a little over the years to better reflect the applications that are being developed.

1992

Category 1. Best Implementation of a Distributed Application Using Object-Oriented Tools

Winner Returns Processing Center Damaged Processing System, Kash n' Karry, Inc.

Finalists Custom Application Suite, Alain Pinel Realtors, Inc.;
Total Benefit Administration, Hewitt Associates

Category 2. Best Implementation of a Reusable Development Environment for Company Development

Winner   LYMB, General Electric

Finalists   Helios, Broussais University Hospital;
OOA Analyst, Boeing Defense and Space Group

Category 3. Best Object-Based Application Developed Using Non-Object-Oriented Tools

Winner   Software Configuration Management System, Landschaftsverband, Rheinland

Finalists   Linkup, Westinghouse Savannah River Company;
Smelter Information System, Alumax Primary Division

Category 4. Best Cost-Saving Implementation Using an Object Approach

Winner   CZ Protocol Print, Wacker Siltronic Corp.

Finalists   Gas Purchase Accounting and Administration, Southern California Gas Company;
"Just the Facts," San Jose Police Department

Category 5. Best Use of Object Technology within an Enterprise or Large Systems Environment

Winner   Concession Management, United Artists Theatre Circuit, Inc.

Finalists   Business and Management Support System, Civil Aviation Authority (UK);
Order Management Network Integration System, Seimens Energy and Automation

1993

Category 1. Best Distributed Application Using Object Technology with Legacy Systems

Winner   Avanti Systems, Inc., Automated Routing and Implementing System

Finalists   Airport of the Future, NCR, AT&T, Objective Inc.;
Network Configuration Facility, Bank of America

Category 2. Best Application Utilizing Reusable Components Leveraged from or for Use in Other Projects

Winner   Financial Risk Management System, Creditanstalt Bankverein

Finalists   TRADE Trading Management System, Anderson Financial Systems;
BILL/800, Bellcore

Category 3. Best Object-Based Application Developed Using Non-Object Tools

Winner   Residence Halls Assignment and Billing, University of Wisconsin, Madison

Finalists   ULLS-A/AdaSAGE, EG&G Idaho, Inc.;
Home Office Life Insurance Conversion Object Workbench, Trillium Resources Corporation

Category 4. Best Application that Demonstrates the Cost/Benefit of Using Object Technology

Winner   Civil Aviation Authority (UK), Sector Information System

Finalists   Potential ARARS Screening Tool, Computer Sciences Corporation;

Global Management Information System and
Customer PC Reporting System, The Thomas
Cook Group

Category 5. Best Use of Object Technology within an Enterprise or Large Systems Environment

Winner   Network Configuration Facility, Bank of America

Finalists   Visual Intelligence and Electronic Warfare
Simulations Workbench, Argonne National Lab;
CareVue 9000, Hewlett-Packard,

1994

Category 1. Best Object-Based Application Developed Using Non-Object Tools

Winner   Type Commander Readiness Management
System (TRMS), The Naval Computer and
Telecommunications Area Master Station

Finalists   State Transition Application Controller (STAC),
Pacific Bell

Category 2. Best Distributed Application Using Object Technology with Legacy Systems

Winner   Forging Steel Planning & Problem Resolution,
Caterpillar, Inc.

Finalists   Automotive Kiosk (Electronic Parts Look-Up),
Canadian Tire;
DISCUS, National Exploitation Lab.

Category 3. Best Application That Demonstrates the Cost/Benefit of Using Object Technology

Winner   State Transition Application Controller (STAC),
Pacific Bell

Finalists   ResMark, MarkAir;
Branch Automation System, Chrysler Financial
Corp.

Category 4. Best Use of Object Technology within an Enterprise or Large Systems Environment

Winner   Document Analysis & Requirements Traceability
(DART), Boeing Defense & Space Group

Finalists   COGEMO V2, Euriware;
Mount Clemens Patient Care System, Mount
Clemens General Hospital

Category 5. Best Application Utilizing Reusable Components Leveraged from or for Use in Other Projects

Winner   Handelsregister (Commercial Register), IBM
Switzerland's Special Business Unit for
Government Solutions

Finalists   State Transition Application Controller (STAC),
Pacific Bell;
Medical Examiner System, Palm Beach County
Information System Services

1995

Category 1. Best Distributed Application Using Object Technology

Winner   AirTraffic Control Framework (AF), The Mitre
Corporation—Center for Advanced Aviation
System Development

Finalists   Weighmaster Automated Transaction System
(WATS), Los Angeles County Sanitation Districts;
Telecommunications Repair and Diagnostic
System (TRaDS), MPR Teltech, Ltd.

Category 2. Best Use of Object Technology to Integrate Legacy Systems

Winner   Financial Marketing Workbench (FMW), IBM Credit Corporation

Finalists   Design Automation/Pre-Competitive Advanced Manufacturing Process (PreAmp), Boeing Defense & Space Group; Telecommunications Repair and Diagnostic System (TRaDS), MPR Teltech Ltd.

Category 3. Best Application Utilizing Reusable Components Leveraged from or for Use in Other Projects

Winner   Message Text Format Editor V4.0 (MTF), Naval Computer and Telecommunications Station, San Diego

Finalists   Human Resources Application, Canadian Imperial Bank of Commerce; Professional Forms Application (ProFormA), IBM Switzerland—Business Unit Government Solutions

Category 4. Best Application That Demonstrates the Cost/Benefit of Using Object Technology

Winner   Supply Management Specialist Tool (SMST), AlliedSignal Aerospace Company

Finalists   Information Services/Customer On-line Order Request System (COORS), Bell Sygma; Electronic Media Claims (EMC), Blue Cross/Blue Shield of Oregon

Category 5. Best Use of Object Technology within an Enterprise or Large Systems Environment

Winner   Boeing Defense & Space Group—Design Automation/Pre-Competitive Advanced Manufacturing Process (PreAmp)

Finalists   Information Services/Customer On-line Order Request System (COORS), Bell Sygma; Remuneration Packaging System, National Australia Bank

Winners at Frankfurt 1995

The Frankfurt Object World show in Germany is not as large as the U.S. Object World shows in Boston and San Francisco, but it is enthusiastic and the crowds are growing. Like the San Francisco Object World show, Frankfurt conducts a contest to determine the best object-oriented applications and gives awards in five different categories. The contest is open to firms from the United States as well as Europe, just as the U.S. contest is, but Frankfurt, naturally, attracts more European entries just as the reverse happens in the United States. We would like to have included some applications from the Frankfurt show in this book, but time was too short. Instead, to give readers a feeling for the types of object-oriented applications that were given awards in Frankfurt in 1995, we have included this brief overview.

Category 1. Best Implementation of a Distributed Application Using Object Technology

Winner: RATP/ Department Bus, France. SPARTACUS

SPARTACUS is a training simulation software system designed to teach the regulation of buses (service, management, frequency, and schedule control). The whole application is based on the analysis of line coding (OOA/OOD, Ptech, Object Store and C++). SPARTACUS' main benefit is in training. It provides RATP employees with simulations of daily traffic and allows them to practice making decisions.

Finalists

Daimler Benz AG, Germany. OPUS-IV.

OPUS-IV (Operative Planning and Variance Comparison) is used for a cost-center-specific, multiyear planning effort that includes budgets, human resources, investments, and areas and variance comparison. Because the users are located at several subsidiaries and the planning coordination is central, the system was realized as a client/server application with an object-oriented client (Smalltalk-80), a central relational database, and communication via TCP/IP RPC.

OPUS-IV ensures faster planning processes, because every role in the process is well supported; increased transparency of planning, because a great number of reports are used; higher information quality, because of central data keeping and relieving the planning departments of many secondary tasks like data administration.

IBM Schweiz, Switzerland. Control PC for Label Scanning Systems.

This application is an open distributed environment for handling parcels at Swiss PPT. It integrates the existing systems for bar-code processing, conveyer belt operation and central track-and-trace functions. The main benefit of this application is the enabling of automated parcel processing with the flexibility to easily include further functionality, which results from the use of object technology.

Category 2: Best Application Utilizing Reusable Components Leveraged from or for Use in Other Projects

Winner: NASA, USA. Telemetry Processing Control Environment (TPCE)

TPCE is a toolkit of reusable software components that can be combined to form an autonomous control and monitoring capability for configurable telemetry processing systems. TPCE had to be easily and quickly adaptable to varying hardware component configurations as well as to varying user requirements from project to project. The reusable TPCE toolkit is built from components and yielded significant cost savings in both development and in ongoing operations.

Finalists

Mannesmann Datenverarbeitung GmbH, Germany. GUIMAN V2.4 Editor.

GUIMAN is a graphical user interface management system designed for industrial automation. It was implemented as a generic framework and is highly adaptable, reusable software that drastically reduces the development expenses for complex software systems with varying customer demands.

SWISS PTT Telecom, Switzerland. PrM Process Manager.

This system supports system recycling using a CORBA approach and provides faster customer service because of the object-oriented integration that results.

Category 3. Best Use of Object Technology within an Enterprise or Large System Environment

Winner: SWISS PTT Telecom, Switzerland. PrM Process Manager.

Already described.

Finalists

IBM Informationssysteme GmbH, Germany. TMN-BFU: Customer Administration of the ISDB Network.

Deutsche Telekom's ISDN-Network, which provides tele and bearer services to analog or ISDN subscribers, operates with

Siemens and Alcatel switch technology in the access network. TMN-BFU provides a direct link between the administrative customer management center, KONTES, and switches from Siemens and Alcatel. TMN-BFU converts the received KONTES orders—that is, new network access, call redirection, three party service, closed user group—into a sequence of management operations (Q3, CMISE) that are sent to the specific switch.

TMN-BFU, the first implementation of an application based on TMN standards in a large production environment, is now deployed nationwide (21 servers and 240 clients). It integrates switch technology, Unix platforms (RS6000, AIX, BFU) and the MVS-mainframe (KONTES). The processing of work orders for subscriber configuration is done automatically in seconds versus days in the past. It runs 24 hours a day and leads to an immense reduction of wrong configuration caused by manual data entry. Because of object-oriented end-user interface, BFU operators can now handle problems without resort to technical personnel.

NASA, USA, *Telemetry Processing Control Environment (TPCE)*.
Already described.

Category 4: Best Cost-Saving Implementation Using an Object Approach

Winner   Debis Systemhaus GmbH, Germany. LOGIS, Logistics Information System.

The Management Information System, LOGIS, is an instrument for the analysis of logistic information concerning the parts of Mercedes Benz. LOGIS provides a tool aiming to ensure better quality of information for warehouse planning and management, and monitoring of agreed boundary conditions for target agreements and performance agreements.

Finalists

BIW Beratung und Informationssysteme GmbH, Germany. OSA (Object-Oriented Sales Application).

The OSA application has a complete CAD integration and an open interface to the PPC software BIW BRAIN and SAP R/3 for field sales services on Nextstep framework. It can be used in field sales services through object orientation and graphic user interfaces with a high degree of acceptance, and it takes into account the increasing significance of the sales engineer at the point of sale. OSA fulfills the requirements of the sales organization, improves customer care and customer services, and reduces the sales business process from more than one week to one day.

IBM Netherlands, Netherlands. SWOPI (Software Ordering and Price Information).

SWOPI provides the user with a clear view of the available software products and of the pricing mechanism.

Category 5. Best Application Combining Object Technology with Legacy Systems

Winner: Swiss PTT, Switzerland. PrM Process Manager.

Already described.

Finalists

IBM Informationssysteme GmbH, Germany. TMN-BFU: Customer Administration in the ISDN Network. Already described.

Systor AG, Switzerland. Documentary Collections.

Documentary Collections is a client/server application developed with IBM's VisualAge/Smalltalk and OS/2 Warp that enables the processing of business documentary collection, including data entry, printing output, processing payments, and feeding the management information system for an international Swiss bank. The main benefit is Documentary Collection's total integration into the mainframe legacy environment of the customer, thus allowing a faster, more efficient, and redundancy-free handling of daily business.

Bibliography

Here is a brief list of books that can provide a manager with a good introduction to object technology and some of the special niches within object technology.

Booch, Grady. *Object-oriented analysis and design with applications* (2nd Ed.). Redwood City, CA: Benjamin Cummings, 1994.

Cattell, R.G.G. (Ed.). *The object database standard: ODMG-93.* San Francisco, CA: Morgan Kaufmann Publishers, 1994. ISBN 1-55860-302-6.

Goldberg, Adele, and Kenneth S. Rubin. *Succeeding with objects: Decision frameworks for project management.* New York: Addison-Wesley, 1995. ISBN 0-201-62878-3.

> This is the best book available on the ins and outs of object-oriented project management. It walks you through the decisions you have to make to get started and then provides lots of good guidelines for succeeding.

Harmon, Paul, and David A. Taylor (with the assistance of William Morrissey). *Objects in action: Commercial applications of object-oriented technologies.* New York: Addison-Wesley, 1993. ISBN 0-201-63336-1.

> This book describes the Object World winners in the 1992 contest.

Jacobson, Ivar, et al. *Object-oriented software engineering: A use case driven approach* (4th revised printing). New York: Addison-Wesley, 1992. ISBN 0-201-54435-0.

Kamran Parsaye, Mark Chignell, Setrag Khoshafian, and Harry Wong. *Intelligent databases: Object-oriented, deductive hypermedia technologies.* New York: John Wiley, 1989. ISBN 0-471-50345-2.

Khoshafian, Setrag. *Object-oriented databases.* New York: John Wiley, 1993. ISBN 0471-57058-3.

Loomis, Mary E.S. *Object databases: The essentials.* New York: Addison-Wesley, 1995. ISBN 0201-56341-X.

Moore, Geoffrey. *Crossing the chasm.* New York: HarperBusiness, 1991.

> This book provides a general overview of how new technologies work their way into the mainstream or fail to be adopted and disappear.

Orfali, Robert, Dan Harkey, and Jeri Edwards. *The essential distributed objects survival guide.* New York: John Wiley, 1996.

> There are other books that explain CORBA, OLE, and OpenDoc, but this is the best for beginners.

Object Management Group. *The common object request broker.* New York: John Wiley, 1992.

Rumbaugh, J. et al. *Object-oriented modeling and design.* Englewood Cliffs, NJ: Prentice-Hall, 1991.

Taylor, David A. *Object-oriented information systems: Planning and implementation.* New York: John Wiley, 1992.

Taylor, David A. *Object-oriented technology: A manager's guide.* New York: Addison-Wesley, 1990.

Monthly Newsletter

Object-Oriented Strategies (Paul Harmon, editor). OOS is published by Cutter Information Systems in Arlington, MA. For more information, contact Cutter at 1 617 648 8702.

Index